DEC 2 9 1998

PROFITING FROM IPOS & SMALL CAP STOCKS

NORMAN BROWN

NEW YORK INSTITUTE OF FINANCE

NEW YORK • TORONTO • SYDNEY • TOKYO • SINGAPORE

Library of Congress Cataloging-in-Publication Data

Brown, Norman H.
    Profiting from IPOs and small cap stocks / Norman Brown.
      p. cm.
    Includes index.
    ISBN 0-7352-0029-7 (cloth)
    1. Small capitalization stocks—United States. I. Title.
  HG4963.B76   1998
  332.63'2044—dc21   98-17862
                                           CIP

Printed in the United States of America

10 9 8 7 6 5 4 3 2 1

This publication is designed to provide accurate and authoritative information in regard to the subject matter covered. It is sold with the understanding that the publisher is not engaged in rendering legal, accounting, or other professional service. If legal advice or other expert assistance is required, the services of a competent professional person should be sought.

> *. . . From the Declaration of Principles jointly adopted by a Committee of
> the American Bar Association and a Committee of Publishers and Associations.*

Netscape Communications Corporation has not authorized, sponsored, or endorsed, or approved this publication and is not responsible for its content. Netscape and the Netscape Communications Corporate Logos, are trademarks and trade names of Netscape Communications Corporation. All other product names and/or logos are trademarks of their respective owners.

ISBN 0-7352-0029-7

ATTENTION: CORPORATIONS AND SCHOOLS

Prentice Hall Books are available at quantity discounts with bulk purchase for educational, business, or sales promotional use. For information, please write to: Prentice Hall Special Sales, 240 Frisch Court, Paramus, New Jersey 07652. Please supply: title of book, ISBN, quantity, how the book will be used, date needed.

New York Institute of Finance
An Imprint of Prentice Hall Press
Paramus, NJ 07652
A Simon & Schuster Company

Prentice Hall International (UK) Limited, *London*
Prentice Hall of Australia Pty. Limited, *Sydney*
Prentice Hall Canada, Inc., *Toronto*
Prentice Hall Hispanoamericana, S.A., *Mexico*
Prentice Hall of India Private Limited, *New Delhi*
Prentice Hall of Japan, Inc., *Tokyo*
Simon & Schuster Asia Pte. Ltd., *Singapore*
Editora Prentice Hall do Brasil, Ltda., *Rio de Janeiro*

For my wife Freda and children Amy, Burt, and Toby,
who allowed me time and sometimes space to pursue my dreams.

Acknowledgments

My thanks to the many people who encouraged me to write this book and contributed ideas, provided important information, and made hundreds of helpful and often candid comments. Too numerous to mention here, they include brokerage officials, mutual fund managers, college professors, government regulators, individual investors, and other industry observers.

Grateful acknowledgment is also made to Morningstar Inc. for permission to reprint their list of Small Cap Mutual Funds and to the *Hulbert Financial Digest* for the use of their Newsletter Directory. Both appear as Appendixes to this book.

Sincere thanks also to my editor, Ellen Schneid Coleman, for her professional assistance, support, and long-distance friendship. And to Sybil Grace, who attended to clarity, precision, and content in the preparation of this book.

Contents

Introduction
xiii

4

In Your Own Backyard
39

5

Fishing for Red Herrings
53

6

When to Buy or Sell
69

7

Ventures and Partnerships
83

8

Seek Out Special Situations
95

9

Margin Trading and Options
107

10

Going Global with Stocks
119

11

Consider Mutual Funds
131

12

Reading Annual Reports
147

13

Finding the Right Broker
161

14

Investing By Computer
175

15

Penny Stocks and Other Scams
189

16

Thinking About Taxes?
201

Appendix A

Leading Indexes and Indicators
215

Appendix B

Newsletters and Advisory Services
217

Appendix C

Regional and Discount Brokers
225

Appendix D

Small Cap Mutual Funds
229

Index
245

Introduction

Forget bonds. Most mutual funds, too. Only about 20 percent of them even do as well as the market—the rest underperform it. If you want to get rich, you have to buy individual stocks. That's not just my opinion. Legendary stock pickers from Peter Lynch to Warren Buffett have shown that the way to wealth is by building your portfolio with the stocks of companies big and small.

The sole purpose of this book is to help you make money by picking stocks that will appreciate in value and avoiding those that won't. Historically, those have been the stocks of small cap companies. Small cap companies typically have a capitalization of $150 million or less. And with blue chips way up in price, they are considered the single best investment for the next several years as well as a pleasant alternative to paying high premiums for larger companies.

The premise, simply, is that it's a lot easier for a half-billion dollar company to double in size than for a $30 billion behemoth to get to $60 billion. And in periods of rising growth, such small or new companies can make you rich a lot faster than anything else.

It's easier and cheaper than ever to join the ranks of investors looking for better returns—thanks to discount brokers, on-line trading, and free financial information on the Internet (once available only to professionals). But be ready to invest some time before you invest your money. The small cap universe is a stock picker's domain—and to make money you have to separate the hots from the dogs.

In this book, you'll find out:

❑ how small cap companies tap into new or niche markets;

❑ why they have better growth prospects than their blue-chip cousins; and

❑ how initial public offerings (IPOs) can bring you gains of 50 percent or more in a matter of months, not years.

You may even want to put a sizable chunk into one of these new issues, but you have to be rigorously selective. A lot of real junk is brought to market, along with youthful trailblazers of real substance. You'll learn how to tell the difference.

You'll meet the smart players and the big losers in the high-stakes world of IPOs, venture capital, and thinly traded stocks, and learn from them:

❑ how to find quality small cap stocks in your own backyard;

❑ rate them using the latest market indexes and indicators; and

❑ the best time to buy—or sell.

While some Fortune 500 companies fit the small cap category (Chiquita, Amdahl), those that aren't listed on the New York and American Stock Exchanges, preferring to trade on Nasdaq (the automated quotation system of the National Association of Security Dealers) are the ones savvy professionals are talking about.

But small cap stocks are not "pink chips," stocks of little-known companies whose shares are quoted on pink sheets and traded over-the-counter, not in the Nasdaq market. Nor are they penny stocks—illiquid, speculative securities shunned by serious investors unless they happen to know the company well.

In addition, you'll discover how to use regional and discount brokers to find small cap stocks that aren't as closely followed by Wall Street as their larger rivals—companies that constitute the fastest-growing and most profitable part of the economy. You'll find practical advice and professional tips on

❑ using options, rights, and warrants that can put extra dollars in your pocket;

❑ reading prospectuses and annual reports the right way (backwards); and

❑ researching or buying stocks using a personal computer.

You'll also find the latest information on avoiding penny stock scams and how to save on taxes (under the new rules). By owning individual stocks instead of mutual funds, you can elect when to pay taxes and avoid paying management fees. It takes only a little more sophistication, and can add to your bottom line.

Best of all, you'll develop a solid, working knowledge of the market forces that drive new or emerging companies (Staples, Microsoft) to succeed or fail in our superheated economy, and learn first-hand about tomorrow's growth stocks from industry observers. As fans of Warren Buffett's investment strategy know, he didn't become wealthy by throwing darts. He does exhaustive research on companies before buying their shares.

Not long ago, investors seeking to duplicate his success had to send for annual reports or spend hours at the public library. Today, anyone with access to the Internet can find valuable information on thousands of public companies at hundreds of Web sites.

The rich menu from which you can choose has something for everybody—from steakhouses (Logan's Roadhouse) and designer jeans (Ralph Lauren) to tiny companies (as yet unnamed) that exist only to bring to market an idea lurking in some scientist's mind. The dynamics of our economy, the world's largest and most influential, keeps that market buzzing with activity, and our securities laws and enforcement agencies make it safer to invest in the world's most open market. Nobody can guarantee profits, but there's no better place to give it your best shot.

At the end of the book, there are handy appendixes to help you further:

❏ leading indexes and indicators;

❏ newsletters and advisory services;

❏ addresses of regional and discount brokers; and

❏ a list of mutual funds that specialize in small cap stocks.

All the information you'll need to win big on your own.

CHAPTER 1

What Are Small Caps?

A stock's capitalization is the value of all its shares, equal to price times shares outstanding. While there's no universal rule, most small cap stocks have a capitalization of less than $1 billion and usually much less.

The menu of small cap stocks from which an investor can choose is huge. The New York Stock Exchange lists some 2,200 issues of which about one-fifth are considered small stocks. Another 800 or so are traded on the American Stock Exchange. And the rapidly growing National Association of Securities Dealers Automated Quotation System (Nasdaq) carries 5,000 stocks.

Several thousand more are listed in the "pink sheets," which is jargon for small, thinly traded stocks whose prices used to be published on pink paper. And that's just in the United States. Most other nations have their own stock exchanges with hundreds or thousands of listed stocks.

Money managers try to make sense of that vast menu by subdividing stocks into various categories such as size or market capitalization. They refer to the assortment of big, medium-sized and little stocks as large caps, mid-caps and small caps. How does an investor make sense of all this?

Large caps are companies with a market capitalization that starts at $1 billion and keeps climbing. They are often companies you know—established leaders who have achieved their stature by possessing the right products, marketing strategies and management. Many are also multinational with the capacity to produce earnings from opportunities overseas. Large cap stocks may not offer the rapid growth of their smaller counterparts, but they tend to be less risky.

Mid-caps are equally expensive, with capitalizations of between $168 million and $8 billion according to the S&P Mid-Cap 400 Index. Though not "fledglings," many are still small enough to make some adroit maneuvers that large companies often can't pull off. They can be opportunistic and respond to economic turns or market trends quickly, but that potential for growth does come with some risk. Mid-cap stock prices are generally more volatile than their larger counter parts.

Small caps are those "little gems" you hear about and regret you didn't know about sooner. They could be start-up operations with bright promise, or new public offerings. Some are established businesses turning out a single product that's in high demand. Their small size can also be a big asset, giving them an agility and earnings growth potential that other companies lack. Small caps are vulnerable to unforeseen market changes and cash flow squeezes, but holding on to them can often take the edge off such risks.

DOING THE RESEARCH

Everyone wants to own the next Microsoft or Staples, and those who find it will do very well. Unfortunately, many small companies that look appealing in the beginning soon lose their luster as they become bigger and more clumsy. Rewards are bigger, but so is the competition.

The premise, simply, is that it's a lot easier for a half-billion dollar company to double in size than for a $30 billion behemoth like PepsiCo to get to $60 billion. In periods of economic growth, such small or new companies can make you rich a lot faster. But you should know that the small cap universe is a stock picker's domain—and you have to separate the hots from the dogs.

Start with this homily: Do your homework. While some Fortune 500 companies fit the small cap category (Chiquita, Amdahl), those that aren't listed on the New York or American Stock Exchanges, preferring to trade electronically on Nasdaq, are the ones savvy professionals are talking about.

But small cap is not synonymous with "pink chips," companies whose shares are not traded in the more formal Nasdaq market. Nor are they penny stocks (illiquid, speculative securities shunned by serious investors unless they happen to know such a company well.) More representative are companies such as Williams-Sonoma, the San Francisco merchant of kitchen equipment, with more than 250 retail outlets and a market capitalization of $500 million; and Glenayre Technology, a New York manufacturer of telecommunications equipment and software, valued at $690 million.

There's no easy way to track down issues as obscure as Glenayre or Keane, a Boston-area developer of computer software for the hospital industry. So investors without specialized knowledge tend to invest in small caps via mutual funds. But as investment legends Peter Lynch and Warren Buffet have proved, to get really rich you have to purchase individual stocks, not mutual funds.

"We're firm believers that people ought to look at stocks directly," says Thomas O'Hara, chairman of the National Association of Investors Corporation (NAIC). Its members, organized into local investment clubs, seek to double their investment in five years by pooling their time, talent and money to research and invest in big and small stocks.

If that isn't enough, the famed Beardstown Ladies investment club in rural Illinois has parlayed its homework into returns averaging 23 percent annually for the past ten years, outperforming the $52 billion Fidelity Magellan, the world's largest stock fund, which returned an average 17 percent for the same period.

Some money managers specializing in small cap stocks may hold them no more than a year and sometimes for only a few weeks. The reason: A small company stock can drop by half or double in price in a single day's trading, and these investors are looking to make their names and fortunes with 30-, 40- or 50-percent annual gains.

Wall Street's ignorance or greed can be bliss for small stock investors. A report by Prudential Securities found that the less a small stock is followed by brokerage firm analysts, the more it rallies when it beats those analysts' expectations. That buttresses the belief that one of the best ways to beat passive indexes like the Dow is to hunt for neglected stocks whose value has yet to be discovered by hordes of analysts and investors.

"Relatively underfollowed small companies have tended to show good performance," says Claudia Mott, director of small stock research at Prudential. "It might have been a highflyer that fell on hard times, and analysts quit covering it. Or an IPO that didn't generate enough interest for an analyst to start covering it, but turned out to be a good investment for the long haul."

Blue-chip companies commonly have 20 or more analysts following them. Even small, actively traded "growth stocks" are followed by half a dozen analysts. The truly neglected are small issues with just one or two analysts covering them—or none. Among several thousand of these,

Prudential found average gains of 32 percent compared with just 23 percent for companies followed by five or more analysts.

CLOSELY HELD COMPANIES

Where do you find such stocks? Most new companies are started by individuals with an idea and a small pool of money, either their own or borrowed. The few that survive go on to the next step, in which they find a bigger pile of capital—often from venture capital investors who are given partial ownership in exchange for their money.

As management builds a track record, the need grows for more capital. It's at this stage that the company sells stock for the first time in an initial public offering, or IPO. Once the stock is sold, the company looks for fast and predictable growth. As more investors buy into the action, the price soars—at least for a while.

Regional brokers try to exploit the "neglect factor" by targeting undercovered stocks. "Less coverage is definitely a plus from our perspective," says Thomas Pence, vice president at Conseco Capital Management in Carmel, Indiana. While that requires more of his own research, and often includes visiting a company, it also means others are less likely to have realized its value, he says.

Conseco bought Fairfield Communities, a vacation-property developer, partly because only two analysts covered the company. After struggling for a few months, the stock began to rally and doubled in price in little over a year.

Lack of scrutiny, of course, can give companies the opportunity to gloss over shortcomings more easily, putting more onus on investors to watch out for window-dressing. "People who don't do their homework can get burned," says Pence. He tries to stick to stocks where he has some unique insight. Then the prospect of future analyst coverage is a nice catalyst to the rise in stock price.

Profiting from neglect doesn't mean you should buy any uncovered stock, however. Prudential excluded thousands of companies with no coverage at all, many of which are speculative, infrequently traded issues. And while intense coverage may subtract from the performance of small cap stocks, most undercovered companies don't intend to stay that way. Financial officers spend a lot of time on the road pitching the company's story to analysts and investors.

Your research on a stock—before you buy it—should definitely include reading the prospectus. It's among the most important documents for investors deciding whether to buy a stock. Initial public offerings, or "new issues" as they are sometimes called, are for the pros and serious investors.

Start by getting from your broker the prospectus of a company that will soon be going public. Study it and watch the price moves when the stock is finally sold. Wait a few weeks for the price to settle down or to establish a solid pattern of gains. Only then do you want to own the stock. Resist the temptation to "get in on the ground floor" the first time out. Sooner or later, greed always gets punished in the stock market.

Eventually, the growth rate must slow. No company can double in size every year. As growth slows, the "smart money" crowd sells the stock and goes shopping for another more youthful and faster-growing company. And a different kind of value investor takes over—one who hangs in as long as the company continues to produce predictable growth, albeit not nearly as fast as it once did.

BULL AND BEAR MARKETS

Additional research should be aimed at understanding the economic environment in which you're investing. Don't worry; it won't take long. Both the economy and the stock market tend to move in cycles (hence the inclusion of stock prices in the government index of *Leading Economic Indicators,* a forecasting tool you might want to start keeping an eye on). A list of stock indexes and key indicators is given in Appendix A.

Unfortunately, the record of economists has been as dismal as their science in recent years. Indeed, studies have shown that an investor would have fared better by flipping a coin, or by betting *against* the economists' predictions. Peter Lynch, probably the world's best-known stock picker, has this to say about economics and the stock market: "If you spend more than 15 minutes a year on economics, you've wasted 12."

What we do know is that bulls romp in smaller pastures, and the key to longevity may well be whether investors look for value in the stocks of small companies, or choose to bid the blue chips even higher. That seems to be the case, as mutual funds and individual investors have rediscovered small stocks, after virtually ignoring them since the Crash of 1987.

At this writing stocks are also in the midst of one of the strongest bull markets of this century, with the Dow Jones industrial average up nearly 4200 points, or 108 percent, in just two years. And the higher it goes, the greater the fear that it will fall hard. But for those daring enough, there are riches yet to be claimed.

"The small cap market generally moves in cycles of about seven to nine years," says William O'Hearn, portfolio manager at Navellier & Associates, a money management firm in Incline Village, Nevada, that specializes in small companies. "Only within the last three years has small cap investing been growing in vogue, which suggests the trend should last for at least another four to six years."

Even those skeptics who say that investors are getting too rich, too fast, admit that bearish indicators like inflation just aren't there. And most of the news out of Washington has encouraged investors to buy more stocks. The powerful forces underpinning the stock market, at least for the foreseeable future, remain in place.

GROWTH AND INFLATION. Over the last ten years, the economy has been marked by steady growth and little inflation, providing long-term confidence in the stock market. Small stocks usually outperform all other types of assets in such markets.

BANG FOR YOUR BUCK. When small stocks take off on a tear, as they've done recently, the gains can be terrific for years at a time. And these are *extra* profits over and above what you'd get from an index fund.

THE STRONGER DOLLAR. A weak dollar helps large companies while a strong dollar helps small ones. That's because global giants like Coca-Cola can earn 70 percent of revenues outside the United States. But when they lose that advantage, savvy investors switch to smaller firms.

There's more to this market than high-tech and global stocks. There's cash, and plenty of it. Mutual funds have been far and away the major buyers of stocks, along with individuals and institutions. And that can be a powerful prescription for higher stock prices.

MEASURING PERFORMANCE

The most important thing to manage in any market is your own expectations. Bear in mind that every year of huge gains raises the odds for one of subpar returns and even occasional losses. Some tips for dealing with a superheated market:

❏ *Don't get too greedy.* If you've been in the market the past four years, you've been handed a bonanza. You may even have reached financial goals you didn't expect to hit for ten years. Cash in some stocks that are overvalued, and put the money in a tax-deferred account.

❏ *Don't be overly naive.* If you've got the money and you're bent on investing it in stocks, do so slowly to lower the odds of a big dip occurring right after you invest your wad. And don't buy stocks that are sky-high. Instead, consider a higher cash position so you'll have funds available to buy stocks after a decline.

❏ *Rebalance your portfolio.* Those blue-chip stocks could be up 50 percent since you last checked. If so, you may have a greater weighting in big stocks relative to small stocks than you ever intended. Sell some blue chips to buy small stocks and foreign stocks.

Once you own a few stocks, you have to keep track of them. That doesn't mean calling your broker every day to get a quote. Small companies aren't followed as closely by Wall Street as their larger rivals, so you have to work harder to learn about them. The other side of that coin: They're probably still low in price.

To supplement what's offered by your broker, advisory services like Standard & Poor's and Value Line can be enormously helpful. Their reports are expensive, so you may want to use them at your library or broker's office before buying your own copies.

Stock indexes like those listed in the Appendix can also be helpful. Standard & Poor's, for example, has a *Small Cap 600* that complements its mid-cap and large cap indexes. As a group, the 1,500 stocks in the three indexes represent about 80 percent of the total market capitalization of stocks traded in the United States.

Moody's Investors Service, while not an advisory service, also publishes updated manuals that describe American and foreign companies, including financial and operating data, company histories, product descriptions, and plant and property locations. One of these covers 2,200 unlisted or hard-to-find companies not listed on Nasdaq's National Market System or on regional exchanges. A Dun & Bradstreet company, Moody's is known throughout the world for its bond ratings and factual publications, and its materials are used by investors as well as the professional and business community.

As a rule, brokerage firms and institutions ignore small caps: They're too small to research, and too thinly traded to generate significant commissions. "Yet that is exactly what makes them so attractive," says Jim Collins, publisher of the *OTC Insight* newsletter. "Most are obscure firms or new issues that over time offer some of the best returns an investor can earn."

One reason: Small companies often constitute the fastest-growing and most profitable part of the economy. And that's making believers out of fund managers as well as individual investors. Small firms tap into new markets and have richer growth prospects than many of their bigger brethren. Since 1925, according to researchers at Chicago's Ibbotson Associates, small cap stocks have delivered average annual returns of 12.4 percent versus 10.3 percent for large-company stocks.

With bigger potential gains come bigger risks. The securities of small companies are more volatile than those of larger, more stable companies. That's a boon when they surge, but dips can be heart-stopping. There's no foolproof method for avoiding such dangers; however, there are sensible ways to capture the huge profit potential of small stocks while dramatically lowering your risk.

Collins offers this advice on separating the hots from the dogs among small cap stocks:

❏ Get a report from your broker and make sure the company is traded by at least three *market makers*, or dealers who buy and sell securities at publicly quoted prices for their own accounts, and who are subject to Nasdaq rules.

❏ Stay away from any bankrupt firms and from penny stocks with huge capitalizations. The letters "VJ" in the listings mean the company is in bankruptcy or receivership or being reorganized under the Bankruptcy Act.

❏ Winnow the list of potential candidates to a dozen, and write to each company for a copy of its annual report. You can obtain the addresses from either the Standard & Poor's or Moody's directories.

❏ Eliminate any companies with excessive long-term debt, too much emphasis on so-called "good will," negative working capital, or serious legal problems. Growing companies in promising markets selling at low multiples, often at a discount from book value, are your best bets.

The bottom line, say small stock experts, is that investors in small companies often have to be long-term investors—because you have to be able to withstand the short-term ups and downs that can whipsaw any small stock. But if you can hold on—and pick right—history indicates the payout can be phenomenal.

Buy only those companies you know well, and figure on holding most of them for the long haul. Whichever way you go, individual stocks or mutual funds, the bulls agree on one thing: "This is the best place to be invested for the next several years," says Michael DiCarlo, manager of John Hancock Special Equities Fund. "They really are the only alternative."

SPOTTING NICHE COMPANIES

They are the stars of the small cap universe—companies whose drive, ingenuity and agility keep them charging ahead faster than much bigger rivals. Many are cashing in on high technology, but others are profiting from such diverse ventures as pizza, bicycle gear, and small-arms training.

Even though small, they are strongly entrenched in their market niche. They've made themselves so indispensable, so knowledgeable about their little corners of the business world, and so hard to compete with on their home turf, that they've come to dominate their niches the way big companies like Wal-Mart dominate their industries.

Earnings of Encad, for example, the $210 million manufacturer of quality ink-jet printers used in graphic arts and computer-aided design, are expected to grow 30 percent a year through 2002, say analysts, yet the stock trades at a reasonable 19 times earnings. The industry leader is Hewlett-Packard, but "Encad is two years ahead of Hewlett-Packard in developing new wide-format printers," says John Rossi, analyst at Banc-America Robertson Stephens in San Francisco.

Analysts following $390 million Showbiz Pizza, known for its Chuck E. Cheese pizza parlors, rate the stock a buy despite a low of $5 in 1995. The drop was a result of turf wars with Discovery Zone, a glitzy upstart that went into bankruptcy a year later. The Irving, Texas company plans to add at least 30 new stores, and facelifts to the existing 312 should boost earnings by an average 20 percent for the next five years, according to Dennis Telzrow, analyst at Principal Financial.

Mining a trend isn't the only route to profits. Others have found lucrative niches by following entrepreneurial instincts. One is Apollo Group, parent of the University of Phoenix, a chain of adult education programs that has seen a total return of 342 percent in two years. "That niche (adult education or retraining) is a big market that has been woefully under-served," says Peter Appert of Alex Brown & Sons in Baltimore.

Niche companies are the safest kind of small stocks to buy. To find them, you may have to screen out hundreds of small firms or new issues that make up the small cap universe. You can't count on a rising tide to lift all boats, because that tide can ebb as much as it flows.

A way to simplify the task is to look at industries or sectors that have performed well in the general market (health care, temp services, telecommunications). They could spawn the best deals as private companies in those fields go public.

"But be wary of IPOs touted as extra hot," warns Robert Natale, editor of the *Emerging & Special Situations* newsletter, published by Standard & Poor's. "They can be vastly overpriced." The easiest way to spot an overpriced offering? Compare the price-earnings ratio with the P-E's of other companies in the same industry. The P-E of a new issue should not be hugely greater than those of the rest of the industry.

Michael DiCarlo uses computers to identify high-growth companies whose shares are rising in value faster than the market itself. Then he or someone else evaluates the fundamentals to see if they meet four criteria: annual growth of 25 percent for at least two years, little or no debt, position as a market leader, and a high degree of insider ownership.

A company that DiCarlo cites as meeting all his criteria is Bell Sports, the leading manufacturer of bicycle helmets. "It's benefiting from the increased popularity of mountain bikes and the concern over safety," he says. Several states and municipalities have made wearing helmets mandatory for children, and the trend could extend to skateboarders and in-line skaters.

DEFYING COMMON MYTHS

The common belief is that small cap stocks are golden when the bull is afoot, but mighty dangerous when the market turns. That's true for some issues, but a lot more simply become mid-caps with predictable growth and a lot less risk.

A recent study published by Wilshire Associates in Santa Monica, California, shows that over the past 20 years, the very smallest of 2,500 stocks it tracks returned an average of 17 percent a year, while the very largest stocks had an average return of 11.5 percent a year. Other analysts show similar gains and agree that the next ten years will be good ones for small stocks.

Experts admit that buying individual stocks even in a bull market can be a big gamble. Warns L. Keith Mullins, research director for small stocks at Salomon Smith Barney, "It's financial suicide for individual investors to buy one or two small stocks. You have to diversify, and that means a dozen stocks or a small cap mutual fund."

Then if one or two really take off, you're going to do a lot better than you would with blue chips. "If you buy a stock at $137 a share, where's it going to go? To $140?" asks Mullins. But whether you're taking the plunge directly or through a mutual fund, a few myths about small stocks need exploding:

❑ *Small stocks are short-term buys; large stocks are for the long-term.* Reverse that. As you've read, you need to take a long-term view with most of these securities because they are so volatile. The proven method of reducing the risk of volatility is to invest for the long term and diversify

❑ *Small cap mutual funds are very aggressive, buying and selling shares frequently.* In truth, some small cap funds are downright sleepy, with portfolio turnovers of only 20 or 30 percent each year.

❑ *Small stocks are all technology issues.* Not so, even though the Nasdaq index is loaded with them, sometimes skewing key indicators. Some big gainers for 1997 are shown in Figure 1.1:

FIGURE 1.1. BIG GAINERS IN 1997

	Return on Capital	Market Value
Gradall Industries (GRDL) Construction equipment manufacturer	73%	$112M
Rockshox (RSHX) Bicycle suspension systems	63%	$211M
Firearm Training Systems (FATS) Small-arms simulators	52%	$286M
PJ America (PJAM) Take-out pizza	50%	$71M
General Employment Enterprises (JOB) Staffing for technology firms	44%	$29M
Logan's Roadhouse (RDHS) Steak and seafood restaurants	40%	$104M

Source: Business Week.

DIVERSITY IN SMALL STOCKS

Bulldozers, steak houses and temp services may not seem very exciting, but there's nothing humdrum about a stock that promises explosive growth—and delivers. And while the average small stock may not be overpriced, some sectors sure seem to be. Many technology companies are trading at astronomical price-earnings ratios. "They are accidents waiting to happen," says John Jensen, portfolio manager at Cadence Capital Management in Boston.

You can lessen that risk by diversifying among a dozen different stocks, he says. And that may only take a minimum outlay of about $100,000, given the low share price of most companies or new issues. It helps to have some inside knowledge as well, and to buy stocks one at a time and not all at once.

"Give yourself another advantage," advises Jensen. "Only buy stocks of local companies, where you have knowledge the analysts or institutions can't possibly hope to acquire."

Historically, cycles of small stocks outperforming large ones have lasted until their price-earnings ratios soared to twice those of their bigger rivals. But right now they are not much above those stocks in the Standard & Poor's 500. So there's opportunity for those daring enough to claim more of the riches.

INVESTOR INFORMATION

Many brokerage firms, government agencies and mutual funds have materials available free of charge that explain stocks and how to invest in them. Sometimes, all you really need is to get in touch with the right person.

You can start by obtaining a copy of *Stock Market Investing: The Definitive Guide* available from PaineWebber, 5151 Beltline Rd., Dallas, TX 75248 (800-288-1515); and the booklet *What Every Investor Should Know,* published by the Securities and Exchange Commission, Office of Investor Education, 450 Fifth St. NW, Washington, DC 20549 (800-342-5647).

Investors who wish to dig deeper can also inquire at the library about the quarterly and annual handbooks on small companies published by Moody's Investor Service, 99 Church St., New York, NY 10007 (800-342-5647).

And if you want to move slowly, consider joining an investment club where the emphasis is heavily on stocks. You can find out about investment clubs, and purchase a subscription to *Better Investing* by contacting the National Association of Investors Corporation, 1515 E. Eleven Mile Rd., Royal Oak, MI 48067.

CHAPTER 2

Step Up to the Counter

The menu of stocks from which an investor can choose is huge—and constantly growing as more companies sell shares to raise capital. But few understand how stocks trade on the exchanges or over-the-counter and how brokers profit when novice investors buy or sell shares. Stock orders are handled differently depending on whether the shares are traded in an auction market, such as the New York Stock Exchange, or a dealer market (such as Nasdaq) where the orders can go to many persons rather than just one. Here's how it works:

Auction market

A customer like yourself places an order with his broker to buy 100 shares of General Motors (GM) "at the market" or the going price. The broker then sends the order to the floor of the New York Stock Exchange where it is routed to a specialist who supervises trading in that stock.

Basically an auctioneer, the specialist offers to buy shares of GM for $56.75 (the bid) and sell shares for $57.35 (the ask). The difference between the two prices is called the spread.

With the order to buy shares of GM, the specialist will do one of the following:

1. Simultaneously receive a market order to sell GM and match the orders at $57 a share.
2. Have a limit or standing order to sell GM for $57.25 and offer it to the buyer at that price.

3. Hear from a seller that he has shares for $56.75, in which case the buyer pays that amount.

4. If no sellers make offers, the specialist may sell shares from his own inventory for the ask price, or $57.25.

As a result, the buyer pays between $56.75 and $57.25 a share, plus a commission to the specialist (usually a small firm or partnership) of $170. (This is not a cheap broker!)

Dealer market

A customer wants to buy 200 shares of Rockshox, which trades on Nasdaq under the symbol RSHX. A broker takes the order and sends it down to his firm's own over-the-counter desk, where the chief trader looks at his computer screen and sees several different price quotes for Rockshox, which is very actively traded.

Among the quotes from the seven market makers, who buy and sell shares for their own accounts, are the following:

1. Adams & Co. is willing to buy shares of RSHX for $14.25 and sell them for $15.50, for a spread of $1.25.

2. Chance Securities will buy shares for $14.50 and sell them for $15.25, a spread of 75 cents.

3. Wiley & Sons will buy shares of RSHX for $14.25 and sell them at $15.25, a spread of $1.

4. Rich Associates will buy shares for $14.75 and sell them for $15.25, a spread of 50 cents.

The "inside spread" or best bid and ask price, is buying at $14.75 and selling at $15.25. So the customer will pay $15.25 a share—though the broker will probably fill the order itself at that price, rather than send it to the lowest seller.

The fact that Rich Associates does not automatically get the business has in the past discouraged Nasdaq market makers from competing on price (something that has changed somewhat under new rules that took effect in August 1997). A lower price might have been available, but a customer would have no way to know.

The new rules let investors submit limit orders to buy or sell at a specific price rather than at the market and the order must be disclosed to other traders. A second change increases the visibility of orders in electronic markets, like Instinet, and on all of the Nasdaq machines. Small stocks with moderate volume and previously large spreads are most likely to benefit from the new rules.

The customer in our example gets his shares of Rockshox for $15.25 each, or $3,050, and pays a commission of just $40. (Rich Associates is a discount broker!) The firm doing the trading also makes at least 50 cents a share on the trade, or $100.

LISTING REQUIREMENTS

Other ways in which Nasdaq differs from the traditional stock exchanges are its advanced technology, and listing requirements that are less difficult than those of the New York and American Stock Exchanges.

Nasdaq is really an over-the-telephone-and-computer market, and was the world's first electronic stock market when it was created in 1971. Today, with millions of investors around the world, it has more companies listed than any other market. It is also an area traditionally dominated by individual investors looking for bargains or bonanzas among the thousands of smaller or newer companies.

The original over-the-counter market stems from the days when securities were sold in banks and stores right along with money orders and prescriptions. Nowadays the OTC market is distinctly separate from Nasdaq, although both are regulated by the National Association of Securities Dealers (NASD).

Stocks that trade on Nasdaq are listed separately in the financial pages of newspapers under the heading "Nasdaq National Market." Over-the-counter companies tend to be even smaller and less well-known than those trading on Nasdaq, or on the New York and American Stock Exchanges. The stocks of these companies are listed in the "pink sheets" (named for their color) published daily by the National Quotation Bureau, which give the bid and asked prices for 13,000 stocks along with the names of market makers.

An electronic version of the pink sheets, called the OTC Bulletin Board, helps make a market for 5,000 stocks that are too thinly traded to be listed on Nasdaq or any stock exchange. Brokers have access to the Bulletin Board via computer and can match buyers and sellers of the smaller stocks to make trades, says Alfred Berkeley, Nasdaq president. As yet investors can't access the OTC Bulletin Board directly.

Pink sheet stocks usually have much lower prices but higher risk levels because of their volatility. And since they are not owned by institutions or followed by analysts, research on them is not very abundant. However, this can work to your advantage, since it means neither Wall Street nor the public has run up the price.

Even if technology stocks take a dive, many strategists are bullish long term about small cap stocks, especially those listed on Nasdaq. Keith Mullins of Salomon Smith Barney, for example, sees Nasdaq getting a boost from strong-performing financial and service industry stocks. But there are caveats, of course.

Once in a while you'll find a stock that has been delisted for some reason, or is bankrupt. All securities listed on Nasdaq are identified by a four- or five-letter symbol. The fifth letter indicates issues that aren't common or capital shares, or are subject to restrictions or special conditions, including:

C—Exempt from Nasdaq listing for a limited period

D—New issue of an existing stock

E—Delinquent in required filings with Securities and Exchange Commission (SEC)

F—Foreign company

Q—Currently in bankruptcy proceedings

Z—Miscellaneous situations, including any unit that represents a limited partnership interest

Mullins's advice on trading in stocks selling for under $10: Don't buy a pink sheet stock unless you can obtain adequate information on the company from reliable sources. Even then, stick to OTC stocks that trade frequently and are listed either on Nasdaq's Small Order Execution System or on the OTC Bulletin Board.

To qualify for a Nasdaq listing, either for the National Market, which has some 3,200 companies, or the Small Cap Market with 1,300 stocks, a company must have pretax income for the most recent year of only $400,000, and it needs just 100,000 publicly held shares. By comparison, pretax income and shares are $750,000 and 500,000 on the American Stock Exchange, and $2.5 million and 1.1 million on the New York Stock Exchange.

TRADERS AND SPECIALISTS

Trades of small stocks take place mostly on the American Stock Exchange and over Nasdaq's network of computer terminals or screen-based workstations. There are some 250,000 terminals receiving Nasdaq trading information in 55 countries, so your trade and all others can be viewed by brokers and investors around the world.

On the major and regional exchanges, specialists in OTC stocks match buy and sell orders received from brokerage firms. But when you trade on Nasdaq, your broker will fill your order from his inventory or buy the stock from another broker who makes a market in it and then sell it to you. (A market maker is to Nasdaq what a specialist is on the exchanges.)

So trading in small stocks can be an expensive proposition with hidden transaction costs if you don't watch out for them. As we've seen in the description of the dealer market, brokers can receive a payment for funneling orders through one dealer. Clearly, that's an additional cost to the dealer who may recoup that cost by increasing the bid and asked prices for those stocks.

If that's the case, guess who's paying extra? Big traders know this and won't stand for the additional charges. And you can fight this potential abuse yourself by ordering your broker to execute your transactions on Nasdaq's Small Order Execution System or over the OTC Bulletin Board where all trades are viewed by everyone.

On the exchanges, the difference between bid and ask prices, the spread, is just a few pennies. But on Nasdaq, the market makers negotiate the prices, and spreads are typically larger—as much as 25 percent for some highly speculative issues.

How do you find quality small stocks and avoid getting burned? "Start in your own backyard," advises John Jensen of Cadence Capital Management in Boston. Research companies in your region and check with a local broker for ideas. Read annual reports or prospectuses and visit the company yourself if possible.

Get into the habit of sizing up any company with which you have dealings for its investment potential. Fidelity's Peter Lynch made frequent use of this technique. If he stayed at a motel he liked during his many research trips, he'd study up on the stock. And if the financial performance looked good, the debt level wasn't too high, and the growth rate seemed sustainable, he'd buy the stock.

If and when you believe big stocks are overpriced, as many observers believe they are, it may be time to move some of your portfolio into small caps. Many are still undervalued by historical standards, and if analysts become interested it can only boost prices. This is also fertile ground occasionally for takeover candidates.

"We're seeing small company growth stock earnings paralleling, if not exceeding, those of large caps either annually or sequentially," says Gerald Perritt, publisher of the *Mutual Fund Letter*.

Finding the real pearls among the faux could become easier under tougher listing standards being proposed for stocks that trade on the Nasdaq National and Small Cap Markets. The standards, if approved by the Securities and Exchange Commission, would increase the minimum stock value to $1 million, and change the assets measure to $2 million in *tangible* assets—a tougher measure that doesn't count "goodwill" such as value of a franchise or brand names.

For national market stocks, the biggest of small companies, minimum stock value would rise to $5 million and tangible assets to $4 million. The proposal would also require small cap companies to have the same corporate requirements as national market stocks, such as independent directors and an audit committee subject to peer review.

"The goal is to achieve the proper balance," explains Alfred Berkeley, Nasdaq president, "giving small entrepreneurial companies access to capital and providing investors with quality stocks." It should also help address some of the complaints about Nasdaq's order system—namely, that some brokers fail to honor their pledge to stand ready to "make a market" in OTC stocks at all times.

RULES OF THE TRADE

The new rules won't affect the way you do business with your broker, but your broker will find it easier to contact market makers for the stocks you want to buy. Both big and small brokers are enthusiastic. "It's a step to insure that individual investors get a fair shot in OTC trading," says pioneer discount broker Muriel Siebert.

Consider Apollo Group, the company that provides higher-education services to working adults. At one point, market makers were quoting a best bid price of $33.50 and a best ask price of $34. Under the new rules, an investor who chose to submit a limit order between those prices, say $33.75, would see one of two things happen. Either the market maker would do the trade at that price, or post the order for all to see, effectively narrowing the spread to 25 cents.

That would benefit any trader who wanted to sell the stock, and would likely lead to the filling of the limit order. The old way, the market makers did not have to disclose the order to other traders, and did not have to fill it themselves unless they traded the stock for their own accounts. "Finally, we're starting to build a market for the customers," says Junius Peake, professor at the University of Northern Colorado and long-time proponent of more open markets.

The change will mean savings for individual investors as they slice the markup dealers charge when they buy and sell stocks. "Among many stocks, you're going to see 40 to 50 percent reductions in trading costs," says Peake. That can really add up for serious investors interested in small company issues.

It could also calm the "whipsaw volatility" of many small cap stocks, where any news or perception of change can violently swing stock prices in this superheated market. Indeed, most of the *Fortune* 100 fastest-growing companies are relatively small, which is why most (83) call Nasdaq home—at least for now.

While investment advisers downplay the significance of Nasdaq 1500, just as they dismissed Dow 7000, the milestone underscores a stunning ascent for "the market for the next 100 years." Nasdaq has rocketed 209 percent since this bull market began in October 1990, versus 99 percent for the Dow over the same period.

Technology stocks have been leading the Nasdaq charge, as optimism builds about the future of computers and information systems. The huge gains are raising concerns that technology stocks have jumped too high and could all tumble. Even if they do, many strategists still are bullish about the long-term prospects of small cap stocks.

In his book, *A Random Walk Down Wall Street*, Princeton University Professor Burton Malkiel wrote, "A substantial amount (but not all) of the risk of investing can be eliminated by a program of long-term ownership of common stocks." This buy-and-hold philosophy doesn't mean you should stick with companies that have stopped growing or have fallen victim to poor management. Malkiel himself is a speedy seller of losing stocks.

One bellwether: The software giant Microsoft can skew the Nasdaq index if it reports earnings only slightly below analysts' estimates. Other fledgling Nasdaq-listed stocks have also become major companies (Intel, Compaq) but continue to trade on the electronic market.

"We have seen no advantage to other exchanges," says Intel spokesman Howard High. "We started there and it has served us well." In the past, many companies, as they got bigger chose to move to the more prestigious New York Stock Exchange. But that isn't the case anymore. Many like Nasdaq's reputation as a place for emerging or rapidly growing companies and stay there.

The stock market also performs differently now than in the past. The impact of just two sectors—finance and technology—on stock indexes has been enormous. That, analysts argue, may mean the market deserves the heady valuations it has enjoyed in recent years.

"This is not your father's index," says Thomas McManus, investment strategist at NatWest Securities. "The S&P 500 is higher growth, more global, less cyclical and more diversified than it has ever been and merits higher price-earnings ratios."

A similar phenomenon has occurred with the Dow Jones Industrial Average. Recent changes increased the representation of technology, finance and health sectors while reducing cyclical and industrial companies. Like Nasdaq, "stock indexes try to add exciting, liquid companies," notes McManus. "That always applies to growth stocks."

CHOOSING SMALL STOCKS

Now that you know about the markets, you can start looking for those hot stocks. For the serious investor, that means competing with millions of others in a fascinating game of finding the winners. But be careful: There are usually more losers than winners among those hot stocks. Wildly daring investors grab for a fast ride—hoping they can jump off before the crash.

It may seem odd then to suggest that small stocks are the best investment for the next decade. However, over time, they offer the largest total returns of any asset class. Sure, they may be outshone by blue chips one year, and real estate the next. Still, over ten-year spans, small companies are the most profitable and consistent performers.

Latching on to a fast-growing small stock as it shoots for the sky can be an exciting financial experience. Nothing else compares to it. Consider if you had invested $10,000 in any of the following stocks just ten years ago. Here's what you would have made:

Cisco	$744,000
Microsoft	$720,000
Oracle	$564,000

Amgen	$328,000
Intel	$215,000
Sun Microsystems	$170,000

Of course, it's not easy to pick the next Microsoft or Wal-Mart. But your odds have never been better. Economic conditions are perfect for sending the entire small stock category higher, and a few stocks will go skyrocketing on a journey that will make savvy investors wealthy.

The risks in picking the wrong small stock are equally great. When you buy a big stock like General Motors, its size acts as an insurance policy against total disaster. You're not going to double your money in a year or two, but neither are you going to lose it all. You can be virtually certain the company will be in business five or ten years from now.

In contrast, smaller companies are more vulnerable to unsure management, poor marketing and increasing competition. And while a small company may race at full sail over economic waters in good weather, a recessionary storm—or even a single bad quarter—can capsize it.

The risks of stocks, especially those of small companies, shouldn't scare you away. Instead, you should weigh them against your own self-interest and financial need—now and in the future. Some risks you can do nothing but watch: economic growth, interest rates, and market cycles. Take some consolation in the fact that the market tends to move higher over time, big drops notwithstanding.

The risks that are specific to a company are ones you can sort out. Is management competent? Is the product a fad? Do competitors have advantages of one sort or another? Those are just a few of the possible concerns in picking a stock. You may not be able to answer them all. But you should, in most instances, be able to answer enough of them to make an informed decision. If you can't, don't buy the stock.

"Everyone wants to be rich, but few want to work at it," says Richard Driehaus, who manages $1.9 billion not only in small caps but also in mid-cap and foreign stocks. "The question is not how many winners and losers you have, but how much do you make on the winners and how quickly do you cut your losses."

It's fun to find winners and climb aboard for a profitable ride. But you have to keep your eyes open for whatever it is that will bring the train to a screeching halt. You want to get off before that happens. Although the market for small issues is highly volatile, in the long run such stocks tend to produce higher returns than big stocks.

Andrew Lanyi, who heads his own research division at Oppenheimer & Co., has made a name for himself with a mixture of stock-picking acumen and shameless self-promotion. His profile appears in silhouette on coffee mugs, letter openers, tee shirts, and the cover of his book, *Confessions of a Stockbroker*. It's even on his research reports.

Nevertheless, his results are hard to argue with, say clients who entrust him with more than $170 million. Like many others, Lanyi looks for what he thinks are undiscovered blue chips. "The trick is you have to know more than others do," he says.

In that area, Lanyi's tactics are more traditional—and profitable. He looks for sales and earnings growth that meets lofty goals. He grills executives on management strategies. And he talks with outsiders such as suppliers and printers to gauge inventory shifts and customer satisfaction.

WHAT'S WEALTH TO YOU?

However you do your screening, realize that common stocks are the single best investment you can make over time. If you can accept their volatility, small cap stocks are the best way to make (or lose) big bucks in the stock market. The premise: Find a company with a unique product or service, buy the stock cheap, ride it high, and bail out if you have to. You can expect a rougher ride than you would get with those big blue chips.

The task may seem overwhelming at first. Newspapers seldom report on small companies, and Wall Street firms tend to ignore them. Yet this lack of information makes small stocks even more attractive to risk-taking investors, who feel they have a chance of seeing something in a small or new company that no one else sees.

The valuation criteria for small stocks is also different from those of other stocks. Since you are buying future earnings, you can expect a company that produces 40-percent annual gains to carry a higher price tag than one that produces 10-percent gains. That's why you'll find the price-earnings ratios of a few growth companies up in the stratosphere.

For a better value, add the stock to your portfolio on the down tick. Often when a small company comes up short of what money managers expect in quarterly results, the pros will dump the stock. It isn't unheard of for a small stock to drop 30 to 40 percent in one day on an earnings disappointment. If you're following that company, such dips can present an opportunity to add it to your portfolio. Just be sure the slippage was minor and not a prelude to disaster. The stock probably won't recover very fast, so you have some time to do your homework.

Value investing is not the same as growth investing, but it may be more suitable to an individual investor who is managing his own money and not that of others. Of course, you can use either style according to your personality and investment goals. Let's look at how the two differ, whether we're talking about individual stocks or small cap funds.

VALUE INVESTING. Money managers who look for value seek out companies with a low price compared to book value (the company's assets on its balance sheet less any liabilities). Growth is not that big a deal to a value stock manager, and he may even seek out companies whose stocks have fallen on hard times, who have been abandoned by analysts, but whose futures are brighter than others may think.

Historically, when stocks trade below book value, the market will in time recognize a bargain and the shares will be bid up in price. The value investor likes to get in early, when no one is looking. The problems are timing and patience. Other characteristics of value stocks may include low price-earnings ratios and "hidden assets" in the form of property or patents.

GROWTH INVESTING. Most growth managers look for companies they fully expect to grow faster than the economy as a whole. Their emphasis is on a perceived strong trend in sales and earnings for a product or service. They also seek companies in industries showing sustained growth trends.

The most important factor is price. Companies with high rates of growth sell at high price-earnings ratios, and the expectation is that their growth will catch up with the high valuations. Some do, and some don't. And if something goes wrong, you're going to suffer swiftly. Other features of winning growth stocks are strong management, and attractive industry or niche.

Small growth stocks are not for everyone. For those willing to take a bigger than average risk with part of their portfolio, the excitement, challenge and rewards of small cap stocks are unparalleled.

The biggest mistake you can make is not investing at all. The market constantly changes, and no one stock (or any other investment) is right for all seasons. Don't buy a stock, even a blue chip, and never look at it again. The company could be taken over, enter bankruptcy, or just have a bad year. In each case, you should be ready to take some form of action—buy more shares, sell all of your shares, or sell some of your shares.

As we've seen, the best places to start looking for small companies that can make you rich faster, are Nasdaq and the less formal over-the-counter market—home to 4,500 and 13,000 stocks, respectively, and to foreign-based issues and initial public offerings.

Right now, a portion of your portfolio ought to be earmarked for some of these speculative plays. Start slowly by limiting your commitment to no more than 15 percent of your funds. If you are smart enough to make a killing, put half your earnings into some additional small stocks for safety and diversification.

Remember, it's easier to speculate in a rising market. Worthwhile gains will come when more people buy shares—which isn't likely in a down market. Be willing to take quick, small losses, but don't hold on blindly in hope of a recovery. In most cases, small stocks are profitable primarily because of market fluctuations.

Good hunting!

INVESTOR INFORMATION

Two of the more readable treatments of investing in the stock market are *A Random Walk Down Wall Street*, by Princeton Professor Burton Malkiel, and premier stock-picker Andrew Lanyi's *Confessions of a Stock-broker*.

You can also obtain the *Nasdaq Company Directory and Fact Book*, which lists all traded stocks with their symbols, addresses, and telephone numbers, from the National Association of Securities Dealers, Box 9403, Gaithersburg, MD 20898 (202-728-8000).

A list of publications covering stocks and bonds, financial statements, and where to get help when you invest is available from the New York Stock Exchange, 11 Wall St., New York, NY 10005 (212-656-3000).

The Key to Profits

The times are changing, and so are the stock markets. Discount and regional brokers, as close as your Internet provider, have dramatically lowered the cost of trading stocks. Mutual funds now outnumber all of the companies traded on the New York and American Stock Exchanges. And you can screen stocks or funds on your personal computer by the thousands—or watch the markets all day long on CNN or CNBC.

How does all this affect the hoary advice we hear? Buy quality stocks and hold them for the long-term. Don't try to time the market. Use dollar-cost averaging to buy stocks or stock funds. The advice still rings true, according to the experts.

Profitable investing can be remarkably simple. That may sound surprising, given the jargon of Wall Street and its exotic world of options, futures, commodities, penny stocks and limited partnerships. But there is much you can safely ignore—and you won't lose money (or sleep) by avoiding some of the more arcane investments around.

What you need to know at the outset is that saving is not the same thing as investing. Savings accounts, certificates of deposit, money market funds, Treasury bills, and short-term bond funds eschew high returns in favor of safety and security. This is emergency money you can get at easily and quickly.

Investing, on the other hand, is best thought of as a long-term activity. That means years, not months, and high returns that keep you ahead of taxes and inflation. You should not begin investing until you've built up adequate emergency savings. But you should start as early as you can so that you accumulate enough money to pay for long-range goals, such as college for your children or a comfortable retirement for yourself.

If those objectives fall somewhere between five and ten years on your investment horizon, you can afford to step up the risk component of your portfolio, devoting more of it to growth stocks and less to Treasury bills. Then as your objective approaches, you can skew your portfolio increasingly to income investments.

Farther out, you can start to enjoy an investment plan that encompasses the entire range of stocks as well as other interesting, albeit more risky, vehicles such as new issues, warrants, options, and margin trading. Go ahead and take some risks now, when you have time to recover. You'll either get very rich—or have one less regret in your old age.

We've all heard stories about the person who is able to retire comfortably at age 50 or the investor who doubled his or her money in just two years. These stories only add to our feelings of inadequacy. Not to worry. With a little guidance, you, too, can do a lot to improve your finances.

If you can tolerate the ups and downs, it can make good sense to put 15, 25, or even 40 percent of your retirement money in small cap stocks or mutual funds. They usually make money for investors who are willing to hold them for at least five years. With the benefits of compounding, you can reasonably expect to double the value of your money.

FINDING QUALITY STOCKS

In the stock market, quality is determined by a company's acceptance, financial strength, management, profitability, and rate of growth. But don't think it's easy to pick growth stocks from among the thousands of small, unseasoned companies that sell shares to the public.

"If you look at ten companies, you'll find one that's interesting," says famed stock picker Peter Lynch. "If you look at 20, you'll find two. And if you look at 100, you'll find ten. The person who turns over the most rocks wins the game!"

The perils of the stock market are also well known. On any day, you're likely to find a few stocks that have been knocked down 30 percent, or even more. And while the victims are usually the stocks of smaller companies, major corporations are not immune to a selling frenzy.

Sometimes, the fever spreads through the entire market. Those market drops can be nerve-wracking for investors. But while the terror is well known, the virtues of stock market investing do not receive nearly enough attention. Probably more retirees have been pummeled by being too cautious and playing it safe, than have lost big money in overly risky investments.

"Even smart investors panic when they see prices falling rapidly," says Chuck Carlson, editor of the *Dow Theory Forecasts* newsletter. But you should know that market corrections are an inevitable part of investing. This is especially true for those investors who are new to the market—and have only experienced the best of times. As of April 1997, the stock market hadn't experienced a decline of more than 10 percent since the summer of 1990, when Saddam Hussein's forces invaded Kuwait to ignite the Gulf War.

During a selling frenzy, short-sighted investors, along with many Wall Street pros, often throw out good stocks with the bad ones. As a result, shares of some terrific companies may trade at very attractive prices. To spot the bargains, and increase your chances of finding quality stocks, look for the following:

IMPROVING PROFITS. This is an excellent test, because wider profit margins almost always indicate increased earnings within a short period. The gross profit margin shows a company's operating income, before taxes, as a percentage of revenues, and is calculated by dividing income by net sales.

Generally, a gross profit margin of 12 percent or more indicates a company that deserves further study. Anything below that, especially when it is lower than the previous year, is a danger signal. The gross profit margin is very useful in comparing companies within a given industry. But avoid comparison with other sectors, which can be misleading.

PLOWED-BACK EARNINGS. The fastest-growing companies like Microsoft or Staples almost never pay dividends. They reason that by reinvesting a substantial portion of profits, as much as 70 percent, a company can speed expansion and improve production capacity. And corporations that plow back 15 percent or more of invested capital each year will double in real worth in five years.

Growth stocks also come in all sizes, so it's not always easy to spot them. The retailing business, for example, is hardly a growth industry. Margins are often razor-thin, and sales ebb and flow with the economy. But two of them—Wal-Mart and Home Depot—are among the most vital growth stocks in recent memory.

RESEARCH AND DEVELOPMENT. A company that uses earnings largely for new plants and equipment will improve its efficiency and the quality of its products, but it may not grow as fast as a company that spends wisely to develop new or better products.

A prime test for management is whether the company is spending a higher than average percentage of revenues for research and new product development. With good management, this constitutes the most creative, dynamic force for growth available for any corporation. Thousands of dollars used for research often make possible millions of dollars in additional sales and profits.

One caveat: Be particularly wary of companies with no product or revenues, only an idea. The biotech industry is rife with these long shots. Should they ever show promise, it won't be too late to get on the band wagon after they show a profit.

BIG BANG THEORY

If you have a lump sum to invest and won't need the money for a while, the reasoning goes, dump it into stocks or stock funds all at once for a big bang. The thinking is that because stocks rise over the long haul, nearly everyone will almost surely be better off investing all of his or her money immediately rather than gradually.

That advice may have worked during most of the past seven years, but had you followed it in 1976 instead of 1990, the result would have been far different (even without the crash in 1987). Then anyone not fully invested or using *dollar-cost averaging* to buy stocks looked like a genius. And those who sold immediately after the crash, which saw the Dow drop 23 percent in one day, came to regret their cowardice.

The Dow bottomed out rather quickly and has since appreciated fivefold. The lesson from this and subsequent rapid declines, as we've seen, is that any time stock prices fall significantly, it's time to step up your purchases because that signifies a profitable buying opportunity. And if you do so over time, it's impossible to invest it all at the top of the market.

Many investors also go astray because they try to dart in and out of the financial markets at just the right moment to obtain the highest possible returns. This technique, called *market timing*, almost never works over the long run.

DOLLAR-COST AVERAGING. Think of it as investing on the installment plan—something you may already be doing when you make regular contributions to a mutual fund or retirement account where you work. If stock prices go up, you can congratulate yourself for having earned good profits. And if they go down, you pick up some bargains.

Dollar-cost averaging also can be used to buy shares of individual stocks, but brokerage fees on small transactions of less than 100 shares (called odd lots) can be prohibitively high unless you use a discount broker. Better to save until you can make the larger purchase—and do some additional research in the meantime.

Look at dollar-cost averaging as a defensive strategy. It will keep you from getting crushed in the wild up-and-down swings of most small stocks. Also, you'll avoid two common errors: putting all your money into the market when it might be heading for a tumble, and selling out at big losses when stocks are deeply depressed.

MARKET TIMING. As we've said, attempting to figure out when the market is due for a massive rally or steep decline seldom profits even the professional money managers, and they have all day and lots of resources at their command. Rest assured you probably will fail miserably and be sorry that you tried.

Instead, if you think you can assess the market, you may want to "tilt" your portfolio slightly toward undervalued stocks and away from the high-priced ones. If you guess right, you will add substantial profits to your portfolio. And even if you guess wrong, you will understand the market better.

This sort of tacit asset allocation doesn't involve the rapid or large-scale movement of funds among various investment markets. In fact, it can be as simple or complex as you want to make it. The foremost consideration: Knowing when you'll need money to meet expenses or other obligations.

If your goals are long-term, it probably makes sense for at least half or two-thirds of your investments to be made in stocks. That way, you can tap into their potential for inflation-beating returns, and you'll have time to ride out the market turbulence that is likely to occur along the way.

Roger Gibson, Pittsburgh money manager and author of *Asset Allocation*, recommends that investors under age 60 maintain at least a 70-percent stake in stocks. "Even then, your money needs to keep growing faster than inflation," he says. Life expectancy of the typical 60-year-old is now 83 for men and 87 for women.

VALUE OR MOMENTUM?

Price doesn't seem to matter anymore. Momentum investing has been in the limelight for most of this decade. "Buy high and sell higher" has been the watchword. And investors seem to have no qualms about owning stocks selling at 30, 40, even 50 times earnings if a company's growth warrants such high valuation.

Many of today's investors have been weaned on the advice of William O'Neill, in his book, *How to Make Money in Stocks*. Among his tenets: "Price-earnings ratios have very little to do with whether a stock should be bought or not." Over the past forty years, his research suggests that "you probably eliminated all of the outstanding companies in America if you weren't willing to pay 30 or 40 times earnings."

But some fund managers think enough is enough and have bid down prices of small midsize stocks with stratospheric price-earnings ratios. "A company that's growing is more valuable than a company that's not," says Ralph Wanger, who invests in small stocks through his Acorn Fund, "but it's not infinitely more valuable."

Even so, research by Jeremy Siegel, professor at the University of Pennsylvania's Wharton School, shows that his "Nifty 50" premier growth stocks of the early Seventies sported an average price-earnings ratio of 37. Some took a beating, but the more successful companies still generated double-digit returns for the next 20 years. "Avoiding pricey stocks," he says, "means never investing in companies capable of doubling or quadrupling in price in a few years."

In the last 35 years there have been eight cycles of bull and bear markets. The bull markets have lasted longer and produced gains far in excess of the losses sustained during the market downturns. Investors who abandon quality stocks when share prices fall often regret the decision because they fail to get back into the market in time to take advantage of meaningful gains. Just ask those who sold stocks after the crash in 1987.

There are plenty of other ways to ratchet your risk down without unloading your stock market holdings. For starters, make sure you have divided your investments among different sectors of the market. It is not enough to spread your money among a number of stocks if many of those stocks are from companies in the same industry or are affected similarly by economic factors and market conditions.

GO BARGAIN HUNTING. "There are exceptions, but small and mid-cap stocks appear more attractive than large caps," says Charles Crane, value investor and chief market strategist for Key Asset Management, which oversees some $52 billion for its clients.

The sectors he likes are basic industry and natural gas, which have good prospects for positive earnings surprises in an accelerating economy. Crane also thinks international stocks deserve some attention and suggests a mix of emerging foreign markets, such as Russia and China for a long-term investor, along with more mature markets, such as Japan. "If the market tumbles, small caps and international funds shouldn't fall as hard as big company stocks," he says.

"Don't be afraid to sell a stock that has reached its price objective, where it is fully valued," he advises. Take your profits, or at least set stop-loss prices for stocks with price-earnings ratios of 30 or higher. Crane tends to hold his small stock picks for four or five years, in sharp contrast to other money managers who are constantly in and out of high-tech stocks as products change and earnings dip.

What he looks for is undervalued companies, as do most value managers, but he also tries to find the ones that aren't going to stay undervalued very long. The real test: Profits must increase as well as revenues, and you have to ignore the hype that surrounds new companies.

BUYING INTO BOOMLETS

We'd probably all like to have a piece of the profits of businesses that are near-monopolies. In fact, you can. They won't be giants like General Motors or even Microsoft, but more likely unglamorous companies that churn out such products as ice cream cartons, football uniforms, or recycled plastic bottles.

Operating outside Wall Street's glare, they often trade at modest price-earnings ratios. Debt is minimal or nonexistent, and because of their dominance in their respective markets, profits tend to rise steadily. Such companies are called *niche stocks* (remember?), and many combine the ability to make lots of money in good times with the strength to muddle through in hard times.

Don't make the mistake of confusing a niche with a fad. Remember solar heaters? Gasohol refiners? Fads attract "me-too" competitors. So the trick is to separate the enduring from the transitory when buying into the next profitable boomlet.

Your own knowledge about a product line or an industry can lead you to a niche company. So can annual reports and 10-K forms, regional brokers, investment newsletters, or reference sources like Value Line and Standard & Poor's.

Beware of placing heavy emphasis on a brokerage firm's research reports. Analysts often face heavy pressure to see a bright and sunny outlook even when dark clouds may be rolling in rapidly. Negative reports in print are relatively rare, and even then analysts avoid saying "sell" and rely instead on the softer-sounding "hold" advice. One firm even rated poorly performing stocks as "long-term attractive" to its investment banking clients!

SOME FUTURE STOCKS

Let's go afield for what some "futurists" see as tomorrow's products and companies. If you ask the trend experts, along with venture capitalists, business school professors, and owners of small enterprises for their list of the potentially fastest-growing areas of the economy in the coming century, they will usually mention the following:

DATA PROCESSING. Competition has brought a series of failures, but many survivors of the shakeout should do well. The future looks bright for those companies that bring unique products or special capabilities to a crowded field.

"Education is a phenomenally untapped growth industry, from the standpoint of providing all kinds of people with ways to upgrade their skills," says Lowell Catlett, Ph.D., economist and professor at New Mexico State University. "Anything you can do to link technology to careers and lifestyles will have a tremendous impact."

HEALTH AND FITNESS. Americans spend close to $800 billion a year on health care, with much of it going to hospitals or nursing homes. So there will be plentiful opportunities for making, selling or servicing medical equipment used in the home, for exercise equipment, and for "alternative medicine" specialists of all kinds.

"We see a lot of stuff opening in health care," says Faith Popcorn, chairman and strategist at BrainReserve, widely recognized as an expert on business trends. As new kinds of physical therapy come to the fore, demand will rise for yoga practitioners, nutritionists, even aroma therapists. "With so many people doing so many things, the service industry is going to be very important."

GENETICS. Drug stocks and biotech firms with a monopoly in the field of genetic engineering should be leaders in the next century. Genentech's sales, for example, have grown steadily since its start-up in the early 1980's, while similar firms have floundered.

Some of the best possibilities for smaller firms in the area are in support fields—manufacturing laboratory equipment or producing enzymes for use in genetic research and vaccine development.

TELECOMMUNICATIONS. "The Internet is a tool that can take a traditional product or service and change the ways of selling it," notes Professor Catlett. "Every small company will have to look at it as a marketplace, so that when trends change you can respond to them."

The computers in all Wal-Mart stores are already linked to Procter & Gamble, and can actually gauge production based on which products are selling in certain parts of the country or worldwide. It makes them more efficient and responsive.

In all these areas, you have to be particularly careful when selecting stocks. Few of us know enough about technology to judge whether or not any widely hyped product represents a genuine profit-making opportunity. There are ways to become more trend-savvy, though. Every month, buy a magazine that you don't usually read, totally outside your particular field. You'll be surprised at what you find. Pick out an emerging technology and follow it carefully. Once you've done your homework, you can consider putting cash into those companies that are most effectively pioneering new products.

SINS OF INVESTORS

Managing an individual investment portfolio is no easy task. Too many people go astray because they commit one or more of the seven deadly sins of investing. Of the seven, pride and sloth can put you in the poorhouse fastest. But there are savvy ways to avoid them all.

When it comes to personal finances, just about everyone sins a little. "Many have no plan or goal," says Richard Michi, a financial planner in Chicago. "They either rush to follow the herd or procrastinate and do nothing."

Here, from financial advisers, are strategies to avoid pride and sloth as well as the other common sins of investors: avarice, lust, anger, gluttony, and envy.

PRIDE. When you make a mistake don't sit watching your savings dwindle away. Show some true grit by looking at your losses and saying the difficult words, "I was wrong."

Admitting mistakes and rectifying them takes more than humility—it takes courage. Even professional investors often lack the stomach to pull out of a deal that's gone sour, Michi says. Stubborn pride makes them ride a loser all the way down. "Let your winners run and cut your losses short," he says.

SLOTH. To a novice, investing can seem like a magic trick. It's not. The work isn't that difficult, but you need to set some goals and know what types of investments are most appropriate for your situation.

One of the biggest investment mistakes is failing to start early enough. If you invest just $3,900 a year when you are 25, for instance, you can accumulate a $1 million retirement nest egg by the time you're 65—assuming your investments earn at least 8 percent a year.

AVARICE. Some investors are tight-fisted and hold on to a dime even after they've made a dollar. Once you've doubled your money, take a small profit. At that point, you've made back the initial investment. The rest is gravy.

Penny-pinchers also fret a lot over taxes. Sit down and do some figuring. Ask yourself if the return on a tax-free investment is really greater than the after-tax profit on a taxable one. And don't do something really dumb, such as buying municipal bonds for an IRA (which is already tax-exempt).

LUST. You wouldn't buy a $300 leather jacket solely on a salesperson's recommendation. But many investors will spend much more than that on a hot tip that backfires. "If you follow tips, just be sure you're gambling money that you can afford to lose," advises Seattle investment adviser William Donoghue.

"If it looks too good to be true, it probably is," he says. Promotional come-ons that arrive by mail or phone are easy to avoid. But it's harder to resist an inside story from a friend or co-worker. Do your own research and decide for yourself no matter what the investment. "Be skeptical but not cynical," says Michi.

ANGER. It's perfectly natural to get excited about an investment and feel let down when nothing happens—or when you lose money. But it's a mistake to get angry. Patience is an advantage investors have over mutual funds and other institutions.

"They (institutional investors) have to perform *this* year and must drop any losers at year end," Donoghue says. "Individual investors can hold on to slow movers that the institutions can't." The longer the time frame, the more likely you are to show a profit.

GLUTTONY. If avarice involves penny-pinching, gluttony is a more extravagant form of greed. The glutton overreaches and lacks discipline. He needs to go on a financial diet, or at least tighten his belt.

The glutton is so impatient that he frequently trades stocks and buys something from a greener pasture. Such trading can be costly. Say your 100 shares of a $20 stock go up to $22. When you figure in commission, your shares really cost $2,050. If you sell for a $50 commission, you'd get $2,100—a 5-percent gain, pretax (not much better than passbook savings).

ENVY. Many investors are unwilling to wait for long-term results, says Sheldon Jacobs, publisher of the *No-Load Fund Investor* newsletter. They act emotionally rather than rationally.

They jump on the envy bandwagon, chasing what was hot last year, last month, even last week—to their financial ruin. Remember the Aesop fable of the tortoise and the hare? The moral is extremely valuable to even the most experienced investor.

INVESTOR INFORMATION

Check the library before buying any books on investing (except this one). *Beating the Street*, by legendary stock picker Peter Lynch is easy to read and makes it all sound simple. For more insights, check out *Stocks for the Long Run*, by Jeremy Siegel.

Those with a statistical bent, or budding value investors, might consider the classic *Security Analysis*, by Benjamin Graham and David Dodd. It's not as daunting as you might think. "Markets are wrong most of the time," says one of the co-authors.

For the not-too-distant future, read about business trends, new products, and cutting-edge opportunities in *The Popcorn Report*. Best-selling author Faith Popcorn is widely recognized as America's foremost trend expert.

CHAPTER 4

In Your Own Backyard

Put on your investor's hat and consider a little geography. You know, for example, that you can invest in oil companies in Oklahoma, electronics firms in California, ski resorts in New Hampshire, and furniture makers in North Carolina. But unless you live nearby, you probably don't know that Ohio is home to the world's leading supplier of plastic compounds or that Colorado is the hub of the cable television industry, or that Maryland is headquarters for the biggest supplier of spices and flavorings.

Buying stock in companies in your own backyard—like Schulman, Jones Intercable, and McCormick—lets you keep a closer watch on your money. This gives you an edge over all but the biggest brokerage firms or mutual fund companies.

"A lot of portfolio managers don't seem to have much conviction or a lot of in-depth knowledge of their companies," says Lazlo Birinyi, who closely tracks the money flow in and out of stocks. They rush to buy or sell on changing recommendations of Wall Street analysts. But good news or bad news about a company has a way of reaching local folks long before finding its way into analysts' reports.

There are also sound financial reasons to invest close to home: You can often see firsthand how the business is being run, evaluate its products or services, and you may even know its employees or officers. Not everybody gets the same information at the same time—but you also have to know what to look for in small or emerging companies:

FINANCIALLY SOUND. That means a pattern of growth, profitability, and a strong or at least not super-leveraged balance sheet. Many of these companies pay no dividends and instead buy back their own shares.

They usually have aggressive management, a firm grip on their own market niche, and the potential for more profitable products in the future.

To find out whether a company is reeling from only a temporary setback instead of a terminal problem, look for long-term debt that is not greater than 40 percent of the company's total capitalization and less than 10 percent of annual sales. Often you can find hot stocks by making a cool evaluation of the people, products, and services you encounter on Main Street, not on Wall Street.

UNDERSTANDABLE BUSINESS. These are companies any intelligent investor can comprehend and analyze, from spice makers to plastics and antitheft devices. Personal experience can often lead successful small investors to stock market winners. For example, your kids might direct you to a new fast-food chain that is packed with hungry youngsters. Perhaps the stock is worth a nibble.

Ultimately, you should own five or ten stocks. That's a small enough number to be manageable and large enough for diversity. You will want to diversify among industries, too. That will provide extra protection. If, for example, you own only housing stocks and interest rates rise, you could get pummeled.

REASONABLY PRICED. Stock prices are so high today, they're sensitive to the slightest whiff of news or changes in the markets. The upside of this: It's easier for small investors to buy shares in young, unproven, and fast-growing companies. And if the business becomes large enough to attract big investors, the stock's price—and your profits—may jump dramatically.

Prices of these stocks are often low relative to their earnings. But for a better guide, use the ratio based on estimates of *future* earnings in the *Value Line Investment Survey* instead of newspaper stock tables, which are based on the previous 12 months' earnings.

Another reason to favor hometown stocks: They are not the ones you read about in the daily newspapers, nor are they the favorites of large institutions or professional managers. This makes investing in the institutions' relatively few favorites increasingly risky for the rest of us since the bottom could drop out of big stocks that fall from favor.

Unlike the large-scale traders, individual investors do not have to worry about causing market turbulence or justifying their stock picks to a fickle clientele. They can go prospecting in a market of some 10,000 or more stocks that most of the institutions ignore and few, if any, analysts bother with. As a class, these shares produce the biggest profits.

The Leuthold Group, a research firm that follows the historical performance of financial markets, tracks such "neglected" issues in its study of stocks with less than 30-percent institutional ownership. It also follows the "royal blues," stocks most heavily owned by institutions. For a 15-year period, Leuthold's neglected stocks rose 92 percent while the institutional favorites climbed only 54 percent.

THE JOY OF STOCKS

With the Dow setting all-time records, observers are claiming that this is the best economy ever. Stocks and stock funds can do no wrong it seems (unless they bet on bonds as Fidelity's Magellan did, to the chagrin of former manager Jeff Vinik).

"No pain, no gain" describes these financial markets to a tee. But if you want the joy of high returns without all the risks, be shy about investing in businesses you don't understand. "It should be a business you can explain to your teenage son or daughter," says Peter Lynch.

Let the professional money managers draw up their lists. Smart individual investors know that the key to discovering small cap gems is to look around you—at the products you personally find impressive, and the companies you find a cut above in their dealings with consumers. Start with your gut feelings and don't hurry.

Follow up with research on cocktail party stock tips if you want, but never think a small stock opportunity is so hot you'll miss the boat if you don't buy right away. "You didn't have to be there when Sam Walton opened his first Wal-Mart," says Lynch. "You don't need to be in at the moment of conception of any company."

Perhaps the biggest myth is that the way you rack up big gains is by trading in and out of small stocks quickly. Except for some very lucky speculators, that's a sure path to financial ruin. Most portfolio managers buy small stocks based on the company's potential and current value. Then they hang on for three to five years or longer, because it can take that long for a small company to bloom. The longer horizon also helps you deal with the fact that small stocks, with their lower prices and fewer shares outstanding, can be subject to dizzying short-term volatility.

Part of the beauty of small stocks is that they are low priced, often trading for $15 or $20 a share. That makes it possible to own ten or more small stocks in different industries, which lessens the pain if one of them flops. It is also one of the guidelines set down by the National Association of Investors Corporation, which suggests member clubs try to put 25 percent of their portfolios in small cap stocks with sales of $400 million or less.

"To beat the market you have to be patient," says Debbie Wilson, an accountant who started an investment club with ten of her clients in Darien, Wisconsin, almost ten years ago. "Some of my friends find that boring. But to watch your money grow is downright exciting in my book."

She recalls the club's first investment was Oracle Corporation, maker of computer software. After the $18-per-share purchase, the stock plummeted to $9. Some members wanted to unload, but Wilson thought it was best to ride it out, and they did. After two years, Oracle's stock price rebounded and the club eventually sold at $35, doubling its investment.

THE RICH HAVE A STRATEGY

In the previous century, the world's richest man was always someone associated with oil, from John D. Rockefeller to the Sultan of Brunei. But today, for the first time in human history, the world's richest man is a knowledge worker (see Figure 4.1). "We are at the onset of an era that might be better called man-made brainpower industries," says Lester Thurow, professor of economics and former dean of MIT's Sloan School of Management.

FIGURE 4.1. THE TEN RICHEST AMERICANS TODAY

Name	Industry
Bill Gates	Software
Warren Buffett	Investment
Paul Allen	Software
John Kluge	Media
Lawrence Ellison	Software
Philip Knight	Shoes
Sam Walton family	Retailing
Newhouse family	Media
Cox family	Media
Ronald Perelman	Leveraged buyouts

Source: Forbes

A third industrial revolution is creating big, new industries—computers and software, microelectronics, biotechnology, telecommunications, and designer-made materials. As with the advent of electrification, older industries are now being transformed by small or emerging companies.

Even the oil business has become a knowledge industry with four-dimensional acoustic sounding, horizontal drilling, and oil platforms working in water thousands of feet deep. Supercomputers are at the site of the Aramco geophysical center in Saudi Arabia. And "wildcat" success rates have quickly risen to the 40- to 50-percent range, and recovery rates have doubled when oil is found.

"The key distinguishing characteristic or common denominator is not information," says Thurow, "but rather a world in which skills and knowledge are the dominant sources of wealth. Microsoft's Bill Gates, now the world's richest man, is perhaps the best symbol of this shift."

Electronic retailing is going to produce very different shopping patterns, just as computerized ticketing has changed business travel plans. More movies are now watched at home than in movie theaters. And biotechnology is going to alter plants, animals, and human beings. "We can like it, or dislike it, but it is going to happen," says Thurow.

The creators of all this change and their fortunes can have an effect on the spirit, and not just Bill Gates and Warren Buffett ($15 billion each and counting), but also the incessant news of lesser lights, from Michael Eisner's $180 million from Disney to Rick Pitino's $70 million from the Boston Celtics.

What strategy do you need to join the ranks at least of the 70,000 households filing tax returns reporting incomes in excess of $1 million in 1997? As it turns out, their nest eggs were secured not by real estate but by the long upward march of stock prices. And larger fortunes were made not from thin air, but from technology or financial wizardry.

Lawrence Ellison, head of Oracle, and notoriously rivalrous with Bill Gates, was asked what feelings he had toward the other software mogul. When Ellison declined to answer, a friend in the industry ventured, "Well, there may not be a word for it. How many times in history has somebody with $7 billion been unhappy because he doesn't have $15 billion?"

Something has changed about the way we think about money. Entrepreneurial virtues dominate our culture, and it is hard to resist them. Chief executives of some of the largest companies, perhaps the most secure of positions, like to style themselves as "risk takers" and justify their pay accordingly.

Consider the Korean-born software entrepreneur about to take his fledgling company public. He speaks of the hopeful engineers who came to him willing to work for stock options. It is another heartening story of wealth being created by knowledge, initiative, and energy. And if we can't have the dream then at least we can share in it.

What other characteristics besides "vision" should we look for in the managers of small growth companies (since the ones with huge Wall Street followings tend to be hideously expensive)? According to a poll of people with at least $250,000 in income or $2.5 million in assets, some of the keys to success are determination, ability or talent, and intelligence (see Figure 4.2).

FIGURE 4.2. KEYS TO GREAT WEALTH

	Very Important	Somewhat Important	Total
Determination	82%	16%	98%
Ability or talent	49	46	95
Intelligence	45	46	91
Willing to take risks	54	37	91
Supportive spouse	72	18	90
Good luck	27	41	68
Knowing right people	20	46	66
Being ruthless	2	9	11

Source: Worth magazine

A manager with vision is simply someone who knows precisely where he wants his company to go and how to get there, said many of the stock pickers we spoke to about company management. "The difficulty," says Charles Allmon, publisher of the Growth Stock Outlook newsletter, "lies in knowing if growth is sustainable, or was it due to lucky acquisitions, a one-time hot product, or an accounting fiction?"

These days most executives get stock options as part of their pay packages. But Allmon hunts out those who are buying shares with their own money. Insider purchases are what sold him on insurer Jefferson-Pilot, a pick that is up more than 70 percent in two years.

WHAT TYPE ARE YOU?

Never confuse a bull market with brilliance, however. All of us want to know whether the choices we have made as investors were the best we could do. Could we have gained more by taking more risks with small stocks or an initial public offering?

Investors fall into three broad categories: conservative, aggressive, and speculative. And your portfolio should reflect something of each, the emphasis shifting with market conditions, how much money you have to invest, your age, and any family responsibilities.

Conservative investors have a lot in common with longtime clay court tennis ace Thomas Muster of Austria, known for his dogged persistence. They believe that patience pays—and that a financial portfolio ought to aim for a steady-going blend of capital growth and income, with low risk. "Quick, spectacular gains aren't what the conservative investor is looking for," says Thurman Smith, editor of the *Equity Fund Outlook* newsletter. The emphasis is on blue-chip stocks, growth and income funds, and usually a hefty portion of money-market funds or short-term bonds.

Such a recipe might produce average annual returns of 10 to 14 percent, with the investor's income needs being satisfied by the money-market and dividend-producing stocks and mutual funds (considered safer investments than the capital-gains stocks of upstart companies). In most cases, conservative investors look at yield and pay little heed to the impact of taxes and inflation on their money.

The only problem with that is being ultraconservative—stashing large amounts of money in fixed assets like Treasury bills or certificates of deposit or, even worse, holding on to stocks until forced to sell because of the need for cash or income. Conservative investments can be included in any portfolio, but are most appropriate for people who are retired or soon to be, living on a fixed income, or who earn low or modest salaries.

Aggressive investors are more comfortable moving money about and are hungry for the super high returns provided by growth stocks or stock funds. Such an investor does not hesitate to sell in order to take profits. And he or she feels comfortable having a sizable amount in small or mid-cap stocks as well as international funds.

Those younger than 50 probably should be aggressive and not conservative investors, according to financial advisers. One top planner recommends that they put no more than 15 percent of their spare cash into investments that promise steady income returns from dividends and interest. He says that 85 percent or more of their portfolios should be aimed at growth.

The aggressive investor is also likely to have substantial income, and may not require investment income for day-to-day living. But it's also important to assess your tolerance for risk-taking. If your fear of losing money is stronger than your desire to make large profits, stick with a more conservative philosophy.

Speculative investors may not be casino gamblers, but they often try to time the market or outwit the pros. And if they research their stock choices carefully and use only money they can afford to lose, speculative investors can make money—lots of it.

They often favor takeover candidates, initial public offerings of new or spin-off companies, leveraged buyouts or stocks they expect to split, and they buy on margin or plunge into small company stocks that seem to be scoring huge gains. Market peaks often are marked by clear signs of speculation and can mean disaster if stocks are held too long.

The reason: Speculative stocks don't pass the usual tests of quality, but for some reason or another attract investors anyway. Some may even be erratic or down-at-the-heels old companies exhibiting some sort of spark, such as the promise of an imminent technology breakthrough. Many don't do well, so it takes big gains by a few to offset your losses.

Whether you're a new investor or a sophisticated veteran who has weathered bull and bear markets, you should have a sensible risk-reducing strategy. It can be a pyramid, obelisk, tower, or anything you want it to be. The object is to have a solid base of cash or money-market funds; some Treasury bills, tax-exempt bonds and real estate (your home); and blue chip stocks or mutual funds for growth and income.

Then should you get a raise, bonus, inheritance or other windfall, you can consider more risk-oriented investments like small cap stocks, initial public offerings, special situations, takeover candidates, options and futures.

FORGET WALL STREET!

Whatever you do, you should know that out there in the boondocks, regional brokers are turning up plenty of valuable tips on up-and-comers in their areas—stocks that are less picked over by the institutions, and all but ignored by the Wall Street brokerage houses.

The big blue chips may well be sound investments. But often they don't yield the kind of returns an aggressive investor looks for. Their very size and success limits their rate of growth. That's why so many investors seek out brokers who specialize in young, entrepreneurial companies that offer extraordinary growth opportunities. And they find them more often than you might think.

It was a transportation analyst for Memphis's Morgan Keegan who discovered Federal Express soon after it went public in 1978. Other regional firms also have developed expertise in industries concentrated nearby. Thus, Wheat First Securities in Richmond, Virginia, is known for its coverage of carpet and furniture companies; Ragen MacKenzie in Seattle for technology and financial firms; and Blunt Ellis & Loewi in Milwaukee for catalog retailers.

A list of regional brokers appears in Appendix C, and you can find more of them by checking *Nelson's Directory of Investment Research* or special issues of the *Wall Street Transcript,* both fairly expensive trade publications available in some libraries. Opening an account with a broker will also get you access to its research reports, although you'll probably get them a bit later than big customers.

Some of the regional analysts come highly recommended by respected money managers like John Templeton of Franklin Templeton Funds and Ralph Wanger of Acorn Fund. And one study by *Venture Capital Journal* showed that in a 13-year period, when the stocks in the Standard & Poor's 500 appreciated 260 percent, the small, entrepreneurial companies in the Venture Capital 100 went up 1,632 percent.

Of course, it goes without saying that where the opportunities for rewards are so great, there's much higher risk. But when one of these companies does succeed, the upside potential is virtually unlimited. What's more, most of the regional brokers interviewed, like Stuart-James in Houston, research all prospects exhaustively. And only one company in fifty or a hundred survives the scrutiny.

The goal of regional brokers is to get to companies before Wall Street discovers them and bids up prices. As a rule, analysts at the big brokerage firms can't be bothered to follow more than a handful of emerging growth stocks. The rest of these small companies don't have analyst meetings, nor do they employ "financial relations" officials to talk to stockholders or the media. They usually don't bother to send out press releases—they are too busy making money.

Once Wall Street finds a stock, and hordes of analysts follow it, most of its explosive growth is over and it's no longer a bargain, says Peter Lynch in *One Up on Wall Street.* To be on the safe side of any hot tip, he adds this aphorism: When in doubt, wait it out.

If your broker tells you of a company that has a sure-fire product that allows people to lose fifty pounds without dieting, there will be plenty of time to buy the stock at $20, instead of $10, on its way to $50. You might even wait a little longer, until some of those profits actually do begin to trickle in. Don't follow your broker off to oblivion.

Some other Lynch rules: Don't have lots of different stocks in your portfolio just because you are afraid that something bad will happen to some of them. If you believe that one or more stocks are about to slide, don't increase the number of issues—sell the ones you don't like. Diversity for its own sake is self-defeating.

FINDING HOT STOCKS

Where do you find hot small stocks? By looking at what people are buying. Pet owners spent $20 billion last year to feed, groom and tend to the health of their critters. And PetsMart has grown from a kitten to a fat cat since its initial public offering in 1993, which raised $120 million and fueled an acquisition binge resulting in 450 stores in Canada, the United States and the United Kingdom.

Competition from Petco in San Diego and recent problems with inventory and pricing have sent the former high-flyer to under $10 a share. But insiders are buying because they expect new services, such as obedience training and veterinary care, will boost margins to the 17.5-percent annual revenue growth recorded in the past four years.

Often, the market does not bid up shares adequately to reflect a company's improved outlook. A product launch, a large contract, or a lucrative marketing alliance can boost earnings as it did for Molecular Devices. Before a biotech giant such as Amgen can push its latest wonder drug through the FDA and onto drugstore shelves, it must test for contaminants and measure biochemical reactions.

To do so, Amgen and other biotech firms turn to a $50,000 machine developed by Molecular Devices. Another product, Cytosensor, enables scientists to investigate metabolic processes without causing cell damage. And once the company's machines are in place, biotech firms typically buy an additional $15,000 worth of replaceable items, such as filters. That lifted revenues some 30 percent from a year ago, says William Plovanic, analyst with Madison Securities.

Who else is bullish on small stocks? Abby Cohen, the superstar strategist for Goldman Sachs, thinks small and mid-size stocks will do better than their blue-chip cousins, which are fully priced. Her favorite sectors are technology and financial services.

Her advice: Do your homework before you invest. Study the company and the industry before you make stock selections, and keep your eyes open for investment ideas—the company that owns the popular fast-food place, the company that makes products sold in your hometown, and the company that makes the hot items on your local grocery store shelves.

The fact is, you have some advantages that Wall Street doesn't. But look at individual stocks, not at the market. Don't worry about where the market will be next year, what interest rates will be, or what the balance of trade will be. Instead, spend time learning about local companies. "The average person can watch six or seven stocks with no problem," says Peter Lynch.

You probably know quite a bit about several companies. And you may have an edge that Wall Street doesn't. If you're in a town where Friendly's has plants and they keep expanding, you could make $25,000 on a $5,000 investment over three years. But if you don't have a couple of hours for researching individual stocks, buy small cap mutual funds.

The financial media have convinced people they can't pick small stocks, but that's dead wrong. Taco Bell, Chili's, and Kentucky Fried Chicken are massive stocks that when smaller were up 40 and even 50 percent. So you have all sorts of natural advantages in local companies. Why not use them?

INVESTORS NEVER RETIRE

The good news is that you probably have a long retirement ahead of you. The bad news, from a financial standpoint at least, is that you will have to make your money last all those years. Besides picking the right investments, you have to watch how fast you draw upon accumulated savings. Early on, you should try to use only a portion of your investment income for living expenses. The rest should be reinvested.

One rule of thumb for how much of your investments to put in stocks: Subtract your age from 100 and add a percentage sign to the result. You might even want to be more aggressive than that. If you can tolerate the ups and downs of the market, it actually can make good sense to put 70 or 80 percent of your retirement money in stocks or stock mutual funds.

But that advice is anathema to many retirees, who fear their savings will be devoured in a market crash. It's not going to happen. In fact, history suggests that a portfolio that is 75 percent in stocks and 25 percent in bonds is no more risky than the other way around. That's because stocks and bonds do not always rise and fall in tandem. When bond prices are hit, as they have been in recent years, stocks provide offsetting gains.

A successful strategy for getting income from your portfolio that works for some is to take three years' worth of spending money and pop it into a money-market mutual fund. If you intend to spend 5 percent each year, you could tuck away 15 percent of your money as a cushion.

Then you can be as aggressive as you want with the other 85 percent, putting much or all of it into all types of stocks. Every year, you should cash in a portion of your stocks to replenish that three-year supply. Even if the market crashes, you have three years to wait for the recovery. That recovery has happened after every crash but one (1973–74) in this century.

If you truly enjoy picking stocks and have the skill it takes to be good at it, you may want to "cherry pick" some additional issues in an effort to enhance your portfolio. But be leery of betting too much money on any one stock. You could end up owning a fistful of worthless shares.

Stocks of more established dividend-paying companies (often called "growth and income" or "equity and income" stocks by mutual funds) can be smart choices for a retirement portfolio because they tend to be less prone to short-term losses than other more aggressive stocks. But do not entirely ignore small or mid-cap companies, or foreign stocks in developed or emerging markets such as Germany or China.

When adding to an existing portfolio, some basic decisions are important to your success. To pick the best possible investments, you should apply four equally simple tests before parting with your money:

❑ The investment should be reasonably easy to understand.

❑ There should be a good chance of making money.

❑ There ought to be a ready market should you need to sell in a hurry.

❑ The investment should be *relatively* inexpensive to buy, hold, or sell.

NEXT STOP, PROSPERITY

If there is one certainty in this changing world, it's simply this: Those who anticipate the changes and sensibly act upon them stand to prosper. But you will have to act—or react—rapidly to anticipate and respond to developments and novel ideas. In this age of information and technology, everything happens more quickly than ever.

To appreciate the magnitude of change, consider that the Dow Jones average was heading toward an awesome closing high of 1051 as recently as the early 1970s. Yet to appear were money-market funds, stock futures, junk bonds, and discount brokers—not to mention the billions of dollars entrepreneurs and investors would make from computers and software, cable television, and home medical tests.

People like Warren Buffett who consistently have anticipated the turns in the economy have usually managed to cope better than those who have not. They know, for example, that the stock market will be higher two years from now, and significantly higher five years from now, than it is today. They expect the long bull market to continue for several reasons: speculation is not excessive, no recession is in sight, inflation and interest rates show no sign of surging, and productivity is at an all-time high.

INVESTOR INFORMATION

One of the most detailed treatments of this subject is *The Hometown Investor: How to Find Investment Treasures in Your Own Backyard,* by Richard Moduri. The business pages of most daily newspapers also list stocks of local interest, and write stories about their operations.

Investors who are serious about prospecting for stocks can also get additional tips from the likes of Peter Lynch, Richard Driehaus, and Mario Gabelli by dipping into the book *Investment Gurus.* Author Peter Tanous interviews them and a dozen others and provides a "road map" to wealth through personal investing.

Fishing for Red Herrings

Many investors dream of getting in on the ground floor of a new high-flying company—of discovering the next Microsoft or Home Depot. And there are plenty of them to choose from: Last year, 790 businesses raised more than $50 billion by selling shares on the two stock exchanges or over-the-counter through initial public offerings, or IPOs. And in the first half of 1997, 220 hot new issues of stocks came to the market for the first time.

Are you itching to latch on to an IPO yourself? Before plunging in, examine them very closely. Otherwise you might wind up taking a bath. Offering prices are often inflated, and not all of the companies have the financial support of blue-ribbon underwriters, often finding less exacting sponsors.

Companies making their debuts in recent years are also a seductive bunch. They include marketers of such venerable brand names as Polo Ralph Lauren and Estee Lauder, along with Boston Beer, brewer of the popular Sam Adams label, and such high-tech superstars as Netscape Communications, the young company that allows computer users to browse the Internet.

The hype surrounding the most visible newly listed companies makes them seem like surefire winners, and turns many of the entrepreneurs who founded them into multimillion dollar celebrities. But investors thinking about buying their stock should remember that IPOs are highly risky. "Anyone who ventures into new issues needs to be rigorously selective," warns Tom Stephens, director of equity sales at Tucker Anthony in Washington, D.C. "The truth is, in bull markets people believe in bullshit."

That's one reason Renaissance Capital simply ignores issues priced at $5 or less in the *IPO Intelligence* subscription service it sells to newspapers and institutions. But a few of these micro-cap stocks sometimes prove even the experts wrong and beat the year-end averages of other bigger IPOs.

Whatever the future has in store for small company stocks, it's certain that an important rite of passage will continue to be public offerings to raise the capital a company needs to finance its growth. The investment bankers who underwrite the new issues and help sell the shares know that investor enthusiasm for most IPOs is strongest during a bull market.

Sometimes excitement over a new issue can soar—and then plummet. For example, on the day in August 1995 when Netscape went public, its shares closed at $58—better than twice the initial offering price of $28. It has since seen big increases of $157 and lows currently of $37; prices that in many cases reflect the triumph of hope over experience.

Profits of young companies like Netscape are still scant relative to their stock prices, so investors are gambling heavily on the company's future—and still unproven—prospects. At the first sign that those double-digit earnings may not materialize, the highly volatile stock will probably take a dive as disappointed investors sell shares.

FINDING NEW ISSUES

Any foray into the new-issues market has to be based on selectivity, and reflected in the performance statistics of the company. In Polo Ralph Lauren, for example, analysts are looking at the staying power of a menswear line that has weathered the whims of fashion for years—an industry where a bad guess or management missteps can trigger a savage toll.

"The depth and strength of management is the name of the game," says Dana Telsey, stock analyst for Bear Stearns in New York. "While the consumer is entranced by a designer name, getting investors interested means meeting and beating expectations."

That's not always easy with start-up companies like Netscape or others in computer software, medical instruments or genetic engineering. But getting the cold hard facts about hot new stocks is not as difficult as it once was—and it's a lot safer. As one long-established underwriter puts it, "Back in the eighties, if you had an over-priced deal, you got it public quickly so the venture guys could get rid of the thing."

Getting information now is not as difficult. Some brokerage houses publish weekly calendars of forthcoming offerings. Most brokers subscribe to *Investment Dealers Digest,* a weekly that covers the new issues market. The prospective investor should also ask for the stock's prospectus, the so-called "red herring," and scrutinize it carefully.

It's possible to make a lot of money in IPOs, but it requires far more research than most investments, as well as an understanding of the market. To help spot the winners and avoid the losers when firms go public, you may want to read one or more advisory newsletters such as Norman Fosback's *New Issues* and *Emerging & Special Situations* (Standard & Poor's).

Many brokers will let their clients know about new issues that their firm either knows about or is underwriting. Make certain your broker knows of your interest. In addition, check out magazines such as *Barron's* and *USA Today,* which cover IPOs along with all types of financial news. Their roundups give various tallies of the number of deals in any one year, from fewer than 400 to as many as 800. The discrepancy is to some degree attributable to a custom dating back to the boiler-room days of the early eighties, when financial advisers felt obliged to ignore offerings they deemed unsuitable for small investors (with good reason, considering that some underwriters actually went to jail).

In 1996, one of the best years ever for IPOs, some 200 companies with revenues of $10 million or less went public. But you wouldn't know it by the celebrity lavished on Lucent, Gucci, and the big-deal end of the market. There were also new issues that came with sweeteners attached (warrants, convertibles), real estate investment trusts, oil-and-gas explorers, financial institutions, closed-end funds, foreign companies, and nonlisted stocks.

None of these could be considered emerging growth companies, which encompass everything from cigar rollers to biotech firms. They are the stocks that observers expect to prosper and reward investors with outstanding returns while others fail to match expectations. How do you separate the turn-ons from the turn-offs among these hot new issues?

According to W. Keith Schilit, venture capital expert and coauthor of *Blue Chips & Hot Tips,* identifying those emerging growth companies most likely to succeed requires these predictive factors:

❏ Look for companies that have a clearly defined focus and market niche.

❏ Seek out low-tech companies with significant competitive advantages.

❏ Value management over technology.

❏ Search for companies with strong earnings growth.

❑ Look beyond net income to "quality of earnings."

❑ Use the balance sheet to predict future revenues.

❑ Watch for unusual or unexplained increases in accounts receivable or inventory.

❑ Constantly monitor the debt-equity ratio.

❑ Be wary of companies that fail to generate enough cash to fuel their growth.

❑ Look for companies that use the proceeds from an IPO to foster future growth.

❑ Avoid companies with outrageous valuations.

RATING THE UNDERWRITERS

Your chances for success will be increased if you select IPOs from reputable investment bankers. Even the best underwriters make errors of judgment, but they will not knowingly market the stock of a company that is likely to damage their reputation.

Some of the highest-quality new issues among emerging growth companies are brought to market by such blue-chip investment firms as Robertson, Stevens & Co., Alex. Brown & Sons, Hambrecht & Quist, Montgomery Securities, and Cowen & Co. Yet even these companies can fall victim to downturns in the market or unexpected competition from lesser-known firms, and can suddenly find their deals souring. The bottom line is to be careful not to depend too heavily on any one underwriter.

See who is providing the venture capital financing, advises Schilit. Strong backing by venture capital entrepreneurs suggests that the new company has been well groomed to go public and probably has real promise. "Our research has shown that investing in early-stage companies is not a crapshoot," he says, "rather it takes skill to find the gems."

Over the short term, just about any underwriter can take a company public and hype it enough to prompt an immediate increase in the price of the stock. Over time, however, quality will win out. Certainly, any underwriter has had its share of losers, but the better ones have strong research departments and are extremely selective about the companies they choose to represent.

Some well known investment firms account for many of the now-familiar success stories: Microsoft and Goldman Sachs, Home Depot and

Bear Stearns, Adobe Systems and Hambrecht & Quist. More important, each of these firms has a strong *overall* track record when it comes to IPOs. The worst performers are certainly not household names, and a few are no longer in business.

The pleasures and pitfalls of IPOs are that they act like stocks on steroids, and are likely to quickly rise in price. For one example, Standard & Poor's New Issues Index, which tracks stocks during their first six months of life, nearly doubled in 1995, while the S&P 500 rose only 34 percent.

"You can beat the market with IPOs as long as you're disciplined about selling," says Robert Natale, editor of the *Emerging & Special Situations* newsletter. He says the best time to sell is after three to six months, when they begin to lose the support of the underwriting firm and company insiders may legally sell their shares. (A "lockup" agreement with the underwriter prevents early investors from dumping their suddenly enhanced holdings into the aftermarket.)

But individual investors have rarely had the chance to buy new issues at their offering price. And buying during the first few days of trading—usually after the price has soared—can be treacherous. That is changing, however.

Fidelity Brokerage Services and Donaldson, Lufkin & Jenrette are selling IPOs to customers, and Charles Schwab also is considering such a move. Fidelity gets 10 percent of every Salomon Brothers IPO to parcel out to its clients, who pay no commission for the stock, and has already served up a half-dozen new issues. Donaldson expects to do the same through its Website, but you'll probably need $100,000 to gain admission.

If you don't buy an IPO when it's first issued, you can pick up shares in the aftermarket when they trade over-the-counter. If it's a hot market, expect a 20- to 25-percent increase in price. Better yet, follow the progress of any stock you like, and move in when it takes a small tumble. Often a new company will lose its initial luster or report lower than expected earnings, pushing the price down temporarily.

TOMBSTONES AND PROSPECTUSES

Whenever a company goes public, the financial community is notified through advertisements in the financial press. These advertisements are commonly called *tombstones,* because of their traditional black border and heavy print. They all look alike, but each provides information of interest to potential investors (see Figure 5.1).

Figure 5.1. ADVERTISEMENT (TOMBSTONE) FOR INITIAL PUBLIC OFFER-
ING OF NETSCAPE COMMUNICATIONS CORPORATION IN AUGUST 1995.

Common Stock

Price $28 a Share

Copies of the Prospectus may be obtained in any State from only such of the undersigned as may legally offer these Securities in compliance with the securities laws of such State.

5,000,000 Shares

This portion of the offering is being offered in the United States and Canada by the undersigned.

MORGAN STANLEY & CO.
Incorporated

HAMBRECHT & QUIST LLC

ALEX. BROWN & SONS
Incorporated

A.G. EDWARDS & SONS, INC.

GOLDMAN, SACHS & CO.

MERRILL LYNCH & CO.

BEAR, STEARNS & CO. INC.

MONTGOMERY SECURITIES

J.P. MORGAN SECURITIES INC.

PAINEWEBBER INCORPORATED

SALOMON BROTHERS INC

COWEN & COMPANY

FIRST OF MICHIGAN CORPORATION

JANNEY MONTGOMERY SCOTT INC.

KEMPER SECURITIES, INC.

LEGG MASON WOOD WALKER
Incorporated

McDONALD & COMPANY
Securities, Inc.

MORGAN KEEGAN & COMPANY, INC.

NEEDHAM & COMPANY, INC.

PUNK, ZIEGEL & KNOELL

RAUSCHER PIERCE REFSNES, INC.

RAYMOND JAMES & ASSOCIATES, INC.

SOUNDVIEW FINANCIAL GROUP, INC.

SUTRO & CO. INCORPORATED

VAN KASPER & COMPANY

VOLPE, WELTY & COMPANY

WESSELS, ARNOLD & HENDERSON, L.L.C.

WHEAT FIRST BUTCHER SINGER

750,000 Shares

This portion of the offering is being offered outside the United States and Canada by the undersigned.

MORGAN STANLEY & CO.
International

HAMBRECHT & QUIST LLC

August 16, 1995

A disclaimer, required by the Securities and Exchange Commission, says that the ad is not an offer to sell, which can only be made through the prospectus. It's followed by the number of shares being offered for sale, name of the company issuing the stock, and the type of issue (usually common stock).

Next is the *market value,* or price per share, of the stock. Once the shares begin trading, even during the very first day, the price may rise or fall depending on the stock's popularity. The *prospectus* being offered must, by law, be available to anyone interested in investing, and provides detailed financial information not given in the advertisement.

The *lead underwriter* is the investment firm handling the offering and has its name displayed most prominently. Other firms, with smaller roles, are then listed below. The underwriters buy up all the shares for sale from the company and then sell them on the market—to the public—at the best possible price.

The number of tombstones for IPOs reached record highs in 1995 and 1996, so chances are you've seen some of them. You may have noticed that it wasn't just technology companies that experienced a boom. Among those with market valuations over $50 million in the first half of 1997 were a maker of Mexican food products, a day-care provider for corporations, a pump and valve manufacturer, and a California vineyard.

Those of you who want to take part in the IPO process vicariously might want to check out these and other public offerings listed in *USA Today* and the *Wall Street Journal.* Check the initial share price of any company against the current price. Then, if you're interested, ask your broker or the lead underwriter for the stock's prospectus.

Examine the balance sheet in the prospectus. Are the new company's finances strong enough to keep it going even if profits do not meet expectations—or, if profit growth is on target, to provide capital for continued expansion? If you don't trust your own judgment on these matters, don't invest in new issues at all.

But if you do, watch the price moves for a few weeks or even months to see if the price settles down or establishes a solid pattern of gains. Only then should you buy the stock. And because the market pendulum continually swings, you could do better than those who bought IPOs in 1997 or 1996. The only caveat: "It's difficult to predict technology." says Bill Marbach, managing editor of *Venture Finance.*

Once you have a copy of the prospectus (called a "red herring" because of the red-ink warning that the contents are not final), look for the
section that lays bare the holdings of top officers of the company that is
offering to sell you stock. If they are unloading a lot of their own shares,
you should shun the issue.

The officers and directors should have experience with the company
or with a similar organization, and be fully involved in the firm's operations. That's especially important with new ventures in growth areas,
such as telecommunications, specialty retailing, computer software, and
biotechnology. Fledgling companies have a lot to prove to investors—
demonstrating that they can make products that will sell or putting some
figures on the bottom line. Try to invest in an area you know something
about or a company located near you.

Despite its many caveats, the prospectus will help you form an opinion on your own. It typically contains a detailed business plan, describing
the company's history, future plans, competition, and its financial condition. It also outlines how the company plans to use the proceeds from the
offering as well as any important risks facing investors.

Schilit, in his astute analysis of IPOs and corporate financial games,
suggests that potential investors apply these criteria to the prospectus and
balance sheet:

❏ Expanding market and rapid revenue growth

❏ Outstanding managers and directors

❏ Strong earnings and cash flow from operations

❏ Fair financial arrangement for new investors

Investors clearly are hungry for IPOs, adds Jay Ritter, finance professor at the University of Florida. Two factors, among others, make this
boom noteworthy: It has run longer than any other, starting in 1991.
They usually last only a year or two. And past booms centered around a
single industry, such as energy or pollution control. Today's IPOs are
coming from an array of industries.

Will all these new shares glut the market? Not likely, says Ritter.
Many of the IPOs include big companies trying to raise money to pay
down debt, like Revlon, and some are spin-offs from industry giants (Lucent) that have deep pockets. Many companies are also using excess cash
to buy back shares of their own stock.

WATCHING THE INSIDERS

Mention insiders and most people think of whispered secrets and ill-gotten gains by the likes of Michael Milken and Ivan Boesky. But much insider trading is perfectly legal, and worth watching if you have the time and patience. It's not foolproof, but if you follow the buying patterns of officers, directors and major shareholders, you may unearth some special situations.

"It may not be possible to know what insiders know," says Norman Fosback, publisher of *The Insiders* newsletter, "but it is feasible to do what they do." Analysts such as Fosback believe that such buying shows that insiders have confidence that their companies' stocks will rise long-term. And if there's a big enough wave of insider buying, that should be good news for the overall market.

Right now, buying by corporate insiders has reached one of the highest levels ever, says Fosback. This, he says, has "enormously bullish implications for market trading." Others have also noticed the bullish vibes being radiated by company insiders.

You shouldn't try to act on everything every insider does. Transactions by chief executives often precede a merger or takeover, and such deals can spark a sharp but temporary move in a company's stock price. Buying by vice-presidents or directors is a better way to gauge a company's long-term prospects, says Fosback.

Another way is to follow the purchases of large investors who make bold bids to take over entire companies. Their names are often in the headlines, making it fairly easy to follow trades. By law, any investor who acquires more than 5 percent of a company's shares must report that transaction to the SEC within 10 days. The commission publishes a daily summary of these Form 13D filings in its *News Digest*.

For a fee, one can obtain this information from newsletters or computer services that closely study this smart-money crowd. One who does is Kiril Sokoloff, publisher of *Street Smart Investing*. In a five-year study, he measured the investment results of 150 of these big capitalists and found that of nearly 300 stocks in which they took major positions, 95 percent of them rose in price. The insiders' stocks, including IPOs, also beat the market over a ten-year period.

But when insiders sell, watch out. Heavy sales by big investors, directors or officers of a company often precede many of the aftermarket disasters, from Genex to Donna Karan. "If they sell shares the first day, you should probably stay away," says Kent Womack of the Amos Tuck School at Dartmouth College. The situation is particularly dangerous when insider selling suddenly increases after a stock has started to decline.

Most investors can buy IPOs only after their first-day price run-ups, but that doesn't mean you have to stay out of the market, says Womack. In a study of 1,200 stocks that hit the market from 1988–1995, he found that buying those that do well (defined as gains of under 60 percent) exceeded the returns of "extra-hot" offerings—new issues with first-day gains of 60 percent or more. See Figure 5.2 for a list of winners and losers among recent IPOs.

That category did well because underwriters try to price offerings about 15 to 30 percent below what they think the stock is worth, explains Womack. And the offerings seem to be just right for investors since the best performers over a year were issues that jumped roughly that amount their first day, hitting what Womack calls the "sweet spot."

FIGURE 5.2. WORTH A LOOK

Here's how some of the best and worst performing IPOs fared in 1996.*

Company (symbol)	Offer date	Return %
Strong gainers		
Cymer (CYMI) Laser business	September 18	+313
Outdoor Systems (OSIA) Advertising	April 24	283
Sipex (SIPX) Integrated circuits	April 2	249
Sykes Enterprises (SYKE) Computer consulting firm	April 29	229
Pacific Gateway Exchange (PGEX) Long-distance phone service	July 19	201
Siebel Systems (SEBL) Marketing software	June 27	200
Big losers		
Riscorp (RISC) Compensation consulting	February 28	-80
Dignity Partners (DPNR) Life insurance	February 14	79
Infonautics (INFO) On-line reference services	April 29	71
Softquad (SWEB) Internet consulting	February 13	70
Vocaltec (VOCLF) Internet audio products	February 6	69
Housecall Medical Resources (HSCL) Home health care	April 3	68

*Excludes issues under $5 a share or $10 million market value.

Source: Securities Data Company

Insiders also sell their shares for many different reasons other than the declining fortunes of their companies. Want an insider tip? Buys are obviously a better indication of take-over possibilities than insider sales. But be suspicious of huge run-ups in stock prices—even now when many dethroned insiders are in jail or have served time.

Edwin Buck, editor of the *Weekly Insider Report* (Vickers Stock Research), admits a brazen few attempt it illegally, but notes that insider trading is more than a wishful fantasy and it's overlooked by both investors and analysts. "They should pay more attention to what corporate insiders do rather than what they say," he says.

Officers, directors, and large shareholders have up to 40 days after any transaction to report it to the SEC, and tardiness is common. Advisory services like Value Line also note insider activity as do some computer databases and financial periodicals such as *Barron's*. Just be careful to stay within the legal limits—there is still a very real "Club Fed," complete with securities lawyers looking to fill it up with those who defy the law.

BE YOUR OWN ANALYST

If investors take the time to sift through all these new stocks, they are likely to find some good investments at close to their original offering prices. But even the most promising purchases are unlikely to turn a quick profit. "Underwriters danced in the aisles in 1996, and it was an even better environment for investors in 1997," says Robert Natale, editor of *Emerging & Special Situations*.

If you want to follow-up on a new issue or listed stock, remember that subsequent to its IPO, a company traded publicly is required to file additional information with the SEC. Of these, the 10-Q and 10-K financial statements due 45 days after the end of a quarter, and 90 days after the year-end, are useful to serious investors. Both documents are readily available from the investor relations department of any publicly traded company or from the SEC.

While much of the discussion in this chapter centers on the prospectus, it is only a snapshot of a company at a single point in time, before it issues stock to the public. To evaluate a company properly, you must continue to analyze new information. And subsequent 10-Qs and 10-Ks, in addition to the company's annual reports (discussed in Chapter 12), should form the basis of that evaluation.

It's also important to check out or dismiss rumors when making your investment choices, especially those that surround many hot new issues. "Investors who trade in rumor stocks traditionally lose money," says Thomas Burnett of Merger Insight Research, "because there are many more rumor stories out there than facts."

The outstanding stock pickers are successful, not because they rely solely on sophisticated statistical models, but because they are alert to clues all around them that are readily available to all of us. Peter Lynch, for example, likes to give his wife credit for discovering L'Eggs, one of his best-performing investments. Likewise, it didn't take complex mathematical or computer models to forecast that Wal-Mart, Home Depot, and Microsoft would be great investments.

Of course, spotting a potential success story—like Toys "R" Us or Federal Express—simply by noticing their stores or trucks, is only the starting point in selecting a stock. That is where more analysis by the investor is needed, and for those willing to spend some time doing their homework, they can expect returns significantly better than stock funds.

They can also expect more help from the Securities and Exchange Commission, which is trying to get lawyers to use "plain English" when preparing statements to go into IPOs. The SEC is not simply legislating clarity, but attempting to show companies how to achieve it.

"George Orwell once blamed the demise of the English language on politics. It's quite possible he never read a prospectus," says Arthur Levitt Jr., SEC chairman, who has worked to create a user-friendly financial community. He admits the SEC does a good job of requiring disclosure, but not in a form investors can readily understand.

Others simply want initial public offerings to be more accessible to those who aren't ultra-wealthy, politically connected, or officers of major institutions. These big players are usually the only ones allowed in at the offering price, while ordinary investors get creamed buying at the top and watching their money melt away.

Nevertheless, there can be profits even for those who buy on the second day or a week or month later, but only among companies with real rather than invented futures, says Gerri Detweiler, policy director for the National Council of Individual Investors (NCII). It's for this reason that NCII seeks a larger slice of the IPO pie for individual investors (estimated at only 10 to 15 percent of shares right now).

If you want to boost your ability to pick new issues or listed stocks for a winning portfolio, look for companies with at least 5 million shares outstanding. That will ensure liquidity and marketability, because mutual funds and others will be trading in these stocks. In a smaller company, or micro-cap, your exposure to sharp price fluctuations is greater.

Anyone can analyze a stock by looking at financial statements and by using the following six reliable and proven analytic tools discussed earlier:

- ❏ Earnings per share
- ❏ Price-earnings ratio
- ❏ Book value
- ❏ Return on equity
- ❏ Total return
- ❏ Shares outstanding

ONE STEP AT A TIME

The big stock averages are at new highs, but we haven't seen the last of the carnage in hot stocks and initial public offerings. Many have already come down, but not far enough to correct the severe overvaluations. Even the sizzlers like Yahoo! and Boston Chicken have been doused.

Why would anyone want to play these wretched games when you can get above-average returns and keep up with the market with an index fund? Mob psychology, says Tucker Anthony's Stephens. "Young bankers and money managers caught up in the momentum of markets do things no gray-hair would think of doing. A lot of them buy weird stuff. They haven't experienced how bad it can get when it gets bad."

Even the big technology underwriters such as Hambrecht & Quist, and Alex. Brown, along with other blue-chip IPO firms, have had their share of losers. The good news? There are bargains to be found among companies whose IPOs are trading close to their offering prices. Some that analysts say are worth consideration: Donnelley Enterprise, Panavision and Sabre Group.

Take your time. There will be other bargains next week and next month. Above all, don't despair. Savvy investors position themselves for the long term, and will do well if they don't become greedy and rush to buy when markets surge to their tops, or rush to sell out when markets plunge. The discipline of dollar-cost averging also helps you avoid these two common errors.

Keep up with the news that affects your money, not just the market averages and stock indicators, but events close to home and in Asia, Europe or Latin America that can lead to sharp gyrations in the values of your investments. This information can be found in the daily financial pages and business magazines or summarized in books like this one.

When you buy common stocks, you become part owner of a corporation. A stock can increase your wealth in two ways: by paying you regular dividends and by rising in price. If it does indeed rise, you can sell at a profit. And it is this growth, not the dividends, that gives small stocks their investment edge.

"For a while it was just the top 50 or 100 companies in the Standard & Poor's 500 that were trouncing everything else," says Rick Jandrain, chief investment officer for equities at Banc One Investment Advisors. "Now, the rest of the market is catching up, and that's healthy."

INVESTOR INFORMATION

Many brokerage and accounting firms have materials available free of charge that explain initial public offerings. One of the best books on the subject is *Blue Chips & Hot Tips,* by W. Keith Schilit and Howard Schilit.

For the dedicated stock picker who wants to go beyond the lists provided in *Barron's* or other publications, a number of financial newsletters feature new issues and emerging growth companies (check the list in the Appendix for addresses and phone numbers). But they are no substitute for doing your own homework!

If you want a copy of *Getting Your Share: An Investor's Guide to the Profits and Pitfalls in Initial Public Offerings,* write or call the National Council of Individual Investors, 1900 L St. NW, Washington, DC 20036 (888-624-4111). The cost is $5, but it's free on the Internet Website at www.ncii.org.

When to Buy or Sell

Are you ready for a five-digit Dow? Ralph Acampora, chief technical analyst at Prudential, predicts the Dow Jones Industrial Average will hit 10,000 as early as June 1998 because of a "buying panic" by investors who sat out much of the current bull market. A colleague, Claudia Mott, director of small cap research at Prudential, differs only on timing. "We probably won't have to wait that long," she says.

Lest anyone accuse either analyst of "irrational exuberance," Acampora says there are still plenty of high-quality stocks left to buy. "Bull markets end when speculative junk is overvalued," he explains. "Not when companies are hitting all-time highs."

Although nobody can be certain whether the stock market will go up or down, you should try to recognize the really major, long-term points in the market, such as the crash of October 1987 and the huge rebound that began in January 1990 and was interrupted only by the huge corrrection in October 1997.

Stocks generally move in expectation of changes in the economy and in corporate profits. The market is always looking ahead—not backward. If both inflation and interest rates are low, that's bullish news. But when interest rates on Treasury bonds show sustained increases, better watch out. It's a clear and present danger signal.

Fortunately, your own decisions about the stock market do not have to be perfect to be profitable. Just watch for the major turns in the market. You can always buy somewhere above the bottom and sell out some time after the market has hit its peak. You'll still make a lot more money than the investor who ignores the market's long-term growth.

An old adage about the stock market holds that all new information about any stock spreads too quickly for ordinary investors to profit when the stock rises. But that's not really so, according to a study by the Institutional Brokers Estimate System, a service of the brokerage firm Lynch Jones & Ryan. It found that after several analysts sharply increase their earnings estimates for a company, its stock probably will do better than the major market averages *for the next six months.* In other words, you can benefit from any good news.

At the other extreme, you also can do well buying stocks that recently have plunged as a result of disappointing earnings or other sour news. And a number of them can become real bargains. In fact, some of the shrewdest investment professionals study each day's stock market tables just to find shares that have hit new lows. (See Figure 6.1.) They figure that if these stocks have intrinsic value, they may have nowhere to go but up.

Once you have picked out some undervalued stocks, don't buy right away. It is axiomatic that turnarounds generally take longer to materialize than anyone expects. Spend some time watching those stocks. But don't plan to wait until a stock hits its very bottom. Nobody is smart enough to do that. Instead, set "target prices" and buy if and when the stock reaches them. By doing that, you might profit very well buying bad-news stocks.

PROFITABLE INVESTING

Even though it's important to sleep at night, you should also avoid taking the path of least resistance—stashing large amounts of money in savings accounts or money market funds, or buying a few stocks and holding them until forced to sell.

The conservative approach may provide peace of mind, but it's very poor protection against inflation and high interest rates. Instead, use these proven techniques to reduce your risk quotient and enable you to weather any declines in the market:

Investigate before you invest

Don't buy on impulse, hunches, or rumors heard on the golf course. Make investments according to your goals for growth and/or income. Having the right information about a company and knowing how to in-

FIGURE 6.1. HOW TO READ STOCK TABLES

Stock listings look like an endless sea of numbers and letters. But this has more to do with the volume of stocks and the use of small type than with the complexity of the information.

Bold type marks stocks that rose or fell at least 8 percent, but only if the change was at least $1 a share. Stock prices are given in fractions. Thus, 8½ equals $8.50.

Underlining means stock traded more than 3 percent of shares (on the New York and American Stock Exchanges) and more than 6 percent on Nasdaq.

52-Week High and Low. Highest and lowest prices for a stock over the last year.

Stock name is abbreviated by the Associated Press. It is followed by the official ticker symbol.

Dividend is based on the last quarterly or semi-annual declaration. Special or extra dividends or payments are identified in the footnotes below the listings.

P-E. The price-earnings ratio is the share price divided by earnings per share.

Sales. Number of shares, in hundreds, that were traded unless preceded by a footnote z which means sales in full. Figures are unofficial.

Yield is the ratio of the annual dividend to the closing price, expressed as a percentage.

High Low. The highest and lowest prices the stock traded last week.

Last. This is the last price the stock traded, or the closing price.

Chg. The change between the closing price listed and the previous closing price.

Footnotes:

ec	Listed on American Stock Exchange's Emerging Company Marketplace.
n	New issue in the past 52 weeks.
s	Stock has split at least 20 percent within the last year.
pf	Preferred rather than common stock.
rt	Rights to buy security at a specified price.
wt	Warrants, allowing puchase of additional stock.
vj	Company in bankruptcy or receivership, or being reorganized under bankruptcy law.

Source: Associated Press

terpret it are more important than any of the other factors you might hear credited for the success of the latest market genius.

Information is even more important than timing. When you find a small company that looks promising, you don't have to buy the stock today or this week or even this month. Good stocks tend to stay good, so you can take the time to research them. You can get the information you need to size up a company's prospects in many places, and a lot of it is free.

Limit purchases until your forecast is confirmed

When you feel you have latched on to a winner, buy only half the amount of shares you can afford. You may lose a few points of profit by waiting, but you will also minimize your losses. Watch the action in the marketplace, and when your judgment appears accurate, buy the other half of your position.

Aside from the numbers-crunching, balance-sheet approach to finding value in the stock market, you should look for a company that is a leader in big or growing markets, and that invests in research and development (usually a key to future competitiveness).

Continue your research after you invest

There's no such thing as a permanent winner. Plenty of blue-chips like IBM have bounced up and down over the years. This caveat applies especially to small companies that show great promise at the outset but may fall by the wayside.

Watch for trends in the economy, stock market, industry groups, and the stocks in which you are interested. Market leaders change almost monthly, so what was favorable in January may be sliding in June. The stock listings of the *Wall Street Journal, Barron's,* and *Investor's Daily* are similar to those in most daily newspapers. What sets these three apart is the accompanying depth of coverage of the investment markets.

Diversify, but carefully

As a rule of thumb, a portfolio of $100,000 should have at least 10 securities, with no more than 20 percent in any one company or industry. Above $100,000, add one new security for each additional $10,000. And don't be afraid to put 10 percent of your assets in high-risk stocks.

Keep a list of prospects and review them often to determine whether any offer greater opportunities for faster rewards than the stocks you now own. But don't switch as long as your original investments are profitable and appear to have reasonable prospects of reaching your goals.

Don't be in a hurry

If you miss one opportunity, there will be another soon. And don't flit from one stock to another all the time. This may make your broker rich, but will cut into your profits and even decrease capital. Consider: Four trades a year, at an *average* cost of 1 percent of stock value, equals 4 percent of income.

Review all holdings quarterly and replace the weakest securities with those on your review list. Be slow to sell winners, because this will leave you with less profitable holdings. On average, a profitable portfolio will be turned over every five years, or about 20 percent annually.

CHECK EARNINGS REPORTS

Beware of falling stars—at least in the stock market. If you keep that in mind, you will avoid the mistake of buying a stock just because it recently had a spectacular gain. Quite often last year's overhyped superstars become this year's disappointing dogs.

Look at how well a company has done in the last two or three years for an idea of what it is capable of earning. If the most recent results are at the low end of the range, ask a broker for his firm's estimates of earnings for the next six to 12 months. If a turnaround is expected, consider buying the stock.

Many news sources, including the Associated Press and *The New York Times*, use earnings for the most recent four quarters. But the *Wall Street Journal* and *Barron's* use earnings before write-offs and other one-time "extraordinary" events. Many investors feel this gives a truer picture of a company's ongoing business. And some organizations, such as Standard & Poor's and Value Line as well as brokerage firms, also use projected earnings on the theory that stocks trade on expectations rather than on history.

"The value of a price-earnings ratio is a slippery thing," says Arnold Kaufman, editor of Standard & Poor's *Outlook* newsletter. "It's an imprecise measurement that changes under different economic and market conditions." His advice: Be consistent. Stick with the same source and apply the ratios in a uniform way.

Use key facts about a company to size up prospects for a stock. The following list shows where you can find those facts, in addition to daily newspapers. In most cases, you won't need more than two or three of the sources listed.

ANNUAL AND QUARTERLY REPORTS. Basic information about the company, including audited financial data for the most recent year and summaries of prior years. Available free from brokers and from the company directly.

FORM 10K. More extensive financial data, required to be filed with the Securities and Exchange Commission, showing assets, liabilities, equity revenues, expenses, and other items. Available from the SEC (800-638-8241) for a modest copying charge.

FORM 8K. Report required to be filed with the SEC if a certain specified event occurs, such as a change in control of the company, acquisition or disposition of assets, bankruptcy or receivership. Form 8K must be filed within 15 days of the event. Also available from the SEC.

ANALYSTS REPORTS. Commentaries by the research departments of brokerage firms, containing varying amounts of hard data to accompany buy or sell recommendations for stocks followed by the firm. Available from brokers.

VALUE LINE. Vast collection of data, including prices and earnings, along with analysis of 1,700 stocks. Available in libraries or from Value Line, 711 Third Ave., New York, NY 10017 (800-633-2252). Ask for a trial subscription.

STANDARD & POOR'S. Reports offer a wealth of current and historical information. The monthly *Stock Guide* contains similar data on more than 5,000 stocks, but with no analysis. Available in libraries, or from S&P, 25 Broadway, New York, NY 10004 (800-221-5277).

COMPUTER DATABASES. There are several, which provide current and historical data, information on file (at the SEC), market news, and analysts reports. Users pay about $2 a minute, plus a search charge. For a complete list, see Chapter 14, Investing by Computer.

LIMIT AND STOP ORDERS

Now that you've found the stock you want to buy, it's time to think about protecting the not-so-small gains you may have picked up in the stock market in recent years. Stop-loss orders, which tell brokers how low you will follow a stock before dumping it, are one way to do that.

A stop-loss order tells a broker to sell a stock when its price drops to a certain level. Investors can put a stop on a stock when they buy it to limit losses should the company head south. Or they can put stops on stocks that already have gains to protect them from eroding in a down market.

Even investors who might not ordinarily use stop orders at all can put stops on stocks in their portfolios if they are taking an extended trip and will be out of touch with their broker. "It's an invaluable strategy," says Bruce Poliquin, vice president of Avatar Associates, a New York firm that uses stops on every trade it does in managing over $1 billion in investments.

Other financial managers are concerned that investors can get bumped out of good stocks if they are overly reliant on stop orders. When stock prices fall, it can provide an opportunity to buy more shares in an otherwise good company. But some stops are probably warranted in this overheated market—especially for investors who take gains and then want to buy back in at a lower price. "It's pretty important to think about protecting portfolios right now," adds Poliquin.

Stop-loss orders don't cost anything, but they are not fail-safe. Once a stop price is reached, the sell order is automatically triggered. And in a market that is spiraling down fast, a stock can fall below the stop price before it is actually sold.

"You'll get a market price but it may not be the one you want," explains John Markese, research director of the American Association of Individual Investors. His point, which even advocates concede, is that stop orders "sound great but are very hard to implement."

Put simply, a stop order must be set close enough to the stock's current price to protect existing profits, but not so close that an investor gets dumped out of a good company because of one bad day. Poliquin handles this issue by setting stop prices with a formula that is based on a stock's volatility. Thus, a very volatile stock might have a stop set at 20 percent or more below its price.

Probably the most widely used measure of price volatility is called the *beta*. It's calculated from past price patterns and tells how much a stock can be expected to move in relation to a change in the Standard & Poor's 500, which is assigned a beta of 1. A stock with a beta of 1.5 historically rises or falls one and a half times as much as the index.

Betas are published by several stock-tracking services such as Value Line and are usually available from a broker. The key thing to remember about betas is that the higher the number the bigger the risk. If you're going to assume the risk that goes with an oversized beta, it should be in the expectation of an oversized reward.

SPREADS AND SPECIALISTS

Most buy orders refer to "block trades" or round numbers of shares (multiples of 100). But what if you have a fixed sum of money to invest—say, a bonus of $500? The number of shares that $500 will buy is likely to be an *odd lot* and not a multiple of 100 shares.

It's better to wait until you have the amount needed for a block trade (also called a round lot). This is the preferred number for buying and selling and the most economical unit when commissions are calculated.

What happens when a broker can't fill your order even for a round lot? This is where the *specialist* or match-maker comes in. Specialists concentrate on trading particular stocks and stay at their post on the exchange floor where those stocks trade. If a broker can't fill your order immediately, the order will be left with the specialist.

The specialist keeps lists of the unfilled orders and, as the market price moves up or down, looks for opportunities to fill each order. In this way, the specialist acts as a broker to other brokers, charging them commissions for every order successfully carried out.

When the *spread* between the bid and ask prices for a stock is wide, specialists turn into dealers and buy or sell some stock themselves. This has the effect of narrowing the spread and stimulating more trading activity—a good thing for the exchange and the specialist, but not always of benefit to the investor who pays more commissions.

By contrast, the thousands of stocks traded on Nasdaq or over-the-counter are sold through dealers or from broker to broker who monitor the activity of stocks on their computer screens. Nasdaq is also where you find the smallest, youngest companies. Many of them are high-technology and financial service stocks that have boomed in recent years. But you'll have to research them carefully to avoid the falling stars among the high-flyers.

You'll have no trouble finding candidates. Brokers are full of suggestions, of course, and you may come across intriguing products or companies while walking through a store or leafing through a magazine. Most of the information you need to check out these possibilities is readily available from the sources listed in the chapters and appendixes of this book, or calculated from the data you find there.

There's also practical advice for choosing good common stocks in Chapter 12, Reading Annual Reports. And if the techniques don't work all the time, they work often enough to be of great use to successful investors. Aside from price-earnings ratios and volatility, you'll want to check out the following:

BOOK VALUE. Normally, the price of a company's stock is higher than its book value (the difference between assets and liabilities), and stocks may be recommended as cheap because they are selling below book value. At any given time, hundreds of stocks will be selling below book value for one reason or another, and they aren't all dogs.

Others may be priced way too far above book value (not uncommon among high technology companies) to merit serious consideration. It's difficult to say what's too high because the standards vary so much depending on the industry (finance and insurance in particular).

DEBT-EQUITY RATIO. This shows how much leverage, or debt, a company is carrying compared with shareholders' equity. In general, the lower this figure the better, although the definition of an acceptable debt load varies from industry to industry.

You'll find data on debt-equity ratios in annual reports, and in publications available from Value Line, Moody's, and Standard & Poor's. As a rule, you should stick with companies whose debt amounts to no more than 35 percent of shareholders' equity.

RETURN ON EQUITY. This number is the company's net profits after taxes divided by its book value. It shows how much the company is earning on the stockholders' stake in the enterprise. If the number is erratic or declining even though profits are steady, there may be debt problems.

Look for a return on equity that is consistently high compared with other companies in the same industry, or that shows a strong pattern of long-term growth. A steady return on equity of more than 15 percent is a sign of a company that knows how to manage itself well.

LEADING MARKET INDICATORS

Like the year before, 1997 was a banner year for corporations, shareholders and chief executives. Corporate profits were up 11 percent, the stock market rose 23 percent, and the median total compensation of top bosses soared 18 percent, to $2.3 million.

Unemployment nationwide continued to drop. Consumer confidence shot up 13 percent. And inflation and interest rates stayed low—good for business and the stock market. But which of these *market indicators* will best help you understand—and forecast—the direction of the economy and the fate of your investments?

Stock indexes are probably the most closely watched indicators of the financial future. When the market rallies, it's a good sign for the economy in general. One measure by which to read the market is the Standard & Poor's 500. Its broader sampling makes it more useful than the Dow Jones Industrial Average, which is based on the stock prices of only 30 blue-chip stocks.

Other stock indexes, like the Russell 2000 and Nasdaq Composite, are weighted measures of small cap stocks and national market securities sold over-the-counter, and give perhaps a better picture of the total economy. These are described in Appendix A, along with key indicators like the *Consumer Price Index* and *Leading Indicators* (representing 11 components of economic growth from stock prices to housing starts).

Together they form the basis of the numbers-crunching discipline known as *technical analysis,* in which stock charts, moving averages, and volatility measures help professional and increasingly amateur investors ferret out buy and sell signals for thousands of stocks.

Unlike fundamental analysis—the Peter Lynch admonition to look at company profits, management, market niche, and the like—tech types focus on the price and trading patterns of stocks, rather than on the balance sheet or features of the underlying companies. And technical analysis may have a special appeal, given the long bull market and availability of sophisticated software.

"This is a revolution in terms of access," says Suzanne Cook, president of Stock Smart, which markets such products via its Internet site (www.stocksmart.com). "We have the opportunity to deliver to a wide audience what was previously available only to brokerage firms and institutional investors."

Nowadays, the serious investor can search through millions of bits of stock data—a capability that was beyond the reach of even those on

Wall Street a few years ago. But critics argue that technical analysis is too much like market timing, or the active trading of stocks in the hope of making quick gains. This is a risky strategy for individual investors, according to industry observers.

"Fundamental analysis is better for most investors," says Jay Kemp Smith, chairman of Leading Market Technologies, a company that sells software to big Wall Street brokerage firms. But many investors are using the new products not as a sole guide, but as a supplement to knowledge of a company's fundamentals.

The new software ranges from simple tutorials to more academic tools with bewildering names like "Option Vega" and "Binary Wave." Basically, they all allow investors to plot the ups and downs of a stock, and then determine whether it is time to buy or sell. "But you've got to be pretty bright or pretty dedicated to use the stuff," says Smith. What's out there is described in Chapter 14, Investing by Computer, which includes information and advice about software packages, major databases, getting stock reports, and tracking small companies using fundamental and/or technical analysis.

WHEN TO BAIL OUT

Despite the stock market's unnerving gyrations the past few years, investors have for the most part heeded the advice to buy stocks for the long term. But blind faith is not always a virtue. There may come a time when you *should* bail out of a stock or mutual fund.

The refusal to sell, whether it's due to unrealistic expectations, stubbornness, lack of interest, or inattention, is the undoing of many an investor. As a long-term investor, you don't want to cash in every time your stock moves up a few dollars. Commissions and taxes would cut into your gain and, besides, you'd have to decide where to put the proceeds. By the same token, you don't want to bail out in a panic in the aftermath of a market correction.

Even money managers admit that it's difficult knowing when to dump a stock. And analysts compound the problem by refusing to pull the plug even when companies fail to meet earnings expectations. When they do get uneasy about a stock, they often hedge with phrases like "weak hold." You should take that to mean, "Don't buy any more shares and if you've got a profit, seriously consider selling this stock."

Small cap guru Claudia Mott suggests that you reexamine your reasons for owning a stock. If you own it because you think it's a good value, it's probably less imperative to sell on a negative earnings surprise. "But if you expect the company to grow steadily, you might want to rethink your position because there's a question whether that growth will be realized." She adds, "It may be a good idea to sell on the first surprise, because there's a good chance you can buy a stock back at a lower price later."

Here are some clues that it's time to consider selling a profitable stock no matter what the analyst's report says, or what's in the most recent quarterly report:

FUNDAMENTALS CHANGE. Whether you own Wal-Mart or a small company most people have never heard of, you need to follow the corporation's prospects, earnings growth and its business success as reflected in market share, unit sales and profit margin. News stories in daily newspapers, investment newsletters, and financial publications like *Money* and *Barron's* are fertile sources of such information.

If the company's fundamentals start to weaken, it's time to reconsider your investment. An example might be a fast-expanding discount chain whose sales per store, after rising for years, suddenly decline. Such problems could signal that the business has peaked.

ECONOMY GOES SOUTH. Don't mess around during slumps caused by changes in the economy, such as the outlook for inflation or interest rates. These changes will affect company profits and investments in new businesses—two crucial drivers of stock prices. "These are situations that you really have to evaluate, because they can take a long time to mend," says Cheryl Rowan, senior strategist at Merrill Lynch.

In other words, try to figure out how much financial pain—that is, stress from the situation—you can handle and why you invested in stocks in the first place. Even a long decline may not matter much if you've got years before you need the money. But if that time is near, you may want to move into investments that aren't affected by market whims.

TARGETS ARE REACHED. If you have set specific target prices, either up or down, sell when the stock reaches that target. A good target is to double or triple your money, or limit losses to 20 percent. Such guidelines can prompt you to take your gains in a timely fashion and to dump losers before the damage gets too painful.

If you don't have stop orders with your broker, keep one in mind when you check the stock listings and sell any stock that hits your mental stop point. Don't fall victim to the Wall Street maxim that, "Bulls make money, bears make money, but pigs get slaughtered."

GRASS IS GREENER. Sell when you've found something better. Let's say you own a $10 stock that has an appraised value of $20. Then you find another $10 stock with a $30 value—50 percent better. That's when to sell.

A word of caution: Fund managers and other professional investors are by nature of their work more active traders than is appropriate for individuals to be. And while you can learn much from them, remember they are using other people's money.

MOMENTUM SLOWS. It's been a favorite catchword on Wall Street for several years, but momentum investing can work both ways. "Buying on rises, on dips, on *anything* has worked over the past decade," says Scott Lummer, managing director of Ibbotson Associates.

But anyone who used that strategy in 1974, when the Standard & Poor's 500 lost 26 percent, would have fared poorly. When growth slows, you should sell. Heavily promoted investments should also send out warning signals. By the time they gain notoriety, the smart money has gotten out.

Many investors also put off selling when it's time because they don't like the idea of paying taxes on their capital gains. But it's much wiser to take a taxable short-term gain then wait and suffer a long-term loss.

Losing some money on stocks is inevitable. Nobody buys only winners. But as Martin Zweig, a top investment adviser and publisher of the *Zweig Performance Ratings Report*, says, "You can be right on your stocks only 40 percent of the time and still do fine—if you cut your losses short."

INVESTOR INFORMATION

It doesn't take an MBA degree to do fundamental or technical analysis. But you have to know which questions to ask, and where to get the answers. Two books that can help are *Securities Analysis* and *Technical Analysis* (part of the personal seminar series available from the New York Institute of Finance).

You might also find useful The *Beardstown Ladies Common-Sense Investment Guide,* especially for the down-to-earth advice on "how we beat the stock market—and how you can too." And to simplify stock tables, dip into *The Wall Street Journal Guide to Understanding Money & Markets.*

Ventures
and Partnerships

Want an investment that returns your money five-fold? Just go back a few years and buy a chunk of a start-up company or new venture. Microsoft and Federal Express exist today because of money provided by "business angels" or venture capitalists. And the firms or funds that sell shares of new or untested companies say they still have a wide appeal for investors, and point to a 50-percent increase in such investments in the past year.

Before you decide to become a venture capitalist, there are a few caveats. About one-third of all venture capital deals are winners. That means some 67 percent are not, according to Stanley Pratt, editor of *Venture Capital Journal*. Most venture capital deals take five to seven years to reach maturity—not a way to make a quick killing. If you don't want to lock up funds over the long-term, look elsewhere.

If you would like to make a personal investment in a start-up company with real prospects, you should know that they are no longer the province of the very rich. You can purchase shares in public venture capital companies, buy into mutual funds that invest in emerging growth companies, or go all the way and take a $50,000 stake in a private placement or an initial public offering.

WHERE TO LOOK

Begin by reviewing a sufficient number of deals to be in a position to separate the hots from the dogs. "Professionals in the field review 400 to 500 prospects in a year," says Chantee Lewis, professor of finance at Bryant College in Rhode Island.

Individual investors needn't cope with so many proposals, he says, just enough to determine whether the deal is a fair risk compared to similar ones. Most important is to become involved in a network of informed investors, bankers and entrepreneurs. Other sources of information about new ventures are trade journals, shows and conventions, accountants, attorneys and business clubs.

And don't forget the 500 or so investment companies licensed and regulated by the Small Business Administration. These companies pool the money they raise by selling shares to the public over-the counter or on the American Stock Exchange. Their results are not always spectacular, but SBIC portfolios are diversified among new companies, second- or third-round financing, and companies with new products.

Venture capital companies are also publicly traded, but have fewer restrictions on the type of investments they make. These companies are generally more speculative and carry greater risk, so a good rule of thumb is to allocate no more than 20 percent of a portfolio to such investments, says Lewis.

Angels in the outfield are another matter. More and more individual investors are beating out venture capitalists and other financiers as a source of funds. And there are several very good reasons:

❏ Banks and funds are reluctant to lend money to start-up companies because they have a high risk of failure.

❏ Entrepreneurs hate venture capitalists—who often demand as much as 51 percent of a firm's stock.

Angels are easier to find, and they make a lot more deals—close to $56 billion in an estimated 450,000 small companies last year alone. That makes them a bigger force than venture capitalists, who invested only $4 billion in the same period. They are also as close as your neighbors or co-workers. Economist Robert Gaston says the typical small company angel is a business owner or manager who invests in companies that are less than 50 miles away from home or office. Angels also are not ultra-rich ($90,000 median income), deal makers putting up less than $50,000, and frequent investors (they make annual trades).

Angels don't give money away, however. They want their investment to grow by at least 25 percent each year for five years, says William Wetzel, professor at the University of New Hampshire. And many times the angel wants an active role in company management or direction.

How do entrepreneurs find angels? A growing number of small companies that want to raise money are bypassing Wall Street in favor of a do-it-yourself approach. Using a DPO, or direct public offering, companies sell shares directly to interested investors including employees, customers, suppliers, distributors, and friends.

"Entrepreneurs are taking control of how money is raised and invested," says Drew Field, a San Francisco securities lawyer who helps take small companies public. Last year, companies raised $455 million in DPOs, up 40 percent from the previous year.

By doing it themselves, they save money in two ways: Document preparation and the average 15 percent in fees and commissions that brokers get for selling the shares. "When a broker is involved, you have three lawyers that you didn't have before, so your cost is going to go up astronomically," says Field. He estimates a DPO is 10 percent of the cost of an IPO done through investment banks where costs can run into the millions.

Critics of direct offerings say they are risky and not easy to sell. "There's no liquidity," says David Menlow, president of IPO Financial Network. Intrastate offerings, for example, can't be resold outside the state in which they are originally sold for nine months. And interstate DPOs of less than $1 million need only be filed with state securities regulators.

Niche companies tend to make the most successful DPOs, analysts say, because individual investors get the chance to support something they know about. Among those filed early in 1997 were the following:

Company/business	Amount (millions)
Real Goods Trading	
Retails alternative energy products	$4.6
Blue Fish Clothing	
Designs and markets women's clothing	4.0
Mendocino Brewing	
Craft brewer	3.6
Summit Savings Bank	
Community bank and mortgage lender	2.0
Annie's Homegrown	
Markets macaroni and cheese dinners	1.5
Thanksgiving Coffee	
Roasts and markets arabica coffee	1.4
Bridge City Tool Works	
Makes and retails tools for woodworkers	1.1
Hahnemann Laboratories	
Manufactures homeopathic remedies	0.5

PUTTING IT ALL TOGETHER

Hardly a week goes by without a major merger that shakes up an industry. But in a quieter way, some companies grow by acquiring one tiny business at a time. Although they lack the drama of a Boeing or Microsoft, these deals can add up to a lucrative opportunity for investors.

The "roll-up" companies, as they are known, are often begun by venture capital firms, which pick managers and provide initial financing. (See Figure 7.1.) "Then we buy and build," says Bruce Rauner, a principal at a Chicago venture capital and buyout firm that has financed more than 55 such deals. Once a company reaches appropriate size, it is taken public, although the venture capitalists may retain a position in it.

But investors in roll-ups should be wary, especially of gobble-them-up outfits. "You want companies with a strategy, not just a consolidator trying to build revenue by buying companies cheaply," explains Richard Dowd, corporate finance partner at the accounting firm of Ernst & Young.

Another sign of a smart roll-up is the cross-marketing of products to newly acquired clients. Lason Holdings, a company that helps businesses manage their paperwork, fits this profile, says Robert Gardiner, portfolio manager of the Wasatch Micro-Cap Fund. In this way, Lason has achieved a growth rate of 20 percent—double that of similar companies in separate markets converting, printing, or distributing documents.

Other companies use roll-ups to broaden product offerings. Cable Design and American Medserve, for example, provide cable for computer, video, audio, and home alarm systems, and fill and deliver prescription drugs to institutions, including nursing homes. Yet even without stock run-ups, such companies are still a good buy considering annual earnings growth in excess of 25 percent.

Trouble is, you have to search hard for these opportunities because they are rarely publicized. Your best leads will come from local bankers or brokers. Ask them what ventures they are looking at and which ones they recommend. And look for companies in businesses you know something about. It's also wise to start with ventures that are near your home so that you can maintain close contact with the people running the company.

But face it: Many people who sink their money into start-ups will lose at least part of it. Even successful ventures rarely show a payoff within five years. But you can improve those odds by buying shares in the small business investment companies, or SBICs, mentioned earlier. These companies raise capital and invest it in businesses with a net worth

FIGURE 7.1. MOST ACTIVE VENTURE CAPITAL FIRMS

The 30 most active venture capital firms, measured by the number of deals in U.S and overseas companies in the first half of 1997:

Company	Location	Total deals
New Enterprise Associates	Baltimore	26
Advent International	Boston	21
Oak Investment Partners	Westport, CT	20
Robertson Stephens & Co.	San Francisco	20
BancBoston Capital	Boston	19
Hambrecht & Quist	San Francisco	19
Accel Partners	San Francisco	18
Atlas Ventures	Boston	18
Bessemer Venture Partners	Boston	18
Norwest Venture Capital	Minneapolis	17
U.S. Venture Partners	Menlo Park, CA	17
Institutional Ventures	Menlo Park	14
Brentwood Venture Capital	Los Angeles	12
Canaan Partners	Norwalk, CT	12
Dominion Ventures	San Francisco	12
Sprout Group	New York	12
Venrock Associates	New York	10
Benchmark Capital	Menlo Park	9
Sierra Ventures	Menlo Park	9
Weiss, Peck & Greer	San Francisco	9
Charles River Partners	Boston	9
Crosspoint Venture Partners	Los Altos, CA	8
NationsBank Capital	Charlotte, NC	8
Partech International	San Francisco	8
Trinity Ventures	San Mateo, CA	8
Ben Franklin Technology	Philadelphia	7
Onset Ventures	Menlo Park	7
Alta Communications	San Francisco	6
Foundation Capital	Menlo Park	6
Menlo Ventures	Menlo Park	6

Source: Coopers & Lybrand

of $6 million or less. Most are owned by banks or groups of private individuals, but some have public shares that can be bought or sold over-the-counter or on the American Stock Exchange.

SBICs concentrate on small businesses that create jobs. They are licensed by the Small Business Administration, which guarantees them up to $4 for every $1 of private capital they raise. Some of the money is invested in start-ups that offer little more than potentially workable concepts. The rest are second and third-round financings to help spur the growth of companies that are already marketing a product or have moved solidly into the black.

A number of SBICs prefer to cut out as much risk as possible. They invest only in companies that are mature enough to provide them with some current income, which they in turn pay out to shareholders. Staples and Federal Express are among the 80,000 companies that have used SBICs in the past.

What kind of SBIC you invest in depends on whether you want immediate income or longer-term capital gains. But whatever kind you select, ask yourself two questions: Do you think that the companies supported by the SBIC are sound businesses? And what is the investment record of the company's management? (For a free directory or more information, write to: Investment Division, Small Business Administration, 409 Third St. SW, Washington, DC 20416. Or visit the Internet site www.sba. gov/inv.)

COPING WITH RISK

Managing risk does not mean dumping all your stocks or other investments when you see storm clouds—or rushing in to buy at the glimpse of a rainbow. To develop a strategy for all seasons, you first must ask yourself if you are more interested in seeing your investments grow in value, or in collecting immediate income. Obviously, betting on future growth is riskier than collecting dividends and interest payments.

The degree of risk that you choose to take should be determined by your age, earning power, net worth, tax bracket—and temperament. A 30-year-old single person with bright career prospects can take larger risks than someone nearing retirement or living on savings.

An aggressive investor who aims for high growth but does not demand immediate income might put all his money into high-growth, high-risk stocks. Or he could pick medium-risk growth stocks, but simultaneously increase both his risks and potential rewards by using leverage or borrowing money from his broker (more on this in Chapter 9, Margin Trading and Options).

When calculating how to manage potential losses, bear in mind that there are three kinds of risk:

MARKET RISK. This refers to the overall behavior of the stock market. The standard yardstick used to measure such risk is volatility—that is, the extent of stock price flucuations in relation to those of the Standard & Poor's 500. A stock that has risen or fallen more sharply that the S&P index is considered riskier that the market as a whole.

To find out a stock's historic record of volatility, ask your broker or look it up in the *Value Line Investment Survey*. If you think it's time to be cautious, you can cut your market risk by reducing the portion of your assets in common stocks, especially the most volatile issues.

DIVERSIFIABLE RISK. Stock prices also fluctuate because of industry and company developments. This type of risk is called "diversifiable" because you can reduce it by diversifying your investments.

It's possible to achieve good diversification by owning only five stocks—provided they are in different industries that are exposed to different types of economic and political risk. For example, some stock groups that are not likely to behave in the same way at the same time are: computers, cosmetics, and hospital management.

INTEREST-RATE RISK. Changes in interest rates apply primarily to bonds, but this can also affect the shares of corporations whose earnings are hurt when interest rates rise—and helped when they fall. These firms include utilities, banks, and finance companies.

Ideally, you should buy these interest-sensitive stocks before interest rates start to turn down, and then switch into other stocks before the next uptrend begins. Calling the turns on interest rates right on target is an impossible dream, but anybody who reads the financial pages carefully should be able to get a handle on which way rates are likely to head.

Almost all investments have some risks, but don't let that stop you from investing. Sometimes the riskiest strategy of all is to do nothing. If you had let your cash sit in a savings account or money market fund for most of the 1990s, you would have drastically cut the gains you could have made. Smart investors analyze their own situations and decide which risks they are willing to take, and which they want most to avoid.

QUESTIONS TO ASK

Before you buy any stock, ask some tough questions. That's the best way to separate the real pearls from the faux. Don't get caught up in the race for quick profits. Most investors do best by picking several stocks as a way of cushioning the loss of one flier that takes a dive. And be prepared to live with the rule of five. It says that out of every five stocks you own, probably one will be a loser, three will do nicely, and one will do much better than expected.

As we've seen, those risks increase even more with IPOs and venture capital shares. That means your chances for success will be increased if you select new issues from reputable investment bankers, and venture capital firms like Sevin Rosen, which took Compaq public in the 1980s.

Once you find out about a new company, your first investigative step is to read the prospectus. Despite its many caveats, the prospectus will help you form a rough opinion about the company and what it may be worth. Look for the following:

MANAGEMENT. Small stocks, by virtue of their high rate of earnings growth, also have a high potential for earnings disappointments. "Make sure you have a management team that has some sort of track record, so they have stability," advises John Rogers of the Ariel Growth Fund.

Depth of management is also important. Small companies' managements tend to be fairly thin. It can often be one or two people that make all the decisions. "That's kind of dangerous," says Rogers.

BUSINESS. What you want are companies with unique products or franchises. The problem is that many of them—like Dell Computer or Microsoft—seem too expensive already. Also seek out companies relatively immune from foreign competition, such as newspapers, restaurant chains, cable television or insurance firms (see Figure 7.2).

The best way to protect against any decline in the stock market is to own stocks that aren't already in the stratosphere—that is, value stocks. They have made a comeback in recent years, and you'll have a better chance of separating the bargains from the bombshells.

FINANCES. The company should be able to service its debt. But because start-ups usually have not had sufficient time to build up profits and earnings, look at the ratio of total earnings price to annual sales. On

FIGURE 7.2. AVERAGE SIZE OF VENTURE DEALS

Business	1997	1996
Consumer products	$11.8M	$7.7M
Radio/television	11.3	3.8
Retail stores	7.0	12.0
Telecommunications	5.5	4.7
Biotechnology	4.9	4.3
Medical devices	4.4	5.4
Electronics	4.2	5.2
Healthcare services	3.8	5.4
Computer software	3.6	3.5
Other	4.5	5.3

Source: Coopers & Lybrand

the whole, this capitalization-to-sales ratio should not be greater than 2 to 7.

Many companies, in their enthusiasm to invest in new plants and larger inventories, often overexpand. Then they have to unload their goods, thus driving down prices and profits. Their revenues stagnate or fall, and profits decline or turn into losses.

DIVERSITY. It's hard to cut your losses short on a small stock if you're following the rule about ignoring short-term price swings. The pros say you should sell only if the company's fundamentals turn sour. But the nature of small firms is that even the best can fail quickly.

So, if you're in small cap stocks for the enormous rewards they offer, you must be prepared to have one or two picks go belly up (remember the rule of five?). "You shouldn't have any favorite stocks," says Peter Coolidge, director of equity trading at Brean Murray & Co. "Have a handful at the barest minimum."

PROSPECTS FOR PROFITS

Another way to get in on a start-up business is through a *limited partnership*. Lately, some brokerage firms have offered for public sale some partnerships that invest in new businesses, among them Merrill Lynch and

Boettcher & Company. Investors can buy into the partnerships for $5,000 plus a sales commission. But unfortunately, there is no aftermarket where you can sell your units if you suddenly should need the money. All Merrill Lynch will do, for example, is try to match up sellers with buyers through brokers.

Limited partnerships aren't new (but they are no longer the tax shelters that gave many investors anxiety attacks). Oil and gas partnerships, for example, use your money to lease land and equipment and then pay for drilling and producing. Naturally, any sharp decline in oil prices can reduce your income and even your capital.

You also can buy shares in an office building, apartment house or shopping mall either as a limited partner or shareholder in a real estate investment trust. These potentially lucrative investments are sold by brokerage firms, insurance companies, and financial planners.

They also ask that you put up at least $5,000. But you can choose from two types of partnerships—those that stress tax breaks and those that emphasize income and the prospect of capital gains when the partnership's properties are sold.

Public partnerships are registered with the Securities and Exchange Commission, which requires the sponsors to disclose their records. Each has scores, and often hundreds, of investors, and some are asked to put up minimums of $10,000 or more, depending on the properties.

Private partnerships do not have to register with the SEC, although they do have to make some disclosures to that agency. They can accept only up to 33 investors, so the stakes are higher, and usually require a minimum investment of $25,000 or more. Your risks of being audited by the IRS are also greater than with a public partnership.

When considering a partnership, make sure it is a strong investment with solid prospects for income or capital gains. Never consider one offered by an unknown caller over the telephone. And check the prospectus to see that the general partners collect their share of the profits at the same time you do—and there is no skimming.

Finally, be particularly cautious of buying limited partnerships toward the end of the year. That's when hustlers tend to unload inferior partnerships on panicky investors trying to reduce taxes. Many of these could be dangerous to your wealth.

Several newsletters evaluate public partnerships and sponsors, and they can point you in the direction of reliable programs. One that assesses deals of all types as well as tax-planning strategies and economic factors is the *Stanger Report,* 1129 Broad St., Shrewsbury, NJ 07701 (800-631-2291).

You might also get help finding partnerships or ventures from interested local investors. Check to see if there is a venture capital club in your area. There are more than 90 such clubs across the country that hold monthly luncheon meetings at which entrepreneurs and investors can discuss ideas for new businesses. Members include venture capitalists, bankers, attorneys and corporate executives as well as individual investors.

VENTURE FUNDS

These are another type of limited partnership where you buy in and don't see any money for several years, or until the company is sold or goes public. Then you realize a handsome profit—or loss, if the fund makes too many bad picks.

Venture funds are not for every income bracket, with minimum investments in some cases of $250,000. As with mutual funds, they tend to be only as good as the portfolio manager. It pays, therefore, to read those quarterly and annual reports to measure performance.

Some venture funds that invested in cable television and phone-paging companies have reaped big rewards. But others chose to back many high-tech and biomedical firms and suffered badly as one after the other disappeared. The upshot: Stick with funds that pay out in five years or less, and where the annual rate of return is 20 to 30 percent.

If you don't have a spare quarter million dollars, consider those mutual funds that invest part or all of their portfolios in start-up ventures. The best-known is the Nautilus Fund in Boston, which helped launch Apple Computer in 1979. Apple soared and made many shareholders happy—notably those who took their profits near the peak before it eventually plunged.

According to Lipper Analytical Services, there are at least 140 of these special funds. They sell shares for as little as $1,000 and will provide you with a free prospectus and past performance records that you can check. Venture capital investment hit a new high in June 1997 of $5.7 billion, compared to $1.5 billion in 1995, according to a survey by Coopers & Lybrand.

A sound method of choosing among the funds that invest chiefly in the stocks of small, promising companies is to get a trial subscription to one of the many newsletters that rate fund performance. Two of them are *No Load Fund X* and *California Technology Stock Letter* (see Appendix B).

Among the funds that invest in start-ups besides Nautilus are the Acorn Fund, Ariel Growth, Founders Discovery, Janus Venture, and Vanguard Explorer. Many of these funds are heavily weighted with high-tech issues. But if you want still more specialization, you might look into Alliance Quasar, Merrill Lynch Phoenix, Montgomery Micro-Cap, and Oppenheimer Discovery.

That's not always a good idea, however. "When you read about a lot of fund managers bragging about all the technology stocks in their portfolio, and shunning the smaller, consumer-oriented companies, that gives me comfort that they should come back into vogue for the next three to five years," says John Rogers, president of Ariel Capital Management.

These are the companies not well researched by analysts, where you can get in, do your homework, evaluate the management and product, and make a difference with your money, notes Rogers. "When we find one of these companies, we'll own them for five, six years, or more, and we won't have all those trading costs or tax losses."

No longer do venture capitalists and fund managers concentrate their dollars on companies that have proven they can make it. Because of the unusual success of some recent new businesses, particularly in the realm of financial services, fastfood chains and home health care, financiers are willing to take greater risks than just a few years ago—if they figure they may also reap greater rewards.

By some standards, this illustrates the best of the American capitalistic system: finding and seizing an opportunity and cashing in on it. But it also indicates a growing trend to safer investments—a strategy born out of all the disappointing technology and biomedical issues that came out in the 1980s before and after the market crash in 1987.

"What changed is that there is much less motivation to do seed investing" says Edward Roberts, professor of management at MIT's Sloan School of Business. "Why take the risk of high tech start-ups when you can double your money with funeral parlors, trail bikes or steak houses?" Only in America can investors see greater profits in coffins than computers.

INVESTOR INFORMATION

Real estate limited partnerships aren't as interesting as investing in stocks, and it shows in the number of books available on the subject. For an overview that isn't deadly dull, look into *The New Dow Jones-Irwin Guide to Real Estate Investing* by Gaylon Greer.

Those interested in finding out about venture capital deals and the companies that make them might want to obtain a copy of the annual *Money Tree Survey* available from the accounting firm of Coopers & Lybrand (888-609-7117).

CHAPTER 8

Seek Out
Special Situations

They aren't for everyone, nor are they easily classified. But for some reason, people expect a stock to do well even if it's been a laggard for years. Sometimes the reason is new management. If the new managers succeed, the stock will indeed soar. If they fail, the stock goes back into the dumpster. It's difficult to call the outcome in such a special situation, but the winners tend to win big. And the losers don't get beaten too badly because the stock usually was priced low enough that it won't sink a lot lower.

"There's very little room for the stocks we buy to fall further because we're buying them so cheaply," explains Robert Perkins, manager of the Berger Small Cap Value Fund. Most mornings he starts his day scanning the newspaper tables for those stocks that have hit 52-week lows, not highs. That's because Perkins is a contrarian, befriending stocks at a time when they have lost all their friends.

When evaluating these stocks, he is looking for firms whose troubles he believes are temporary and cyclical, providing the opportunity to get a stock on the bargain counter. The strategy has paid off for shareholders. In a market led primarily by gains in large cap stocks, the Berger fund's much smaller stocks delivered a total return for 1996 of 26 percent, equal to the Dow's return.

Even bankrupt companies offer investors an opportunity to make money if the company pulls itself together or restructures successfully. But you should buy soon after the firm emerges from Chapter 11. At that point, there's still risk but also a low base for future gains. And since most institutions shy away from stocks of troubled companies, investors can sometimes make large profits in turnarounds.

Mergers and buyouts are also special situations. They were at the heart of the raging bull market that preceded the crash in 1987. Investors then were actually looking to buy shares of poorly run companies on the theory that some other company would want to buy up the assets, throw out the old management, and run the company better.

That happened frequently enough to make the strategy profitable for some savvy investors (or those with insider information on what was going to happen, an entirely legal way to invest, described in Chapter 5). Of course, when no other company came along in this corporate variation of the "greater fool" theory, the investors who decided to buy after the stock had climbed 50 percent, took a bath.

Most fads are based on the greater fool theory—"I'll be foolish and buy it today because I can sell it to a greater fool tomorrow." The fad lasts only until it becomes clear that nobody at all wants the stock.

Splits and spin-offs make more sense—when they are justified by profitable growth. Firms most often declare stock splits when their earnings are strong. And spin-offs provide shareholders in the parent company with price appreciation that "significantly and consistently outperforms the market averages," says Joseph Cornell, CFA, author of *Spin-Off to Pay-Off.*

SIZING UP THE MARKET

For investors who place safety first, the best common stocks are those of companies that have been around for 20 years or more. Many, but not all, have familiar names like Philip Morris or IBM.

Even safer are preferred stocks (indicated by a "pf" or "pr" following the company's name in the newspaper tables). With preferred stock, the dividends are fixed, and the company's obligation to pay them is stronger than for common stock. The down side is that your dividends stay the same even if company profits jump.

If you have common stock, you share directly in the success or failure of the business. If it has large profits, your return increases. You are also legally entitled to a say in major company decisions, such as whether to issue additional stock, sell the company to outside buyers, or change the board of directors. The rule is that each share has the same voting power, so the more shares you own, the greater your power.

You can vote in person by attending a corporation's annual meeting, or you can vote by using an absentee form, called a *proxy ballot,* which is mailed to you before each meeting. The proxy allows a yes or no vote on any number of proposals. Alternatively, shareholders may authorize their votes to be cast consistently with the board of directors who are charged with setting long-term goals for the company.

Secondary issues are the solid, well-established businesses that receive only a little less investor confidence than blue chips. But they are not considered *growth stocks*, which are usually relatively young companies with growth potential but less assurance of success.

Stocks that sell for less than $5 a share are generally known as *penny stocks* (a good example of inflation!). Though cheap, they are highly speculative. Worse, they are sometimes outright scams sold over the phone by clever salespeople to unwary investors. (See Chapter 15 Penny Stocks and Other Scams.)

Like ventures and partnerships discussed earlier, special situations can occur among big and small companies. But you have to seek them out yourself, because nobody except possibly a friendly broker is going to bring them to your attention.

Along with bargain-hunting, special situations are an "acquired taste," involving restructurings, liquidations, mini-stocks, and the like, that can turn wallflowers into sought-after equities almost overnight.

BANKRUPT COMPANIES

Older investors' eyes glaze over at memories of the huge fortunes that were made on bankrupt companies of the past such as Interstate Stores, which eventually became Toys "Я" Us. The potential for such gains springs from the nature of the bankruptcy laws, designed to give companies a new lease on life, or to work out a plan to pay creditors.

Investing in bankrupt companies is not for the faint of heart, however. Even situations that look promising often do not pan out. And since the bankruptcy game is dominated by professionals, it would be foolhardy to jump in without coaching from such experts as those at Bear Stearns or others who invest in bankrupt companies.

If you'd like to take a crack at it, here are some guidelines from the National Institute of Business Management. They identify the traits that indicate a company will make a strong comeback:

❑ A large tax loss carry-forward that can be written off against future earnings, thus sharply boosting after-tax profits.

❑ Substantial salable assets relative to debt, indicating that the securities will appreciate even if the company is partially or completely
liquidated.

❑ A new management team, especially one with turnaround experience that will sell off unprofitable divisions or buy profitable new
ones.

❑ Restructuring of debt to improve cash flow and reduce leverage by
outsiders.

The returns that can be had by investing in businesses going
through corporate restructurings are huge. The reason the strategy works
may be something you don't want to know: It requires old-fashioned securities analysis into obscure companies. There are no index funds, and
no simple ways to buy bankrupt companies.

Some mutual funds also invest in bankrupt companies, but you'll
have to look hard to find them. Three that do are Fidelity Special Situations, Mutual Beacon, and Merrill Lynch Phoenix.

You have to remember that it takes time for improved performance
to be recognized even after restructuring. As a hedge, look for companies
that have a strong position in their field, and diversify with at least three
stocks. If you're lucky, one will prove to be a big winner. Hopefully that
choice will do well enough to make all the risks worthwhile.

SHOULD YOU BECOME A CONTRARIAN?

Money managers are paid to deal with occasional floods of money. But a
tidal wave of money into a particular stock or fund is often a contrary indicator. It shows that a particular stock, sector or type of fund is wildly in
favor with investors—and probably due for a whopping decline. There's
some Wall Street snobbery in contrary indicators—but also a bit of wis-
dom. After all, most people, without intending to, buy at the top of the
market and sell at the bottom.

As we've learned, smart investors buy small cap stocks after a sell-off
in the broad market—when most people are afraid to buy anything that
seems risky. Once the speculative sap rises and your indicators warn that
the market is entering a high-risk area, you can begin to take profits.

"Sell any individual stock if the company's annual rate of earnings
growth slows to less than 10 percent for two consecutive quarters," says

Richard Bang in *Contrarian Investing*. Growth stocks can be savagely un-forgiving if you buy them too high or fail to sell them soon enough. They can fall even faster than they rose, he says, a cruel form of "capital punish-ment" for anyone whose timing is off.

Buy small stocks only if you don't mind watching the market on a daily or weekly basis, can accept short-term fluctuations in the value of your shares, and are willing to own at least five or ten different stocks for diversification. It may be easier to be patient with volatile stocks if you re-strict them to a smaller percentage of your portfolio.

While the contrarian approach seems to take a great deal of courage, for those investors willing to accept additional risk, this may be a way to earn above-average returns. When the shares of a half-dozen semiconductor equipment makers fell 70 percent on a temporary down-turn, Berger's Perkins swooped in to buy them all. And when orders for new computer chips started to rise in 1996, the stocks of the equipment makers bounced back.

Just because something is cheap doesn't mean it can't get cheaper. To take advantage of these situations, analysts and stock pickers use many different methods for calculating a company's intrinsic value, some too complex for most investors. There are much simpler ways to spot bargain stocks—if you keep three caveats in mind:

DIVERSIFY AS MUCH AS POSSIBLE. While depressed stocks consis-tently outperform the market as a group, some individual issues may per-form quite badly. David Dreman, author of *The New Contrarian Invest-ment Strategy*, favors stocks with low price-earnings ratios over more popular issues. "Fads are as prevalent in the stock market as they are in the garment industry," he says. "And when an out-of-favor stock comes back into fashion, its price-earnings can go up surprisingly quickly."

BE A LONG-TERM INVESTOR. Some companies may need two to three years to show capital gains. Instead of looking at earnings, Norman Weinger of Oppenheimer & Co. totals the non-cash charges, such as de-preciation and amortization, and subtracts the amount that will be needed for any capital improvements.

When a stock's price is low relative to its undedicated cash flow, it's a sign that someone could in theory borrow the money for a takeover and pay off the debt with the company's own cash. "Even if that doesn't hap-pen, the stock should rise as others recognize how cheap shares are," says Weinger.

REALIZE THAT STOCKS MAY LAG. During a strong bull market, when investors are exuberant, popular issues usually race ahead of under-valued stocks. Buy the shares of established companies that are selling near their average lows for the past ten years, advises Berger's Perkins.

"That's common sense," he says. "You want to buy a solid company when it's having a terrible year and sell when it's having a great year." When savings and loans were going bankrupt in the early 1990s, Perkins put 35 per-cent of his fund's portfolio into thrifts he figured would survive or be taken over because "they were priced as though they were going out of business."

Bear in mind, junkyards are mean places and any price increases have come in the middle of a long bull market. When markets turn sour, junk can sink pretty fast. But the pros are preparing for the next reces-sion, which they think will be awe-inspiring. And they're buying the wreckage now—cheaply. To take advantage of these special situations, the hardest bitten of Wall Street professionals are even setting up what are ominously called "vulture funds" that will pick at the carcasses.

What they look for when bargain-hunting are shares of companies that have been in business for a while, have very low price-earnings ratios, and can generate cash flows beyond what are needed for existing opera-tions. "Such stocks offer the opportunity to buy the company with no money down and easy payments," says Oppenheimer's Weinger.

MERGERS AND BUYOUTS

Takeovers and buyouts occurred by the thousands in the past few years, and no end appears in sight (see Figure 8.1). The effects aren't felt just on Wall Street. Investors all over the country need to know how to react as well. Suppose you look in the business pages of your daily newspaper, and find that a company in which you own stock is a merger candidate. What should you do?

The first rule: Don't chase rumors. There are many more phony stories out there than real deals. But if a stock you own does become a merger candidate, your choices are many. For example, you may be asked to consider what is known as an "equity buy-back" plan. If you are, hold on to your shares. Maybe even buy some more. When a company an-nounces that it's buying back its own common stock, chances are strong that the price of the shares will rise.

The motives are often clear. Management, fearing a hostile takeover, will try to give shareholders nearly the same benefits by raising

Figure 8.1: Joining Forces

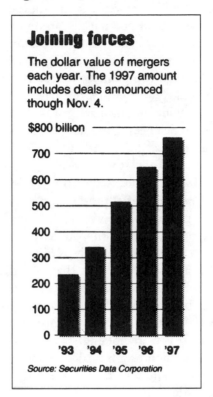

Joining forces

The dollar value of mergers
each year. The 1997 amount
includes deals announced
though Nov. 4.

$800 billion

700

600

500

400

300

200

100

0

'93   '94   '95   '96   '97

Source: Securities Data Corporation

the stock price. Other reasons behind a stock buy-back: The company
may want to increase earnings per share, or boost shareholder values for a
takeover of its own.

More than $418 billion in mergers or acquisitions were made in the
first half of 1997, according to research firm Securities Data Corporation,
on a pace to easily beat the record $648 billion during 1996.

The soaring stock market has made mergers more costly. But that
does not mean the deals are overpriced, say analysts. One reason is that
interest rates are relatively low, reducing the cost to companies that borrow to finance takeovers. Some industries seeing a lot of deals include
computer software, health care, and financial services.

Small stocks also put you into the buy-out game. In one top-per-
forming small cap fund, one company was taken private last year, and ten
others got takeover bids or inquiries—usually at a big gain in price.

But by the time the average investor has heard the news, the pros have probably squeezed the stocks for any short-term gains. The profits that remain "can easily be wiped out just in trading commissions," warns Jay Kaplan, manager of the Prudential Small Company Value fund.

He advises intrepid investors to play a long-term, after-the-fact game—buying into solid companies after the merger, but only when the combination seems likely to yield more than the sum of its parts. Such a strategy will not provide spectacular profits, but according to a recent study by Computer Sciences Corporation, a consulting firm, the approach can substantially beat the market.

One maneuver that investors increasingly must ponder is the *leveraged buyout*. This basically means that the firm's own management or a large investor like Warren Buffet proposes to buy up the shares owned by the public to take the company private. If a leveraged buyout proposal comes your way, do nothing until you have read the official offering statement. Then see what you are really getting for your shares.

Accept the deal if you figure out that over the long term the transaction will yield a substantially higher return than would selling at the current price. But be wary of offers in which you will be paid in low-quality "junk bonds" instead of cash. Often the bonds in these deals are riskier than the stocks you are holding.

If there is a recession or a miscalculation by the deal-makers, some of these corporations could take a dive and drag bondholders with them. In a bankruptcy, a defaulting junk bond could lose more than half its value overnight.

A number of funds take part in leveraged buyouts, but many more could be considered "special situations" funds with 50 percent or more of assets in bankrupt companies or those involved in mergers or spin-offs. "We invest in deals," says Michael Price, president and portfolio manager of Mutual Shares, "but that takes in a lot of territory. We're buyers now even though there aren't that many cheap stocks."

SECTOR STOCKS

The Dow's leap past the 8,000 mark has inspired the more daring market players to step up the hunt for the tantalizing high-return—albeit high-risk—speculative stocks to be found among small companies.

"Tertiary stocks, those selling for $15 and under, have come to life," says Scott Bleier, chief investment strategist at Prime Charter. "One week they want the banks, the next week they want the pharmaceuticals. Lately it's technology, which tends to have a lot of fans," he says.

If you are willing to pay really close attention to your investments and try for spectacular gains, you can specialize—and hedge your bets—by buying so-called *sector stocks* which concentrate on specific areas of the economy. Let's say you are optimistic about technology, but a bit wary about inflation. In that case, you can invest part of your assets in a promising though risky software company. But simultaneously put another 10 percent of your money in retail stores or consumer products. They most likely will jump if inflation threatens.

Keep in mind, too, that stocks in a given group tend to fall in unison. Select stocks in more than one industry so you have some diversification. And study the *Value Line Investment Survey* and Standard & Poor's *Outlook* to keep up-to-date on industry developments.

"There are a lot of stocks around that offer seductive returns and aren't yet discovered," says Scott Black, president and investment manager of Delphi Management in Boston. His favorites are in oil-and-gas producers and out-of-favor suppliers to defense-related markets.

None of these prosaic stocks tend to be hot names like Netscape or Starbucks. Many are companies whose fortunes have yet to be made from their seemingly ordinary operations. And there's no guarantee that these bets will follow their investors' expectations—but that's part of the excitement of the high-spec game.

The playing field has also leveled somewhat, with services such as First Call, IBES, and Zachs Investment Research packaging Wall Street earnings estimates for the public. But the number that matters is the one analysts call in to their best clients as the financial reporting date draws near. That makes patience and the small stocks ignored by Wall Street the way to go for individual investors.

The cut in the capital-gains tax is also going to make investing in small and mid-size companies much more attractive over the next six to eight years, says James Stack, president of InvesTech Research. The reason: Lower capital-gains taxes increase the immediate risks of a 20-percent decline for the glamour stocks that most small investors own directly or through mutual funds. After such a slump, new sectors are likely to thrive.

The current winners among top stock pickers in August 1997, according to *Money* magazine, have generally favored technology and filled out their portfolios with health care stocks and the shares of financial services companies that are profiting from low or falling inflation.

One of them is Bill Martindale, who manages about $2.5 billion for private investors, bank trust accounts, and seven mutual funds (Key Premier). "We hear about promising new companies through regional brokers and underwriters," he says. Indeed, his greatest success has been with small caps.

"The most important thing is whether management actually does what they say they are going to do," says Martindale. "Over time, we sell our mistakes and let the other investments drive the portfolio." Over the past seven years, his firm has earned an average of 31 percent annually compared to a not too shabby 20 percent for the Standard & Poor's 500.

SPLITS AND SPIN-OFFS

When the stock market soars, as it has for the past seven years, it's time to watch for stock splits. A company subdivides its stock to keep it attractive to investors who generally prefer shares in the $15 to $40 range. If a stock rises to, say, $60, then the company may issue three new shares in exchange for two old shares. That usually brings the price down to about $40.

The most recent New York Stock Exchange study shows that stocks splitting at least three shares for two rose an average of 2½ times more than stocks that did not split. The study compared prices three years before the split with those three years after.

Firms most often declare stock splits when their earnings are strong. Thus splits can be good news for shareholders, bringing increased dividends or favorable growth prospects. So it may be wise to ask a broker for his recommendations of stocks that seem likely to split. Other reasons that a company may split their stocks:

❑ Management becomes fearful of a hostile takeover. When the top officials hold only a small percentage of the outstanding shares, a stock split will make more shares available at a lower price and thus lessen the likelihood of a raider buying the company.

❑ Earnings are likely to continue to grow, which means that the price of shares will keep rising. With more stock, the per share profits will appear smaller—but only for a while. It also indicates that directors recognize the advantage of adding shares to keep old stockholders and attract new ones.

❑ A small, growing company, whose shares are traded on Nasdaq, wants to list its stock on an exchange where the rules are far tougher. To trade on the New York Stock Exchange, for example, requires a minimum of 1.1 million shares and at least 2,000 share-holders for a market value of $18 million.

❑ A corporation seeks to make an acquisition with minimal cash or debt. To do that, management needs the additional shares to attract the directors and shareholders of the target company.

There can even be a *reverse split*, where you exchange ten shares for five, with each new share worth twice as much as the old one. Reverse splits can make a stock attractive to many institutional investors who will not buy stocks under $15 per share.

Another special situation where you can pick some stocks with potential returns twice that of Standard & Poor's 500 are spin-offs made during corporate restructurings. The strategy can work even for investors with little appetite for technical analysis. In 1996, there were 31 spin-offs from corporations worth at least $200 million, according to Horizon Asset Management. And the spin-offs presented millions of investors with odd lots of shares whether they wanted them or not.

The trouble investors have deciding what to do with shares they've received from spin-offs is key to what makes them a mother lode of stock market bargains. Shareholders rarely know the spin-off's industry, which is often a niche market. So the easiest decision is to sell. And brokerage firms don't have any vital incentives to promote the stocks since they don't generate significant commissions.

Yet last year, these "castaways" put $34 billion of stock on the market compared with $60 billion added through initial public offerings, an arena of more glitter. And the $34 billion doesn't include tens of billions in deals that were not pure spin-offs, such as Lucent.

Karen Wruck, associate professor at Harvard Business School, cautions that average returns make spin-off investing look deceptively simple. It's the big winners that make the averages look so enticing. The payoff for value investors tends to come in three years as successful small companies post good results, win recognition, and see their stocks rise to typical market valuations. They are most volatile during their first six months of trading.

Beyond basic analysis, Wruck suggests spin-off pickers look for companies that link management's pay to stock performance. But avoiding losers may be more important than picking winners. Veteran investors have known for years that there's money to be made sorting spin-offs. But it remains uncharted water where bargains can surface any time a new company falls into the hands of investors who don't know it and don't want it.

Not every spin-off is a winner. Often the motivation for divesting a unit is that management wants to unload a low-margin or poorly performing business. And even savvy investors can be caught short by a spin-off coming out of left field. "You have to dig out those special situations in which big profits are possible," says Joseph Cornell, president of High Yield Analytics in Chicago.

INVESTOR INFORMATION

For investors who prefer not to wade through hundreds of pages of *Value Line* or Standard & Poor's *Outlook,* there are several outstanding newsletters that focus on special situations. Three of them are *Emerging & Special Situations, Equities Special Situations,* and the *California Technology Stock Letter* (addresses are in the Appendix).

There are also useful case histories from the last five years in *Spin-off to Pay-Off* by Joseph Cornell. And you won't find a better guide to stock bargains than David Dreman's *The New Contrarian Investment Strategy.* His lectures and columns in *Forbes* have earned him a reputation as the consummate value investor.

CHAPTER 9

Margin Trading and Options

Brokers are only too happy to lend you money to buy stocks if you open a margin account. You just sign a couple of forms and your broker runs a routine credit check. Brokerage houses are eager to approve your application because margin accounts lead to additional business and commissions.

They make money on the loans—margin investors are more likely to buy twice as many shares as cash-only investors—and the shares (which are held as collateral by the brokerage firm) are often lent for a fee to other customers, such as *short sellers* who must produce stocks they don't own.

But you can come out ahead in rising markets because you put up only 50 percent of the cost of your stocks, thus making your money work at least twice as hard. If you're an aggressive trader, you can also buy mutual funds on margin the same way you would individual stocks. Among the discount brokerage firms offering fund shares on margin are Charles Schwab & Co., Jack White & Co., and Quick & Reilly.

Another advantage of margin loans is that they can be used for other purposes besides buying stock. Since margin interest rates are typically several points less than those on consumer loans and credit card balances, it can make sense to take out a margin loan to pay off consumer debt. The only hitch is that, unlike home equity loans, the interest is not tax deductible. But you aren't charged fees or points, and you can make your own prepayment schedule.

Sound great? Margin accounts can be a lot riskier than you think. Let's say you want to buy 100 shares of a stock that costs $30 per share. Normally you would pay $3,000 plus commissions. But with a margin account, you put up only 50 percent of the price, or $1,500. Your broker lends you the remaining $1,500, and the stock that you bought acts as collateral for your loan.

If the price of the stock rises—terrific! If it rises enough, you could sell some shares, pay off the loan, and come out ahead. But if the gains in your stock do not cover your net interest payments, then you lose money. And if the stock falls, you could suffer in two ways: Not only would your investment dwindle, but you could receive a *margin call* from your broker.

MARGIN CALLS

When the stock market crashed in October 1987, many investors learned the hard way about the perils of margin accounts. As stock prices plummeted, brokers called clients who had purchased shares on margin, directing them to put up more cash or their stocks would be sold. In many instances the brokerage firms sold the shares without notifying the owners, as they were legally entitled to do.

The stories are legend. There was a shooting at a Miami brokerage firm, a suicide in Wisconsin, and the well-publicized troubles of a British financier. For many investors, the margin calls were a sobering experience—five years of bull market profits were wiped out virtually overnight.

"When you buy a stock, you generally think it will do well over the long term," says John Markese, research director for the American Association of Individual Investors. "But if you buy on margin, you're vulnerable to short-term market conditions that may force you to sell. The risk is beyond what most people can accept."

Yet that sell point—as a number of fearless investors showed during the October 1987 crash—may be precisely the time to *buy more shares.* While margin investors (who couldn't meet their calls) were being pushed out of the market, others moved in and grabbed the suddenly undervalued shares of good stocks.

Bull markets create less risky opportunities for margin investors than do bear markets. "During a surge, it makes sense to buy on margin no matter what stock you select," says Al Frank, publisher of *The Prudent Speculator* newsletter. "But when stocks are extremely volatile and overvalued as they are now, you have to be careful not to be too highly leveraged."

Here are some ways to reduce the risks of borrowing on margin in bull and bear markets:

DON'T BE FULLY MARGINED.   Borrowing less than the 50 percent allowed puts you in a stronger position to weather a temporary price drop. And keep a close watch on your margined stocks. Check the closing prices at least twice a week—more often if the shares tend to fluctuate wildly as do most small stocks. You don't want a margin call to take you by surprise.

"Don't rely on your broker to monitor your stocks," warns Frank. "It's not his money that's at risk." There are brokers out there who never witnessed a real crash. And they have been selling stocks on margin believing the only way the market can go is up.

CHECK YOUR COLLATERAL.   Use mutual funds or blue-chip stocks as collateral for those high-flying and volatile technology issues. And ask about interest costs. When a stock goes down or remains unchanged you incur interest costs without any offsetting gains. Even if the stock price rises, it has to be enough to cover interest payments plus commissions for you to make a profit.

Traditionally, interest is based on the "broker call rate," or what banks charge brokerage firms for lending them the money that's lent to you. To make a profit, they then add one quarter to two percentage points to this rate, depending on how much is borrowed. And the broker call rate can rise and fall spectacularly depending on the banks.

ASK ABOUT TRIGGERS.   Federal regulations set the trigger for margin payments at 25 percent of the purchase price. If the worth of your holdings drops below that level, your broker will demand that you deliver enough cash or other securities to bring your collateral back to the required amount. If you can't—sometimes by the next day—the broker will sell your stock, take back what he lent you and collect interest.

Many brokerage firms let you ante up at higher levels, usually 30 to 35 percent. And you get up to five days to come up with the cash or sell the stock. The problem would come for the brokerage if the investor walked away from the debt and the stock price fell below the loan amount.

USE STOP ORDERS.   For extra insurance, you can instruct your broker to sell your margin stocks automatically if they fall to a certain price. You choose the price at which you no longer want to own the stock and advise your broker to sell at that price. Then, if your shares fall without your noticing, your broker will sell them anyway to prevent a bigger loss.

Stop orders are not foolproof, and there's no guarantee that you will receive all of the target price, but they can be a good way of avoiding runaway losses when a stock's price drops sharply (as often happens with volatile small companies).

OPTIONS TRADING

The use of stock options has been soaring in popularity along with the market. Yet, if you're typical, you may shrink from "puts" and "calls" as exotic investments with an utterly confusing jargon.

Not so. A stock option simply gives you the right to buy or sell the underlying shares at a preset price, known as the *strike price*, any time before the option expires. Investors who made the biggest profits during this long bull market were those who bought call options. Those with put options are the big winners when stocks plunge.

Options made even more news when the 1997 Nobel Prize went to economists Robert Merton of Harvard Business School and Myron Scholes of Stanford University, who devised the breakthrough formula that is used to accurately price and measure the risk in options on a share of stock.

An option is a contract that gives the holder the right, but not the obligation, to buy or sell shares of stock on or before a certain date at a set price. Before the creation of the Scholes-Merton pricing model, options trading was limited to ineffective attempts to hedge the financial risks in farm crops or commodities.

But the Scholes-Merton model revolutionized how options could be used, and spawned the creation of *derivatives*—financial contracts whose value is derived from other instruments (stocks, bonds, currency) that touch nearly everyone. And while most economists agree the options-pricing model has reduced risk and made world markets more efficient, not everyone has been pleased. Program trading and portfolio insurance, made possible by the formula, were blamed in part for the market crash of 1987.

Early warning signals are now in place to keep that from happening again. But it hasn't changed the way options work to profit investors—for a lot less than it would cost to buy the stock.

PUT OPTIONS.   A put gives you the right to sell a stock for a set price during a scheduled period, up to nine months. Put options are traded on the exchanges and in the over-the-counter market. They are of special value if the market declines—offsetting some of the losses in a margined stock.

Dick Donsky, director of options trading at Shearson Lehman Bros., compares buying puts to home mortgages that offer homeowners the chance to prepay if interest rates fall—but not the obligation to pay off the loan before the due date.

For example, say you own 500 shares of a stock that has risen from $42 to $50—a paper profit of $4,000. For $1,125, you could have bought a put option that would allow you to sell those 500 shares for $50 in the next six months. (Puts cost much less than the share price and for a few hundred dollars, you can acquire temporary control of thousands of dollars worth of stock.)

If the stock falls, you still reap your $4,000 gain—minus the cost and commissions (about $250). If you still like the stock over the long haul, you can keep it and sell the put option before it expires. The more the market drops, the more your put is worth.

Options expire on a set date, and lists of them are published in the *Wall Street Journal* with both closing and strike prices. But remember, put options can be in high demand—and more expensive—during market plunges.

When you *sell* a put, you agree to buy a stock at a set price that's usually below market price. Some investors sell puts with the hope of acquiring stock during a market slump at a bargain price. "In the worst case," says Allen Gelb, vice-president at Prudential, "you are buying stock at a deep discount, which is a good way to buy them."

CALL OPTIONS.   These are the opposite of puts, and let you buy a stock at a set price within a certain period. It can make sense to sell stocks and buy call options in a bull market, says Tom Hart, vice-president at Paine Webber. By cashing in your gains, you don't have to fear a price drop. If the stock price rises, your return will be even greater than if you owned the stock. Takeovers have led to spectacular spurts in option prices. For example, when Standard Oil acquired Kennecot, shares of the copper producer rose from $27 to $54 while calls soared from $2 to $24.

Selling stock calls can also be sound strategy. "Too many investors who buy a stock anticipating a long run-up, hold on too long before they unload," says Price Headly, research director at the Investment Research Institute. "You get someone to pay you to take the stock off your hands and you still profit."

As with puts, the important factor in profitable calls is the underlying stock. The best candidates are stocks that: pay small or no dividends, sell at high price-earnings ratios, are unpopular with institutions, and are highly volatile. Stable stocks move more slowly even in an active market.

Options traders (you can call yourself one of them now) unsure about which way a stock will move often use "spreads and straddles" or "strips and straps" to hedge their positions. These are mixtures of puts and calls on the same stock with different expiration dates. These ploys, along with "leaps" or long-term equity anticipation securities, are best left to the experts with computers and other people's money.

Index options are another matter. They are tied to the value of an index rather than a single stock. Index puts may be a good bet if you own a lot of stocks since they rise in value if the overall market drops. Index calls are riskier, and you could wind up losing thousands of dollars without owning any stocks.

If you own small stocks, you may want to consider Nasdaq index options instead of Standard & Poor's 500. "But don't bother unless you own at least 30 diversified stocks," warns Bing Sung, portfolio manager at Harvard Management. "Any less and you'd probably be better off hedging individual stocks with separate options."

RIGHTS AND WARRANTS

When putting together a stock portfolio, you have an unenviable number of choices. Some 19,000 equity securities are listed on the New York Stock Exchange, American Stock Exchange, and Nasdaq or over-the-counter markets. Venture abroad, and the list grows by more than 50,000.

The choice is even more bewildering than it might initially seem. To begin with, there is *common stock*, which gives investors ownership interest in a company. Common stock is what most people mean when they talk about stocks, but some companies also issue other types of securities.

Preferred stock appeals to more conservative investors because they get a higher yield than the company's common shares. Preferred stock gets its name because holders receive preferential treatment in certain areas. For example, shareholders of preferred stock stand in line ahead of common-stock holders in case the company goes bust and its assets are liquidated.

Some preferred shares are also *convertible* into common stock. If a preferred share does not have a conversion feature, it is often more like a bond than a stock, and thus offers little or no chance for capital gains. Very few companies, big or small, issue these half-stock, half-bond securities.

STOCK RIGHTS.   These are a special type of option that permit shareholders to buy more securities, usually common stock, ahead of the public, without commissions or fees, and typically at a discount of 5 to 10 percent. That can put extra dollars in your pocket at little risk.

Rights are a convenient way for companies to raise additional capital at a modest cost. But they have to be exercised within a short time, frequently running only for several weeks. If they are not used by the expiration date, they expire and lose all their value.

If you like a company well enough to continue as a shareholder, check your mail and pick up the rights. Or if your shares are being held by your broker, ask him to keep you informed. Historically, 80 percent of stocks bought with rights have outperformed the market in the year following their issue.

You can also sell the rights in the open market, through your broker or through a bank designated by the company. And if don't own the stock, you can still buy rights either to exercise them or as a speculation. As a rule, it's best to buy rights soon after they are listed in the financial pages (as "rt" following the company name) and sell a day or two before the lapse date.

WARRANTS.   Unlike options, warrants are sold by companies intending to issue stock in the future, or by those seeking to raise cash by selling shares to be held in reserve. For example, a company planning an IPO might sell a number of warrants for those stocks in advance—to make sure the public offering will be bought up.

When you buy a warrant, you're paying a small price now for the right to buy a certain number of shares at a fixed price when the stock is issued—sort of a pay-now and own-later deal. Your broker can tell you what a warrant represents, and when the shares will be issued.

Warrants trade on the exchanges and are most profitable in bull markets, especially during periods of great enthusiasm. Their low prices attract those who trade for quick gains. But there are caveats:

❏ Buy warrants of a stock you would buy anyway. If the stock does not go up, neither will the price of the warrant. Profits come from warrants of companies with high earnings growth, a prospective takeover, or new product or service. It also helps if they are temporarily popular.

❏ Seek out special situations. Warrants of small, growing firms can be profitable since they often rely on the warrants for financing. Anticipated or actual growth can boost the price of warrants rapidly. But be wary of warrants where the stock is limited or closely controlled. If someone decides to dump a large block of shares, the value can fall fast.

❏ Spread out your risks. If you can afford it, buy warrants of five different companies. Your total gains may be less than if you gamble on one warrant that proves a winner, but your losses will be less if you guess wrong.

Except in unusual situations, warrants should be bought to trade or sell, not to exercise. With rapid price changes and a long wait for appreciation, warrants can yield quick gains for those who have time to watch the market. They can be found as part of an initial public offering, intended merger or acquisition, or in newspaper tables (as "wt" after the company name).

SELLING SHORT

Novice investors may not want to start by buying on margin, using options, or selling short. But it's a good idea to know how the veterans do it in bull and bear markets. The lure is you can make 30 to 40 percent—maybe even 100 percent—on your investment in months, not years.
But short sales are not for the faint-hearted. They have even been derided because they're betting on the decline, not growth, of companies. Michael Murphy, publisher of the *California Technology Stock Letter,* bristles at such talk.

"If you can bet on the positive, why not the negative as well?" he says. "What's wrong with capitalizing on a money-making ingredient in a lot of stocks—hype or hot air?" According to Murphy's law, at least two out of every five stocks are overpriced. And in a chaotic market, why not sell short?

In *short selling* you actually sell the stock before you buy it. Here's how it works: You borrow the shares from your broker, sell them in the market and receive the money from the sale. Then you wait for the stock to drop in price, because you will eventually have to replace the stock you borrowed, to repay the loan. If later on, you can buy the stock for less than you originally got from the sale, you'll profit.

But how do you know if a stock is overvalued? It may have future earnings problems, possible write-offs, increased competition, delays in product introductions, questionable accounting practices, or in the case of small airlines, an expected rise in fuel prices. By applying short selling analysis to an entire portfolio, any investor would be less likely to hang on to a loser too long, says Murphy.

What's the risk of selling short? For starters, you pay the broker interest while waiting for the right time to cover your short position. The longer you wait, the more interest you pay. And if the stock price rises, you'll have to pay more to buy it back than you made from selling it.

Short selling is even trickier with warrants since there may be limited markets because of lack of speculator interest, and exchange regulations that prohibit short sales of warrants several months before their expiration date. There's also the possibility that the life of the warrants may be extended—so you may not be able to cover your position at the low price anticipated.

All short sales must be made on a margin account, usually with stock borrowed from another customer of the brokerage firm using a signed agreement. The collateral is generally 50 percent of the market value of the shorted stock. But you can increase the amount to 80 percent of the short sale to eliminate the necessity of coming up with more cash.

Picking stocks for short selling is not that difficult, says Murphy. Ask your broker for recommendations or take a look at these fairly simple indicators:

❑ Insider transactions by officers and directors of the company. If more insiders are selling stock than buying it, the usual assumption is that they believe a decline is ahead.

❑ Volatility as measured by the beta of the stock (price movement in relation to the market). The more volatile the stock, the better it may be for short selling.

❑ How the stock stacks up with other companies in the same industry in growth of earnings and profits. These data are available from statistical services such as *Value Line* and Standard & Poor's *Earnings Forecast*.

The least attractive stocks for short selling are among the micro-caps—thinly traded issues of only a few hundred thousand shares. Because they are so volatile, you could get caught in a squeeze and have to borrow or buy back shares.

WATCHING THE INDEXES

You constantly hear about the latest change in this or that indicator. Unemployment is down. The prime rate is up. But which among all of these pointers will help you understand—and foretell—the direction of the economy and the fate of your investments? These can help:

- ❏ *Interest rate on three-month Treasury bills.* You usually can find it on Tuesday in the business pages of the daily newspapers. It's particularly sensitive because it's based on the rate investors demand in return for putting up their own money.

- ❏ *Major labor contracts.* Settlements like the one made by United Parcel Service in 1997 are danger signs if they increase wages by more than 10 percent, and could indicate that we're heading into an inflationary period.

- ❏ *Strength of the dollar* is another gauge of future inflation. If the dollar drops in value against other currencies, prices for foreign goods will rise. This is sure to cut into corporate profits.

- ❏ *Employment figures,* or the number of people on company payrolls, is another excellent indicator of the overall health of the economy. As this figure rises, so probably will consumer spending and, along with it, the stock market.

- ❏ *Stock market itself.* No statistic is more closely watched as an indicator of the financial future. One index by which to read the market is the Standard & Poor's 500, a much broader sampling than the Dow Jones Industrial Average.

Critics of stock indexes say they add new companies a number of times each year, many of which are involved in mergers or acquisitions, are usually fast-growing and enhance the index's returns. The same cannot be said for the Russell 2000, a leading barometer of small company stocks, which is rebalanced every June according to changes in companies' market capitalizations.

Many companies simply outgrow the Russell 2000 and this can dampen index returns, says Prudential's Claudia Mott. She suspects that the number of IPOs, which often lose steam after a few months, may be partly responsible.

Indicators, charts, and computer programs are used in technical analysis to track price trends of stocks and the market in general. And if you understand the basics of both technical and fundamental analysis, you'll have a great advantage as an investor. But you should never rely on just one indicator or chart service.

REDUCING YOUR RISK

"A novice should start with on-the-money options that are already showing a profit," says Price Headley, director of research at the Investment Research Institute in Cincinnati. They cost more since they are written at an exercise price close to the stock price, but provide a cushion if stock prices go against expectations. "On-the-money options with an expiration date three or more months away combine safety as well as liquidity," says Headley.

Others may prefer to invest in the much cheaper out-of-the-money options (where the strike price is above the market price of the stock) because the profit potential is greater. Either way, "options have become much more of a viable investment and a way to implement strategies," says Headley.

For example, if you are nervous about short-term volatility, the possibility of earnings surprises over coming months, or an interest rate increase, you can hedge market exposure using options rather than selling stock outright. In the first half of 1997, options trading surpassed 152 million contracts compared to 199 million contracts for all of 1996.

It also pays to keep one eye on the tax collector. Option rules are complicated, and the tax status of capital gains can vary according to whether the option is exercised, expires, or is closed out. Most people should avoid strategies like straddles and strips (actually double and triple options) that require constant attention.

INVESTOR INFORMATION

If you want to play, know all the rules. Start with the required booklet *Characteristics and Risks of Standardized Options.* You can get a copy from your brokerage firm, or from the Options Clearing Corp., 440 S. LaSalle St., Chicago, IL 60605 (800-537-4258).

Strategy sheets describing in fairly easy, but detailed terms, how to make money with options are also available from the American Stock Exchange, 86 Trinity Place, New York, NY (212-306-1000).

For an advanced course, check out the third edition of the classic *Options as a Strategic Investment* by Lawrence McMillan. This bible of options trading has been revised to include the latest trading vehicles and stock market derivatives.

CHAPTER 10

Going Global
with Stocks

The huge drop in the Dow on October 27, 1997 made a lot of already nervous investors panicky. Just how do you spread your risks in a lofty, volatile stock market? One way is to look to Europe, where small-company stocks trade at price-earnings multiples 20 percent lower than those of the blue chips—an unusual, near-record discount. In the U.S., small companies now trade at around parity to their larger cousins.

The lesson? Pick stocks, not countries. That should be even more evident after the turmoil in smaller Asian markets that started the October 1997 correction. While it's easier to focus on countries, or emerging markets, there are a lot fewer of them than there are individual stocks.

The continuing expansion of global markets could set a modern record before it's over—and that might not be for quite a while. "Change in Europe is not an isolated event," says John Dessauer, publisher of the *Investor's World* newsletter. "It's the expression of a powerful global trend that represents both opportunity and challenge."

Nevertheless, warnings are being sounded about unbridled "Europhoria" amid dollar gyrations and a soaring trade deficit at home. But even a relatively small investor can build a foreign portfolio—and do it without tremendous risk.

The obvious strategy is to diversify, says Dessauer. That means holding investments in the United States, Europe, and Asia. "Investing with an international perspective may have been a new development in the 1980s," he says, "but it will be a necessity in the next decade."

The critical question for investors: Why bother sending greenbacks to so-called "emerging markets" like Russia and Pakistan when there's a risk the trip will be one way? In fact, why bother with foreign stocks at all, including those in mature markets like France and Japan?

Besides, multinational giants like Coca-Cola and Gillette are doing more business in foreign countries every year, giving shareholders of those domestic blue chips all the foreign exposure they may want. Foreign stocks—who needs them?

You do, perhaps. But the answer depends on how patient you are and how much risk you can stomach. Foreign stocks, especially those traded in faraway and exotic places like Russia and Zimbabwe, are notoriously volatile. But such emerging markets also promise faster growth than anything you can find at home, presenting tantalizing returns of 30 percent a year over long periods.

Interested? Invesco European Small Companies Fund has managed to return 23 percent annually since its inception in February 1995. The $70 million fund tries to keep country weightings pretty close to the Capel Index, Europe's equivalent of the Russell 2000. But managers Claire Griffiths and Andrew Crossley care more about whether a company is in the right business than whether it is in the right country.

"We look for genuine businesses—preferably market leaders—not pseudo-banks getting their income from investments and from currency fluctuations," says Griffiths. Among their holdings are Qiagen, a German supplier of DNA test kits to research labs, and British-based Games Workshop, a producer of war-themed board games.

But with European stocks currently lagging the U.S. market, Invesco has seen nearly half its assets walk out the door in the past year. The reason: Investors tend to go where they think the action is rather than trying to figure out where the action will be. Crossley thinks that an overvalued Dow may sober them up.

"Markets don't go up forever," explains Mark Riepe, vice president with Ibbotson Associates, the Chicago research firm. "The person who is investing only in U.S stocks is actually taking a big risk." If that sounds like you, take heart. Foreign stocks have never been so cheap—at least compared to some of those sky-high issues like Microsoft.

FOREIGN SHARES

Foreign stocks account for 60 percent of world stock markets, so shouldn't you have at least half of your money overseas? Not necessarily, says Laurence Smith, managing director with J.P. Morgan. "There are diminishing benefits as the international equity exposure rises," he says. Once you have a quarter of your portfolio in foreign shares, there's no reason to put in more money unless you believe that an overseas market will outperform U.S. equities.

Risk reduction is not all that reliable either. When stocks get pounded here they also tend to tumble overseas. By itself, a small cap fund like Invesco's is not a low-risk play. But it would be a useful diversification in a portfolio heavily weighted with big company stocks.

Many small foreign companies outperform the U.S stock market. And Michael Howell, chief global strategist at ING Baring in London, predicts that by 2010, emerging markets such as China and India will account for about 45 percent of the world's stock market capitalization, compared to 15 percent now. "Every government wants an airline and a stock market," he says.

The electronic age also makes the flow of money and information almost instantaneous, so whatever happens on the Paris bourse or Hong Kong stock market has a direct impact on investors in Denver or Des Moines. As a result, brokerage firms are handling more foreign stocks for investors than ever before (see Figure 10.1).

Merrill Lynch now trades about 4,000 foreign stocks that aren't listed in the U.S. for retail clients—up from 600 two years ago. Smith Barney trades about 1,000 issues, and a number of discount brokers sell

FIGURE 10.1. FOREIGN STOCK INVESTMENTS, 1985–1995

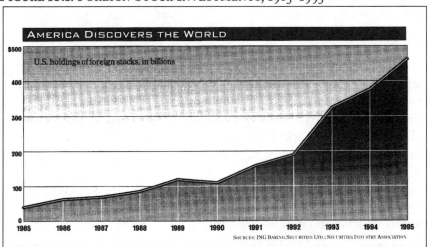

Source: Wall Street Journal

foreign stocks to small investors, but they carry risks beyond those normally associated with domestic stocks.

Annual reports, if they come at all, may not be in English. Foreign markets aren't strictly regulated. In addition, there is the risk that the currency in which they are denominated could rise or drop relative to the U.S. dollar, thereby increasing or decreasing the value of the stock.

"The advantage of buying individual foreign stocks is that you are making your own decisions," says Dessauer. They sell for less, largely due to local conditions, but many of the companies are just as strong and profitable as those in the United States.

One of these is $98 million NACT Telecommunications, which sells integrated switches designed for small companies scrambling in that fragmented $70 billion market, but which do not compete with those sold by such big players as Lucent Technologies or Northern Telecom. "They will sell you the switch and run it for you on their site, so you get to focus on optimizing service," says Reginald King of Hambrecht & Quist in San Francisco.

Opportunities for the small cap firm seem virtually unlimited, as other nations follow the U.S in deregulating telecommunications, creating a host of rapidly growing specialty niches. To get in on that trend, NACT is opening offices in Europe and South America; a first step toward what president A. Lindsay Wallace hopes will be an expansion of foreign sales to 30 percent of revenues within two years.

But if finding a good small stock in your own backyard is difficult, imagine trying to do it in Malaysia or Poland. "Stick to companies with good track records and good management," says Robert Kern, portfolio manager of the Fremont Micro-Cap Fund. "Don't get led to the promised land by some snake oil salesman. Size up the company's potential yourself."

Anyone interested in foreign stocks has to accept the fact that information about them is more difficult to obtain—even from a brokerage firm. In picking them, you probably can benefit from some guides. *The Directory of Investment Research* gives the vital statistics on over 17,000 public companies in the U.S. and overseas. It's available from Nelson Publications, 1 Gateway Plaza, Port Chester, NY 10573 (800-333-6357) for $535 a year.

You can get still more in-depth information from Moody's *International Manual and News Reports,* which gives balance sheets and charts for more than 9,000 foreign corporations along with bi-weekly updates for $3,175. But to save money as well as earn it, remember that these advisory service guides often are available at your public library.

GALLOPING GREENBACKS

When the dollar gallops, as it does constantly, markets all over the world feel the reverberations. When it skids, manufacturers who buy supplies and components overseas find everything more expensive. And when the dollar heads upward, U.S. goods become more expensive abroad, and their sales suffer.

The dollar's movements also affect your investments in foreign stocks, which tend to do well if the dollar drops against that currency. "But currencies don't all move in the same direction at the same time," cautions Dimitri Balatsos, managing director of Furman Selz Capital Management. "While the dollar weakened substantially for most of 1995 against the Japanese yen and German mark, it stabilized against the Italian lira, Spanish peseta, and the currencies of Scandinavian and Pacific Rim countries. And it rose substantially against Canada, Mexico and Latin American currencies."

Right now, Balatsos expects Japan to rebound from its severe five-year recession, making a "basket" of high-tech electronics companies (Hitachi, Kyocera) very attractive. "But you invest in Denmark, Sweden, Finland or Norway on the basis of the excellent return they provide," he says, "not for currency reasons."

Over time, foreign markets get returns as good as, if not better than, U.S. markets. Also, foreign stocks can perform well in years when U.S. markets do poorly—and vice versa. By splitting your portfolio between overseas and domestic stocks, you minimize your risk and get a blended return regardless of the ups and downs of the dollar.

But you have to learn how to speak in currencies, which can be confusing (see Figure 10.2). In fact, just as a strong dollar makes foreign revenues less valuable here, it also makes a U.S. investment more lucrative for an overseas investor by making the payoff more valuable when converted to other currencies.

So, which way should you be rooting? As with most stocks, slow and steady wins the race when it comes to currency considerations. While it can erode the bottom line of blue-chip multinationals, foreign companies that sell to the U.S. get more of their local currency in return.

One way to go global with relative ease and little paperwork, especially if you can't get the research you need, is to purchase shares in one of the no-load funds specializing in foreign investments. In this way, you get risk-adjusted diversification, and can concentrate on picking additional winners among hometown small cap stocks.

Whichever route you choose, be advised that transaction costs are higher for foreign stocks, including those purchased on U.S. stock ex-

FIGURE 10.2. FOREIGN CURRENCY VERSUS THE DOLLAR

Country and currency	October 1997	October 1996
Australia dollar	1.36	1.25
Austria schilling	12.44	10.84
Belgium franc	36.32	31.76
Britain pound	.6186	.6295
Canada dollar	1.38	1.34
France franc	5.94	5.20
Germany mark	1.77	1.54
Greece drachma	277.48	240.95
Hong Kong dollar	7.73	7.73
Ireland punt	.6854	.6247
Israel shekel	3.52	3.24
Italy lira	1729.00	1535.25
Japan yen	120.68	112.47
Mexico peso	7.749	7.725
Netherlands guilder	1.9845	1.7291
Norway krone	7.09	6.53
Singapore dollar	1.5535	1.4140
South Africa rand	4.6935	4.5500
South Korea won	914.80	827.20
Spain peseta	149.25	129.65
Sweden krona	7.639	6.634
Switzerland franc	1.473	1.270
Taiwan dollar	29.21	17.49

Source: J.P. Morgan Index

changes. However, foreign issues generally trade at lower share prices. Any investor should be able to buy a round lot of 100 shares for between $1,500 and $4,000.

You can also purchase options on some foreign stocks, but before you do, go back and review Chapter 9, Margin Trading and Options. Foreign currency options and futures are another matter, and unless you have some special insights, they are better left to experienced bankers. If you guess wrong, you could lose a bundle.

"Fund managers have hurt themselves more than they've helped themselves by trying to manage currencies and stocks," warns Robert Ludwig, chief investment officer at SEI Investments. His advice is to put no more than 20 percent of a portfolio in mature foreign markets, and half that in emerging markets.

MULTINATIONAL COMPANIES

Another way you can profit from global investing is with the shares of American companies that have large overseas operations. Many are well-known and tend to manufacture popular products or necessities like cosmetics, chemicals, industrial equipment, drugs, and foods.

For example, food companies are showing phenomenal growth as the Japanese convert from a rice diet to wheat, says Lipper Analytical Services. And, public works projects in Italy, Spain, and elsewhere in Europe are increasing the demand for construction equipment.

But all multinationals aren't giants. Tiny Larscom in Santa Clara, California makes "inverse multiplexers" that link office computer networks with the world, and bears little resemblance to the company founded in 1970 to manufacture alarm systems. Larscom hopes to generate 25 percent of its sales in Europe in two to three years, thanks to a $73 million initial public offering in December 1996.

Investors willing to ride out the volatile price swings of a company like Larscom could themselves be connected with some fairly substantial returns. "The small companies won't be overlooked," says Christopher Nowakowski, president of Intersec Research Corp. "The officers and directors will make sure that Wall Street hears all about their securities."

Buying shares of foreign companies that export to the U.S can also be a winning strategy. But you'll do better with places like Australia and Taiwan which tie the value of their currencies to the dollar, so stocks won't get hurt by currency moves.

Foreign stocks are sometimes overlooked because they are too small (micro-caps with valuations below $300 million), don't promote themselves, are hard to fit into a simple category—or they could be just plain poor investments. But a number of these neglected stocks often turn out to be big winners.

On the negative side, different accounting standards make it harder to evaluate foreign companies, and information or price quotes are not as quickly available as for U.S. companies.

DEPOSITARY RECEIPTS

You can buy stocks of about 1,500 foreign companies that trade mostly on Nasdaq or on the American and New York Stock Exchanges in the form of American Depositary Receipts. ADRs are generally initiated when a U.S. bank learns there is a great deal of interest in the shares of a foreign firm, or when that firm wants to enter the American market.

They're trickier than other stocks, but ADRs offer bigger gains at lower prices than most American companies. A risk index published by Morgan Stanley shows that a portfolio split equally between foreign and U.S. stocks since 1979 had higher returns and lower volatility than portfolios invested solely overseas or solely in the U.S. That doesn't mean you should send half your money abroad, however.

There's also more information about the companies, which must adhere to stricter accounting and disclosure rules than those not offering ADRs. "It's a lot like buying a U.S. company," says Edward Bousa, senior portfolio manager at Putnam Investments. "These companies could just as easily be headquartered here and nobody would know the difference."

For self-confident investors who want to diversify, ADRs are a welcome addition to the growing list of direct-purchase, or no-commission stocks. And capital gains are paid in dollars, making them easier to buy and sell. The list of ADRs offers choices from every corner of the world, and you can buy many of them from the company directly by filling out an application and mailing a check.

Take note that U.S. banks like J.P. Morgan and Bank of New York charge fees that can eat into returns. Big companies like Sony "can get away with charging fees and having high minimums ($200 to $1,000)," says Eric Fry in *International Investing with ADRs*. But savvy investors can find smaller companies on Nasdaq with fewer fees and the potential of much higher returns.

If you're investigating a foreign company traded on Nasdaq, you probably can get research reports from a broker or elsewhere. But you won't get as much information on a foreign company traded over-the-counter or in the so-called "pink sheets" of thinly traded issues.

Before investing, familiarize yourself with current events in the country, says James Donovan, managing director of depositary receipts at Citibank. Some of things you should be on the lookout for:

- ❏ *Lack of liquidity.* Some ADRs are thinly traded, even when the company has a lot of shares outstanding. You might have a tough time finding a buyer, if you want to sell for any reason.

- ❏ *Political risk.* In some countries, political turmoil can devastate companies and dry up liquidity. And if a government decides to nationalize a company, the ADRs won't be worth much.

- ❏ *Research reports.* They are hard to obtain for small cap companies—if they are available at all. Highly speculative issues in marginal markets create more risks.

- ❏ *Currency risk.* In countries where the dollar is not the standard, you have to worry about fluctuations in the exchange rate.

Each ADR is registered with the Securities and Exchange Commission and certifies that a stated number of shares of the company have been deposited with the American bank's foreign office or custodian and will be kept there as long as the ADR remains outstanding.

EMERGING MARKETS

Ten years from now, you might be glad you bought foreign stocks. No bull market goes on forever, and diversification keeps you in whatever game is going on at that time. But you have to be extra careful in *emerging markets* because they have the potential for failure as well as growth.

These markets include more than just stocks in countries you've never heard of. China, India, Russia, Israel, and Venezuela are considered emerging markets, yet each has a gross national product larger than Canada's. Actually, China's is the world's third-largest economy, trailing only the United States and Japan.

But there are considerable risks in emerging markets, says Gerald Perritt, publisher of the *Mutual Fund Letter*. First, there is the risk of government mismanagement that can cause large deficits and expansive monetary policies that foster inflation and currency devaluation (Brazil, Indonesia).

Second, these emerging stock markets are very small. Any amount of marginal selling by speculators can cause stock prices to decline in double digit numbers. That makes it important to diversify. Single country investing is best left to the pros who have other people's money to spend. If you want, invest in a mutual fund like Montgomery Emerging Markets that invests in several.

If you want any reminders, think Mexico, Thailand, and Indonesia. They all had to be bailed out by the International Monetary Fund (IMF) in recent years, and investors are still waiting for their money. But enthusiasm for many of Asia's "paper tigers" still exists, so you need to approach all of them with caution.

Barton Biggs, global strategist at Morgan Stanley, says he expects even more turmoil. But he advises investors not to rule out all emerging markets, many of which offer better profits and diversification than more developed countries in Europe. In many of them, inflation is down, growth is solid, and trade deficits are mild. "The fundamentals in a lot of emerging markets look better than here," he says.

In fact, as the world heads for the next century, the greatest challenge and opportunity for investors may well be in the emerging markets of Asia, Africa, Latin America, and Eastern Europe. So says Jeffrey Garten, dean of the Yale School of Management and author of *The Big Emerging Markets and How They Will Change Our Lives*.

Garten argues that trade and investment ties with these "sleeping giants" should be a primary concern of foreign policy in the years ahead. "Our current economic success may be making us too complacent," he says. "We could be in for tough times ahead, if we're not prepared for the challenge."

As emerging markets get access to technology and management skills, they are going to change the global industrial structure, says Garten. China now makes computer peripherals as well as toys, and India is fast becoming the world's second-largest exporter of software.

Returns may not be as explosive as they've been in the past few years, but "the trend toward globalization and stronger growth in overseas markets will continue," adds John Dessauer of *Investor's World*. He warns, however, that "you're making bets on the basis of industrial or economic trends that are going to take time to come to the fore."

The obvious strategy is to diversify, says Dessauer. That means holding investments in the United States, Europe, and Asia. There's risk, of course, but it's a tradeoff. In mature markets like Switzerland, you have stability but slower growth; in Singapore and Taiwan, there's tremendous potential for growth along with greater risk.

GLOBAL OR INTERNATIONAL?

Emerging markets investing has been touted by financial advisors because of its great growth potential. But the couple of dozen funds that concentrate their investments in this area have little to show for it to date.

Take Fidelity Emerging Markets Fund, the greybeard of the bunch, which began selling shares in late 1990. A $1,000 investment made at the beginning of 1991 was worth only $1,530 in October 1997, a paltry 6.5 percent annual return. And the record is even worse for some regional or single-country funds.

For anyone who does not have access to research, or the time to evaluate foreign stocks or ADRs, stick with mutual funds specializing in *both* mature and emerging markets and let someone else do the decision-making for you. There are now more than 600 of them, reports Lipper Analytical Services. And many of them outperform the U.S. stock market. There are two basic types:

❏ *International* funds like Oakmark, Scudder, and Warburg Pincus. They deploy their money all over the world, hedging risks by buying into fast-growing companies and countries everywhere.

❏ *Global* funds that offer a mix of United States and foreign equities, such as Fidelity, Lexington, and Templeton. They seek risk reduction by diversification at home and abroad.

But there are also Europe-only and single-country funds that can be highly profitable—and volatile. Closed-end funds such as the Spain Fund have soared 200 percent in recent years. But unlike their open-end cousins, which constantly issue and redeem shares, they trade on the New York and other stock exchanges and can be overvalued or undervalued.

Right now, most are undervalued and sell at discounts of 15 percent or more, making them bargains. "If you can find a country you like, and a fund at a deep discount, you've got an enticing package," says Donald Cassidy, analyst at Lipper Analytical Services.

A safer bet is a no-load global fund like Mutual Discovery, run by premier value investor Michael Price. This fund, which focuses on small, undervalued companies in the U.S. and abroad, has paid out annual returns averaging 23 percent since 1993. In either case, a good start is 15 percent in foreign markets, including 5 percent in emerging markets.

"The person who is only in U.S. stocks is taking a big risk," warns Mark Mobius, who oversees $10 billion in emerging market stocks for Templeton Funds. If that sounds like you, be aware that foreign stocks and funds have rarely been so cheap. And you won't have to buy into sky-high technology issues.

The reorganization of Europe into a single economic market (larger than America's and Japan's combined) will provide savvy investors with many opportunities, adds Mobius. Many of the world's fastest-growing companies are overseas.

You should know all the risks when selecting foreign stocks or funds for even 20 percent of your portfolio. Look for the same things you would in a U.S. stock, including good management and not too much debt, as well as products and/or services that are unique or better than competitors'. Also look for sizable earnings in the U.S. as a cushion against foreign revenue declines, and consider the future growth prospects. Check for good "timeliness" and "safety" rankings in *Value Line Investment Survey*.

INVESTOR INFORMATION

You can add to your list of foreign stocks by studying one of the standard reference books put out by Standard & Poor's, Moody's or Value Line (available at public libraries or brokerage firms).

Or, you may want to check out *Global Bargain Hunting: An Investor's Guide to Profits in Emerging Markets* by Burton Malkiel and J.P. Mei. The authors, professors at Princeton and New York University, are staunch supporters of index funds which they say reduce risks and beat managed funds.

International Strategies for American Investors by John Dessauer covers many of the topics discussed in this chapter in much greater detail. Stephen Eckett's *Investing Online: Dealing in Global Markets on the Internet* tells how to research companies and markets using a directory of 1,500 Websites (disk is included).

Consider Mutual Funds

There are now more mutual funds than there are stocks on the New York and American Stock Exchanges. And while investors struggle with fund choice, managers are bombarding them with more new products—everything from global funds to telephone or online switching and asset allocation.

But there's more than a bull market on the minds of fund managers. Also driving them is increasing competition from banks and insurance companies, trying to regain some of the billions of dollars lost to mutual funds. "The business has become a marketing game," says A. Michael Lipper, president of Lipper Analytical Services. "When you have a lot of products all looking alike, it comes down to who can do a better job of promoting them."

As a result, choosing the "right" fund is becoming just as tough as researching a company's stock. And while you're scanning the pages of tables in your newspaper and wondering which of the more than 6,000 mutual funds meets your needs, consider that its manager may have been a college freshman in 1987.

Chilling thought? A study by the National Bureau of Economic Research reports that younger managers tend to deliver better returns than their colleagues who are older (by at least 20 years). Part of the difference is that younger managers tend to work for smaller funds with lower expense ratios. But they also are more likely to be fired after a down year, and have to work harder to keep returns up.

It's these kinds of complexities that make picking the right funds such a difficult task, and why investors often turn to Lipper's rankings in over

100 newspapers (most influentially in *Barron's* and the *Wall Street Journal*). Fund managers do not take his rankings lightly either—and they have caused some managers to dump low-grade issues to avoid being downgraded.

Here's what you can do to safeguard your money and spread your investment risk: Accept that stock mutual funds are no longer an easy way to invest your money. That's all changed since they blasted through the $2 trillion mark in May, 1997. Sectors of the economy like small caps that had fallen out of favor are being rediscovered. And the decidedly high-flying aggressive growth funds are attracting new interest because they did not fall as fast as technology and large caps.

What's ahead? "Don't try to win back any money you lost by making a big bet on one sector such as emerging markets or gold," says Glen King Parker, publisher of the *Mutual Fund Forecaster*. "This is not the time to go chasing specialized funds." He suggests index funds or a small company growth fund.

If you're reluctant to dive in, get wet slowly. Invest in a top-ranked fund and track what the managers are buying and selling. Both Longleaf Partners Small Cap (currently closed to new investors) and Safeco Growth No Load have impressive one- and three-year records. (A list of small cap mutual funds is included in Appendix D.)

Call the company for copies of the prospectus as well as quarterly and annual reports. At first glance, some funds appear to be a sorry lot. Most fail to beat the stock market averages, not because their managers are incompetent, but because their performance is dragged down by trading costs and annual expenses. So the key decision you must make at the outset is whether you think you can do as well as fund managers in selecting small stocks.

If you want to study them for a while, ignore the fund's stated objectives (which they sometimes ignore themselves) and get right to the nitty gritty: What stocks do they own and in what proportion? A fund that invested primarily in small cap issues in 1993 might be distinctly mid-cap today. Base your decision on the fund's record, not just on size. Some big funds have been consistent winners picking small stocks.

How many funds should you own? "Aggressive investors have the most to gain by diversifying across funds," says Edward O'Neal, assistant professor of finance at the University of New Hampshire. "If you have a long (more than five-year) investment horizon, you should start a portfolio with six growth funds, then add other categories."

LOAD OR NO-LOAD?

Assuming you're willing to do your own research, you're probably better off with a no-load fund (the "load" refers to the sales commission). But don't buy a fund just because it's no-load. Both types charge annual fees for managing your money, and over time some high-fee no-loads may be more expensive than low-fee load funds.

Gray-haired, mustachioed Sheldon Jacobs is sort of the grand old man of no-load funds, having launched his *No-Load Fund Investor* newsletter in 1979. In selecting funds, Jacobs looks most closely at the ones that have outperformed recently. "Even if a fund is a great one, if its performance hasn't been good in the last six months, I'm probably not going to pick it," he says.

But more goes into his fund selection than numbers. Jacobs stays active in the mutual fund world and knows most of the players. He has also been a consistent winner as a *New York Times* panelist and portfolio manager. On average, his portfolios often contain eight or nine funds, which can be cumbersome for investors to mimic. And he hasn't held any cash since 1990. "The long-term odds favor being relatively fully invested," he notes.

Before you invest in any fund, read the prospectus ultra-carefully and be sure you get answers to the following questions:

❑ Is the fund a load or no-load?

❑ How much will it cost me to buy into it? (front load)

❑ How much will it cost me to leave it? (back load)

❑ How large a fee does management charge to supervise the fund?

Buried within the legalese of a fund's prospectus is plenty of valuable information that can help you determine whether a particular fund is right for you, says Susan Pakuch, editor of the *Morningstar Investor* newsletter. Be sure to examine these three key areas:

INVESTMENT OBJECTIVES. This discussion of goals and strategy will enable you to determine whether the fund's approach matches your needs. You'll also want to read the latest annual or quarterly report for the names of holdings, which are rarely found in the prospectus (to see if they match stated objectives).

PORTFOLIO MANAGER.   The prospectus, by law, must provide the name and background of the fund's investment adviser—unless it's a money-market or index fund—and the portfolio manager. If the manager is a novice, you may want to let others be the guinea pigs. And check to see if the old manager was responsible for recent gains (and is now managing a new fund).

RISK STATEMENT.   Not all discussions of risk are equally enlightening. Some fund companies, such as John Hancock, Vanguard, and T. Rowe Price, do a good job explaining how you might lose money. But others seem designed primarily to avoid lawsuits, not to inform investors.

The Securities and Exchange Commission is pushing to make prospectuses more readable, and to spell out potential risks and rewards. But while you're waiting, know that some promise only a bright financial future. The last seven years have been spectacular ones, so many funds have sterling one-, three-, and five-year records. "But a fund with an excellent record may have gotten too big to move quickly in today's global markets, or it may have a new manager who had nothing to do with past success," cautions Lipper.

No mutual fund is forever. Market conditions change or the manager loses his touch. The hard part is knowing when to switch. Then there's the problem of being heard. Toll-free numbers failed thousands of investors in 1987 and again in October 1997, because callers couldn't get through to redeem shares or switch funds.

Here's a smart tip: Send a telegram. "There may still be a delay in the processing, but the date of your request is the trading date," says Jacobs. For funds that require notification in writing, a notarized signature letter is sometimes needed. The Mutual Fund Education Alliance offers a directory of no-load funds along with other information. (They can be reached at (816) 454-9422, or at their Website: www.mfea.com.)

CHOOSING AMONG FUNDS

Small company funds that buy stocks of developing businesses with market values of $1 billion or less are the new leaders of the pack, taking over the top spots in one-year rankings from their large company brethren (see Figure 11.1). One reason for the small cap success is low interest rates, which allow businesses to borrow cash cheaply for continued expansion.

Figure 11.1. Small Caps Are Winners

Fund	Total return* 1997
Royce Total Return	21.6%
Royce Giftshares	22.6
UAM FMA Small Company	30.8
Royce Low-Priced Stocks	20.8
Royce Premier	20.4
Jundt U.S. Emerging Growth A	38.7
Royce PA Mutual Investment	23.6
Average	20.0
*Dividends, gains reinvested	

Source: *Lipper Analytical Services*

And while last year's Asian turmoil left most stock funds nursing losses, the average small cap fund was up 20 percent for the year. That compares favorably with the 17.5 percent for all equity funds during 1997 and mirrors the 20.5 percent gain for the Russell 2000.

But pickings are slimmer among micro-cap funds, which invest in the tiniest companies and often close to investors when the funds themselves are still small. While the 30 micro-cap funds were the best-performing category tracked by Lipper Analytical Services in 1997, at least three have shut their doors.

Micro-cap funds are defined by Lipper as those buying stocks with a market value of $300 million or less, and there's sound reasoning behind their appeal. Most of the academic research that shows small stocks beating large stocks over time has usually looked to micro-cap issues as the small-stock universe.

But even among the hundreds of funds investing in a broader group of smaller stocks, finding good small cap funds that are still open is an ongoing struggle, says Ken Gregory, investment adviser and publisher of the *No-Load Fund Analyst* newsletter. You can take your chances with a brand-new fund or an older one whose rising assets may be increasingly in mid-cap companies (those with a value of up to $6 billion).

The problem, it seems, is that in order to invest large sums, fund managers must load up on hundreds of stocks and thus dilute the advantages of skilled stock picking. That makes it imperative for you to know which stocks are in the fund's portfolio, or you can do your own stock picking.

Russell Kinnel, equity research chief at Morningstar, likes UAM FMA Small Company Fund (one of the winners listed in Figure 11.1) for both its one- and five-year records as well as risk-adjusted performance. But he admits that "the available micro-cap funds all feel like gambles. Some track records are very short, while others aren't impressive." (The fund usually requires a $25,000 minimum investment, but is available for $2,500 through discount broker Charles Schwab.)

If you don't own a small cap fund, and want to test the waters, there's an easy way to do it. Determine how much you want to invest, and spend only a third of it. The following month put in another third, and then the rest of your money if the fund begins to skyrocket. But if you are more value oriented and hate the volatility, consider a low-cost small cap index fund (Vanguard, Schwab) based on the performance of the Russell 2000 Index. Better yet, do your own digging!

Intel once was a micro-cap. So was Amgen. While it's difficult to find an Intel when it is little more than a dream, it's not impossible. The micro-caps are where the entrepreneurial spirit lives. And there hasn't been a better time to scour their small universe for some of these over-looked mighty mites. New rules governing Nasdaq transactions should also deflate some of the trading costs associated with these bargain stocks.

SELECTING SECTOR FUNDS

If you're confident about which industry will do well during the next few years, consider a sector fund that buys stocks in a single industry. Keep in mind, however, that although such funds offer greater profit potential than broader-based funds, they're also far riskier. And this risk factor is reflected in their greater volatility.

One reason is that stocks in a given sector tend to fall in unison. They also tend to stay fully invested or nearly so even when their industry has a slide. And they are less likely to switch out when the industry turns sour. It's also difficult to use past performance to predict future results in most sectors. That said, you shouldn't ignore sector funds but limit your investment to 15 percent or less.

Telecommunications funds have done very well, outpacing the Standard & Poor's Index. But they are not even the best performers, which currently include financial services and computer software. Buying into a fund that holds a number of stocks in one industry also reduces the risk of placing wrong bets on a couple of stocks, says Kevin Gooley, analyst at Standard & Poor's. "Such diversity is particularly valuable right now in the telecommunications industry," he says.

But it didn't help those investors who were in global or international funds when the Asian crash occurred in late 1997. Fallout from that turmoil took its toll on investors in foreign funds—especially those invested in single countries like China and Thailand.

The big winners when Asian markets sank were small stocks, soaring as much as 36 percent for small cap funds and 38 percent for microcaps, according to Lipper Analytical Services. In fact, the smaller the stocks a fund invested in, the better the fund performed. Small company funds beat the performance of both mid-cap and large stock funds to echo the trend that smaller *is* better.

And if Wall Street agrees on anything, it's that this is a stock picker's market. You can no longer count on the broad market to do well—although some stocks certainly will. In such a market, sector funds can be a smart vehicle for investors who want to bet on specific stock groups, and there are hundreds of them, specializing in everything from computers to housing to retail stores (see Figure 11.2).

The only problem is that some sector funds attract "hot" money—speculative investors whose goal is a fast profit. Many of them take a flyer on a particular sector fund "and bail out if the fund drops two weeks in a row," says Craig Callahan, president of Meridian Asset Management. As a result, they lose big money trying to time the market, says Callahan.

FIGURE 11.2. TYPES OF SECTOR FUNDS

Agriculture	Housing
Airlines	International
Automobiles	Leisure
Biotechnology	Paper
Chemicals	Pharmaceuticals
Computers	Precious metals
Defense/aerospace	Real estate
Energy services	Retail
Environment	Technology
Financial services	Telecommunications
Foreign countries	Transportation
Health care	Utilities

But there's money to be made for investors who can anticipate hot stock groups like financial services and chemicals, and who can stick with them. "Industries go through up and down cycles that can last two to five years," says Callahan. "If you expect an industry to do well, stay in a sector fund for two years, not two weeks."

One person who does just that is Ralph Wanger, manager of the Acorn Fund. Turnover at his fund averages less than 30 percent a year, while the average stock fund portfolio turns over completely in that time. Acorn gets many of its best investment ideas from small companies in which it is already invested, and from analysts at regional brokerage firms. The fund especially likes companies and niches not covered heavily by Wall Street.

Sectors that Wanger favors are financial services, health care, and cable television. He argues that the big money does not necessarily go to the technology innovators, but to those who use it to create mass-market businesses.

An example, he says, is International Game Technology, which makes lottery equipment and slot machines. The technology is not complex (special-purpose microprocessors), but the gambling business is growing—and International has 75 percent of the market along with low-cost operations.

Fidelity Investments, a pioneer in the field since 1981, now has three dozen sector funds, ranging from airlines to utilities. Invesco and Vanguard are among the others that offer such specialized portfolios.

Narrowly focused sector funds—especially those investing in a single industry or country—have a tendency to be more volatile than broadly diversified ones. And their names appear often on lists of the quarter's best and worst performers. However, sector funds can make more sense than investing in just one stock in an industry that you want to gain exposure to. The funds diversify within their chosen groups and thus carry no company-specific risk.

Timing purchases and sales is important with these funds. Value investors typically buy when a sector is depressed, while some growth players like Wanger search for the hot industries. Making gradual purchases or *dollar cost averaging* can work well with these volatile funds if you want to accumulate a position over time.

Because of illiquidity, lack of information, and other problems, most global or international funds stick with the larger multinational companies—ones that are easier to find, research, and follow. Yet smaller companies, whether in this country or elsewhere, often have above-average growth potential and can be found in a few foreign funds. (Review Chapter 10, on Going Global with Stocks.)

PICKING FUND COMPANIES

To find the top funds, you have to choose them the same way others pick stocks. Great stock pickers like Warren Buffett love companies whose managers invest heavily in their own stock. Why would anyone choose a small cap fund any differently?

"We really do invest as if the only money we manage is our own," says Leah Zell, top manager at Acorn International. She and her research analysts rustle up fast-growing small stocks in forty countries outside the U.S., looking for firms that can benefit from sweeping changes in technology, financial reform, and higher leisure spending.

Inside ownership

When managers own a lot of their own fund, they're less likely to do things that run counter to your best interests or their own. They won't take giant gambles, charge exorbitant expenses, or trade so much that it generates a huge tax bill. They also can stay small while bigger funds go after larger and larger companies—not in your best interest if you want to stick with small stocks.

Low costs

Unlike future returns, a fund's annual expense ratio is knowable. It's printed on the first pages of every prospectus. On average, funds that charge higher expenses will make you less money than funds with low expenses will. Gerald Perritt, publisher of the *Mutual Fund Letter*, favors no-load funds that have relatively low turnover (such as Mutual Shares, Acorn, and Benham Management).

Tight focus

To beat the market, a fund has to do something different. That means owning fewer stocks, or a lot more of some stocks than the market as a whole. American Heritage, a micro-cap fund, posted gains of 78 percent in 1997 plowing more than half its $18 million in assets into Senetek, a British company that says it has a treatment for male impotence.

Support services

Every fund investment should be a partnership between you and the portfolio manager. "Shareholders should understand there's no quick way to get rich," says Acorn's Zell. By reaching out, funds like Acorn, Longleaf, and Oakmark raise the odds that you'll stick with them if times get tough—which is good for them and for you.

In most cases, you can't approach a mutual fund manager, but with many small cap funds, it's possible to talk with managers individually or at annual meetings. If so, here are some pertinent questions to ask:

❑ Where do you think the market is going, and why? If the fund is beating the market averages, find out whether this reflects investment strategy or a handful of "hot" stocks. If it has underperformed the market, ask why.

❑ Does the manager try to "time" the market, changing the fund's mix of cash and securities based on technical or economic factors? For a value-oriented investor, market timing may not be that important.

❑ What is the manager's investment style? Value investors like John Templeton and Michael Price focus on undervalued but growing companies. Others use fundamental or technical analysis of the market and of particular industry trends.

Investors with portfolios worth $100,000 or more may prefer an *asset manager* to a mutual fund. A manager can be approached for personal discussions and can tailor an individual portfolio, buying and selling to fit a client's tax needs, for example. A fund must pay out all dividends and capital gains by year's end, creating taxable income. An asset manager also may cost less—annual fees are around 1 percent of assets managed plus transaction costs.

FUNDS FOR LAZY INVESTORS

It's hard to imagine controversy over index funds. They cost little to run compared to actively managed funds, so more of the profits are passed on to investors. And they are easy to track since they move in near perfect unison with popular indexes such as the Standard & Poor's 500 or the

Russell 2000. Returns on index funds have also trounced the average stock fund for the last three years.

The drawback is that index funds are a perpetual investment machine, mindlessly buying the stocks that constitute the index without regard to the prices being paid. Critics say the Dow Jones Industrial Average passed the 8000 mark in 1997 in part because index funds are getting so much money to invest. They believe the indexes have become bloated with overpriced stocks and can't help getting hit hardest when the market inevitably turns down.

If you're committed to owning stocks for the long haul, indexing still makes sense. For one thing, there's little evidence that indexes fall harder than most stock funds (see Figure 11.3). Second, there are now dozens of choices in index funds so you don't have to buy just the Standard & Poor's 500, by far the most popular and thus worrisome in the index world.

There are index funds for small companies (Russell 2000), mid-size companies (Standard & Poor's 400) and the broad market (Wilshire 5000). Any one of those offers protection should the big indexes tumble, says Frank Salerno, managing director of index funds at Bankers Trust.

Younger investors who can tolerate their volatility are especially encouraged to consider small-cap index funds for their long-term potential. A good way to time your purchases is to compare the price-earnings ratios of small-cap funds to the Standard & Poor's 500. When this yardstick is close to 100, as it has been in recent years, small stocks can give outstanding value. The best time to buy is when the price-earnings multiples are low relative to those of large caps.

FIGURE 11.3. SMALL-CAP SHOPPING

Of the $2 trillion invested in stock funds, only 6 percent is in index funds. But they have returned 15.3 percent versus 11.9 percent for all stock funds.

Index	Total Investment	Average Return*
Standard & Poor's 500	$85B	20.3%
Wilshire 5000	5B	14.5
Russell 2000	2.4B	22.4
Morgan Stanley International	753M	25.5
Standard & Poor's 100	490M	34.9
Standard & Poor's 400	318M	19.8

*Year-to-date through June 1997

Source: Lipper Analytical Service

Professor Burton Malkiel of Princeton, in his highly acclaimed book *A Random Walk Down Wall Street,* makes a compelling case for index funds. He holds that index funds should obtain better results than those produced by the typical portfolio manager. Why? Because substantial management fees and turnover eat into the bottom line. The transaction costs associated with active management act as a drain on performance, and expenses in general put managers at a disadvantage.

They may be boring, since they will never beat the market, but perhaps it's not an arena where most people should look for fun and excitement. Indeed, many other activities offer more stimulation and less risk than playing the stock market. Index funds may lead to fewer sleepless nights of tossing and turning than individual stocks or funds.

MEASURING PERFORMANCE

It's important to know how to study performance numbers once you've bought mutual funds. Focus on results for the past one, two, and five years. Small cap funds often don't have longer records because they have become mid-cap funds or they are closed to new investors. There are three ways to judge fund performance:

❏ Follow the price of shares, officially known as net asset value, or NAV.

❏ Track the yield or the amount of income the fund is paying out to shareholders.

❏ Look at the total return of the fund.

Although all three figures are important, the total return is the only overall indicator of how well a fund is doing, because it shows the total profit generated by the fund. It's also the best one to use when comparing one fund to another, or one type of fund with another type of fund.

The total return figure over one, three or five years, as well as from the beginning of the year to date, is given in financial publications such as the *Wall Street Journal* and from the funds directly. But keep in mind that in a small cap fund, the yield figure is not terribly important because the stocks in the fund were selected for their potential price appreciation, not for their individual income. In fact, most pay no dividends. What is important is whether the share price (NAV) has been rising steadily for several years (see Figure 11.4).

FIGURE 11.4. HOW TO USE FUND TABLES

The daily performance of mutual funds is measured differently from that of stocks held in the funds. Here's how to use the newspaper tables:

Fund groups come first with separate funds named below. Any funds not in groups are not indented. Capital letters after the fund name designate the type of fund (see Abbreviations below).

Percent return shows total annualized return for five years if available.

NS, fund did not exist at start of period.

NN, fund does not wish to be tracked.

Ranking. Funds are ranked against their peers in their investment group. A, top 20%; E, bottom 20%.

High, Low. The highest and lowest net asset value (NAV) of the fund during the week.

Last, Change. Value of the fund at the close of the last trading day of the week, and the change between the last price listed and the previous week's last price.

Footnotes:

n, No front end load or contingent deferred sales load;

p, Fund assets are used to pay for distribution costs;

r, Redemption fee may apply;

t, both p and r apply.

Abbreviations:

EM	Emerging Markets;
EU	European Region;
GI	Growth & Income;
GL	Global;
GR	Growth;
HB	Health & Biotech;
IL	International;
LT	Latin America;
MC	Mid-Cap;
PR	Pacific Region;
SC	Small Company;
SE	Sector;
TK	Technology

A fund's size, or total assets, is another factor to consider. Funds range in size from under $300 million to more than $10 billion. The largest, Fidelity Magellan, recently had assets in excess of $50 billion. In general, you can classify stock funds into these categories:

- ❏ Micro-cap: Under $300 million.
- ❏ Small cap: $300 million to $1 billion.
- ❏ Mid-cap: $1 billion to $3 billion.
- ❏ Large cap: Over $3 billion.

You also want to compare a particular fund's results with that of other portfolios having the same or similar objectives. For example, small stocks greatly outperformed large cap companies in 1997. The main point to keep in mind is that size alone may affect performance for small cap funds. That's why a number of them close their doors to new investors when they reach a certain size. Some other advantages of small funds:

Easier to maneuver

Small funds are more nimble, making it simpler for management to reshuffle holdings. A $5 billion fund will likely have some individual positions valued at $75 million or more. But it would be difficult for a larger fund to eliminate large positions. To minimize heavy losses, large holdings might have to be reduced gradually.

Limited holdings

In addition to having smaller positions, small funds can also hold fewer stocks. Thus small company and aggressive growth funds can often accomplish their objectives more easily with less diverse portfolios. That's why the managers may close their doors to new investors and even limit additional purchases by existing shareholders if they feel the fund has gotten too large to meet its goals.

Superfluous diversification

Large funds may wind up owning 200 or more stocks, more than is necessary to achieve adequate diversification. Even if a dozen or more turn out to be super performers, their gains will be diluted by the many others that post average results or worse. Big funds simply cannot take meaningful positions in small companies. That's why it's common to see small funds recording abnormally big gains.

Beat the market

A giant fund like Magellan will tend to perform like the market averages or an index fund, except that it has extra management and transaction costs. This cost disadvantage explains why most managed funds trail the popular market averages as well as index funds. It also makes it difficult to sell fund shares when the market is hot—or cold.

Every year, you should review each individual fund and security to see how it has performed compared with similar funds or stocks. Weed out the laggards, aiming to reduce the overall number of poor performers. Most investors buy funds on an ad hoc basis, so that they end up with a host of different funds—many of which have the same investment objectives. If you own more than a dozen funds, you probably own too many!

INVESTOR INFORMATION

What do you do when the stock market gets as wild as it has recently? Don't sell. Read something. A grounding in the history, strategy and how-to techniques of investing can help you prosper even in volatile times.

Start with the *Handbook for No-load Fund Investors.* This annual directory from Sheldon Jacobs has useful ideas on how to pick a no-load fund and performance data on 1,700 funds. Write or call: Box 318, Irvington-on-Hudson, NY 10533 (800-252-2042). Cost: $45.

How Mutual Funds Work, Second Edition, by Albert Fredman and Russ Wiles, covers a broad range of topics, yet treats each thoroughly, including small cap funds. The information is unbiased and nonpromotional—neither author has anything to sell.

CHAPTER 12

Reading Annual Reports

Visit the main branch of your public library just about any evening or Saturday and you'll find the reference room busy with local investors who have decided to take charge of their own portfolios. They may be combing through one or more annual reports for some hint of whether to buy, hold, sell, or skip a particular stock; scanning any of several investment newsletters for the picks and pans of market gurus; or checking the reports of the Securities and Exchange Commission to see if officers and directors are buying or selling shares in their own company.

"Many public libraries now have better research material than a typical brokerage office," says David Strege, senior vice president of Bryton Financial Advisors in Des Moines. "But you will want to keep brokerage or mutual fund statements for the past year. When you receive the annual summary you can toss all of the monthly statements."

Access to financial data won't make you suddenly competent to evaluate or trade stocks, particularly if you've relied on the advice of a broker or left decisions to a mutual fund manager and don't have the time or inclination to do the research yourself. But whether you just want to keep tabs on how your portfolio is faring or make a few of your own trades through a regional or discount broker, there's a treasure trove of resources available to you.

Annual reports, even if "cheerleaderish," are an obvious place to start. If you are considering a stock to buy, look at the annual reports for the past three years as well. They will provide background on a company's fundamentals: what it does, the trend of sales and profits, and management's view of the future.

The most telling nuggets are often found not in the glossy pages up front, but in footnotes at the back of the report—where one reason for glowing profits might be revealed as artful accounting (such as reclassifying accounts receivable as prepaid expenses), or where you may find skeletons, such as pending lawsuits or tax disputes that have yet to be resolved.

WHAT TO LOOK FOR

If you already own stocks, you receive lots of annual reports. They're beautiful to look at, and some get awards for "straight talk" or artwork. But beauty is only skin deep, say financial analysts who were asked recently what they like and dislike about annual reports.

The results of the survey of 50 brokerage and institutional analysts in 15 cities make useful reading for every investor. For example, nearly a third of those surveyed said most annual reports are too long. An Atlanta analyst gave this trenchant comment: "Sixteen pages of baloney before figures that show the company lost its shirt!"

Still, the amount of information you can glean from annual reports is amazing. Scores of figures show earnings of major divisions, foreign activities, plant and equipment leases, depreciation, and tax credits (gained or lost). The text will have explanations of what happened during the year and what is projected for the future.

What should an investor zero in on that would make him or her want to keep or sell stock in a company—and where might it be found? The worst place to start is the letter to shareholders. It has a summary of the year's events and goals for the future, but a reader should discount this as mostly hype.

Watch for double-talk

If there were failures, there should be logical explanations. "Details would be a lot more constructive than some of the snow-job statements now in the reports," said one Chicago analyst. That's why it helps to get reports for past years and compare forecasts to what actually happened.

Most of the analysts complained about the lack of factual information and figures in such areas as production growth, market share, and industry trends. And there was overwhelming approval of three- and five-year statistical summaries (but not misleading graphs) of a company's financial condition. This feeling that annual reports are often less than candid was widespread among analysts *and* investors.

Analysts objected most to double-talk and buzzwords that divert attention from any problems. Ninety-four percent believe that reports "gloss over company problems rather than provide explanations or future plans." Other negatives annual reports may need to address include plant closings, sales of subsidiaries, discontinued products, downsizing, and the need for financing. Not all of these need be adverse, but they can make a significant difference in what happens to a small company in the next few years. If profits were down, was it due to price wars or poor managerial decisions?

Return on equity

So what's the first thing to look for? Analysts study the income statement, where the *really* interesting stuff turns up in those footnotes. Next comes the auditor's opinion. Two paragraphs is standard—otherwise they're hedging. After that, the analyst reads whatever catches his or her eye.

The footnotes are where you can spot problems such as heavy markdowns of inventory, adverse government regulations, rollovers of debt, foreign currency transactions, and other events that the company is required by the Securities and Exchange Commission to disclose. A qualified auditor's opinion doesn't mean that the company is lying, only that the figures may have to be adjusted. The third paragraph usually contains any disclaimers by the auditors who have reservations about the figures.

While analysts rely on annual reports for much investment information, they don't believe everything they read. More important in their buy-and-sell recommendations are factors like industry leadership and price appreciation. Business today is extremely competitive and affected too much by external pressures to ensure swift success.

Return on equity is the best measure of management's ability to make money with your money. Anything above 15 percent is good. Below that, compare the figure with that of previous years and with other firms in the industry. But watch out for accounting maneuvers to "massage" reported earnings, such as including the income from other partly owned companies in total profits. This income cannot be used for expansion or payouts to shareholders. Such tricks are one reason that stocks fall or remain flat after annual profits are reported.

Analysts and savvy investors are smart enough to discover when earnings are more paper than real. And they know that buzzwords like "difficult" and "challenging" probably mean sales and profits were off, but expenses (including management salaries) were up. That's nice for them, but not good for shareholders.

Other positives to note are new plants, products, personnel, and programs. Also look for assets greater and liabilities lower than in previous years. Beware, however, of over-enthusiasm about new products. It usually takes two to three years to translate new operations into sizable sales and profits. But if sales, earnings, and accounts receivable continue to rise, chances are that you've found a winner.

As you review the trends, keep in mind that external pressures can have an impact on the future. Examples include interest rates and small company expansion, cost ceilings on hospital suppliers, and federal legislation on oil and gas companies. "Compare promises made in past reports with the company's subsequent performance," advises William Dunk, doyen of annual reports and longtime industry observer.

They should be available from the company's investor relations department (get the address from *Moody's Manuals* or other reference books at your library). As Dunk sees it, reports in recent years have been full of "feisty talk" for two reasons: All sorts of markets are flat or declining, and management needs chutzpah to swipe market share from the other guys. But he defends annual reports against the familiar rap that they lie. "The majority of companies want to and do tell the truth."

Cheap or flashy

About the overall look of annual reports, most analysts preferred those of standard size over odd shapes or cutouts created for getting attention. One exception was Marvel Entertainment's annual report, fashioned like a comic book. It didn't hurt that net income for Spiderman and company rose 196 percent in its first year as a public company.

But you never know. "Overly flashy reports tend to make me suspicious," said a Baltimore analyst. "Adequate disclosure is the most important thing." Still, companies spend an average of around $3 to publish each snazzy report, not including mailing costs. Sid Cato, publisher of the monthly *Newsletter on Annual Reports,* gives high marks for readability, financial disclosure and straight talk from management. A recent sinner: Glycomed, whose letter from the chairman failed to acknowledge the company's fifth consecutive loss.

Getting insights

All in all, financial analysts agree that reading annual reports can give an investor lots of information about a company. It can help you make a bundle, or save one, but only if you understand a few caveats:

❏ The statements will be factually correct, but the interpretations will naturally attempt to present the most favorable view within legal and accounting limits. You'll have to do some sleuthing to make the words and figures comprehensible and revealing.

❏ Look at the income statement for signs that the company is inflating its earnings to hide management problems. Be suspicious if profits have continued to rise despite a dip in earnings. One way to boost profits is to raise the assumed rate of return on pension-fund investments.

❏ Get out your calculator and figure some ratios. Look for at least twice as many assets as debts, and a habit of reinvesting a third of earnings in expanding the business. But be wary of entries called "extraordinary" or "nonrecurring." Such one-time gains may mean the company is selling off assets to cover up operating losses.

If you still have doubts, obtain the company's Form 10-K. This has extensive financial data not in the annual report and is available from brokers, the company, or the Securities and Exchange Commission. Quarterly reports don't have to be audited, so take them with a grain of salt. And if you really want to dig, ask your broker for Standard & Poor's or Value Line's research reports on the company you're interested in.

PRICE-EARNINGS RATIOS

The price-earnings ratio is probably the single most important thing you can know about a stock. It's the price of a share divided by the company's earnings per share. If a stock sells for $40 a share and the company earned $4 a share in the previous year, the stock has a P-E ratio of 10. Simply put, the price-earnings ratio tells you how much money investors are willing to pay for each dollar of a company's earnings. It's such a significant key to value that it's listed every day in the business pages of newspapers along with every stock's price.

But analysts warn that investors could get hurt if they pay too much for a stock, as many have in this record-setting bull market. As evidence, they point to the bargain hunters that snapped up overvalued stocks when their prices fell during the October 1997 mini-crash. "In a bull market, price-earnings ratios blow past historic norms," says Stan Weinstein, editor of the *Professional Tape Reader.* "If things snowball, they can blow right past those norms again."

The projections appear plausible, especially when accompanied by tables, charts, and computer printouts. But in most cases, they depend a good deal on market conditions and your own investment style. And if you are speculating with "hot" stocks, you should compare the P-E ratio with other companies in the same industry and on some basis decide how reasonable the projection is.

For example, a broker may tell you that the stock of a small company now selling at 40 times its recent earnings will be trading at "only 16 times projected earnings five years from now if the company's earnings growth is 20 percent a year." Not bad, unless another panic or a recession guts earnings. When that happens, stock prices can fall even if price-earnings ratios remain stable.

As you might expect, investors are willing to pay more to own shares of companies they think will increase their profits faster than the average company. But stocks with high P-E ratios also carry the risk that if the company's earnings disappoint investors, its share price may plunge quickly. Just one poor quarter—or the rumor of one—can mean a vicious pounding for a stock with a superhigh multiple.

By contrast, investors don't expect a company with a low P-E ratio to grow as rapidly and are less likely to desert on mildly unfavorable news. And if profits rise faster than expected, other investors can push up both the P-E ratio and the stock price quickly. That's why you have to compare any company's price-earnings ratio with those of similar companies and with broader measures as well.

Market indexes such as the Standard & Poor's 500 and Russell 2000 also have P-E ratios, as do different industry sectors such as computers and biotechnology. Knowing what these are can help you decide on the relative merits of a stock you're considering. In addition, when the Standard & Poor's 500 sports a superhigh multiple, as it did before the stock market crash of October 1987, it may be wise to cut back on new stock purchases or even lighten up on your holdings in expectation of a fall to a more sustainable level.

Arnold Kaufman, editor of Standard & Poor's newsletter, *The Outlook,* doesn't believe that price-earnings ratios are likely to drop very far— unless inflation guts the value of earnings growth. In that case, small companies would probably fall faster than their blue-chip cousins.

He also cautions that a low price-earnings ratio is not by itself a sign of value. A stock's price may be low relative to its earnings because investors have little faith in the reliability of those earnings, and investors could be right. A good example of this was the low premium investors were willing to put on shares of banks just before their earnings evaporated in 1990.

You don't make any money from the stellar performance of a company *before* you buy its stock. You want it to do well *after* you buy it. So look not only at P-E ratios based on previous earnings, but also at those based on analysts' future earnings estimates. Those could be wrong, of course, but they are another piece of information on which to base your decision to buy or not. Brokers will happily provide the forecasts of their firms' analysts.

UNDERSTANDING FINANCIAL STATEMENTS

There are other factors to weigh before deciding which stocks to buy, but price-earnings ratios are the natural starting point because they provide a quick way to separate stocks that seem overpriced from those that don't. Indeed, some value investors have a discipline that doesn't allow them even to consider owning a stock unless its P-E ratio is below 10.

Unlike those who invest in small growth stocks, value investors don't often go for home runs. They don't care what stage of development a company is in. They assume that they can find stocks that are undervalued by the market for some reason, but that have the potential to return to some "fair" value eventually.

By contrast, you'll have to dig deeper to find the gems among the universe of small cap stocks. The following data and explanations are digested from *Understanding Financial Statements*, prepared by the New York Stock Exchange. They are not detailed, but will get you started. For a personal copy, write to the address given at the end of this chapter (or ask your broker to get you one).

Retained earnings

This is the company's bottom line—the profits earned after taxes and payment of any dividends to holders of preferred stock. Dividing earnings by the average number of shares outstanding during the period being measured gives you the *earnings per share*, another key number for evaluating any company.

Earnings are also the company's chief resource for reinvesting in business growth. In the annual report, check to be sure that earnings come from routine operations (sales) and not from one-time occurrences like the sale of a subsidiary or a big award from a patent-infringement suit. Small or new companies generally pay no dividends, and that money gets reinvested in the business.

Sales

These indicate how much business the company did in a year—before deductions for *costs and expenses*. With service organizations and insurance firms, the term "revenues" is often used instead of sales. Check both figures against those of major competitors and the industry as a whole. They may be better (or worse) than they look.

The costs of getting products or services to customers and getting paid will vary with the kind of business: high for consumer goods manufacturers and distributors because of advertising and marketing, and lower for companies selling primarily to industry or government. Caution: Depreciation is a bookkeeping item to provide for wear and tear of machinery and equipment, and can be used to inflate earnings.

Operating profit

The dollars generated from the company's usual operations without regard to income from other sources or financing, is its operating profit. As a percentage of sales, it tells you the *profit margin,* rising or falling in the last year compared to the year before.

Factors that can affect the profit margin include any interest charges paid to bondholders, and provisions for taxes on income (widely variable because of exemptions or special credits). One year's change is interesting, but the true test of management's ability comes over time.

Balance sheet

Use this to determine the financial strength of companies that you own or plan to own. The headings may vary according to the type of industry, but the basic data will be similar—and just as important.

❏ *Current assets* are items that can be converted into cash, such as bank deposits, marketable securities, accounts receivable, and inventories of raw materials, work in process and finished goods.

❏ *Property, plant, and equipment.* This is the land, structures, machinery, tools, and motor vehicles owned by the company. Except for the land, all of these assets have a limited useful life, allowing a deduction from cost as depreciation.

❏ *Other assets* include intangibles such as patents, copyrights, franchises, trademarks or goodwill which cannot be accurately assessed, and are omitted from the computation of *book value* or shareholders' equity.

❏ *Liabilities* are either current (payable within a year) or long-term debt and other obligations due in the future. They include accounts payable, unpaid salaries and commissions, federal, state and local income taxes, any declared dividends, and money needed to finance expansion of the business.

❏ *Stockholders equity* is all money invested in the company by stockholders, as well as reinvested earnings. Common stock is shown on the books at par value, an arbitrary amount having no relation to market value or to what would be received in liquidation. Capital surplus is the amount received from the sale of stock in excess of par value.

DOING YOUR OWN RESEARCH

Howard Schilit, founder of the Center for Financial Research and Analysis in Rockville, Maryland, makes his living "reading documents that no one else is reading." Every week, he and his team of analysts pore over thousands of pages of Securities and Exchange Commission filings looking for accounting gimmicks that are used to hide operational problems. The results are published in a monthly research report for more than 100 institutional investors.

More accessible to you when doing your research on small stocks are the company records in handbooks and manuals put out by research firms or advisory services like Moody's, Value Line or Standard & Poor's, available in many public libraries.

They focus mainly on fundamentals providing earnings estimates, industry and company analyses, investment strategies, stock recommendations and model portfolios—a package of investment materials that you cannot find assembled elsewhere in one place. But they are expensive, costing from $300 to $955 a year, so check the library first. Stocks are no bargain if you spend all your profits collecting reference material—and too much data, or the wrong kind, can be confusing.

Moody's, for example, provides manuals and news reports on over 5,200 Nasdaq and over-the-counter companies that give verified earnings for even unlisted or "pink sheet" stocks. The research firm, owned by Dun & Bradstreet Corp., is not an advisory service and makes no stock recommendations.

Another staple you may find in the library is the *Value Line Special Situations Service,* which provides fundamental and technical analysis of fast-growing smaller companies as well as recommendations. Cost: $390.

To keep abreast of changes in earnings, mergers and other news that can affect a stock's performance, check Standard & Poor's *Corporation Records.* The seven volumes cover financial details, history, and products of over 12,000 companies. And libraries that subscribe to the loose-leaf reference get inserts five days a week for updatings. It's the best place to look for an address or phone number when requesting an annual report.

Newsletters are another story. Almost anyone can do some basic research and publish a stock market advisory letter. In fact, a recent study of 140 independent newsletters (those not put out by brokerage firms) published between 1964 and 1995 came to one conclusion: If you don't know much about the market and have a few thousand dollars to invest, you'd be better off letting mutual funds manage your money.

But a good service might be helpful if you have, say, $10,000 or $15,000 to invest. Mark Hulbert, publisher of *Hulbert Financial Digest,* which tracks newsletter performance, says that over the past 10 years, several have actually beaten the market and adds: "The average mutual fund, economist or Wall Street analyst doesn't beat the market either."

Before committing yourself, sample as many newsletters as you can. Most will offer a trial subscription for a low price, and some will send you a sample copy at no charge. One way to start is to write for the free catalog published by Select Information Exchange (800-743-9346). It describes hundreds of newsletter services and offers a trial five-month subscription to any four you choose for $69. A sampling is also given in Apppendix B, Newsletters and Advisory Services.

Remember, stock or fund rating services are precisely what the people who create them claim they are: tools, not magic wands. The ratings won't solve your investing problems, but they will give you a handle on the big, boisterous world of small stocks, particularly if you use them as part of a sound investment strategy.

Beyond looking into newsletters or advisory services, you would profit from reading about investments in magazines or in daily newspapers. The following are arranged by approximate level of sophistication:

Wall Street Transcript	*Smart Money*
Investor's Business Daily	*Individual Investor*
Value Line Investment survey	*Kiplinger's Personal Finance*
Barron's	*Money*
Outlook (Standard & Poor's)	*Better Investing* (NAIC)
Wall Street Journal	*Your Money*
Business Week	*U.S. News & World Report*
New York Times	*USA Today*
Worth	Local daily newspaper

Subscriptions are available for each, and many of them can be bought at a newsstand. And don't overlook the programs like *Wall Street Week* with Louis Rukeyser that can be viewed on PBS, CNN or CNBC television stations. Know what's going on with the economy as well as individual stocks!

FIGURING DEBT-EQUITY RATIO

The debt-equity ratio shows how much leverage, or debt, a company is carrying compared with shareholders' equity, or book value. In general, the lower this figure the better, although the definition of an acceptable debt load varies from industry to industry. You'll find data on debt in annual reports, Value Line, Moody's, and Standard & Poor's publications.

Stick with companies whose debts amount to no more than a third of shareholders' equity. Look for a return on equity that is consistently high compared with other companies in the same industry, or that shows a strong pattern of growth. A steady return of more than 15 percent is a sign of a company that knows how to manage itself well.

One popular strategy is to concentrate on issues selling for $5 or less. These cheap thrills sometimes turn out to be fast-growing small companies. Another tactic is to catch a fallen star, a stock that has been a victim of bad news. As mentioned, you can spot these "unfortunates" in daily newspaper lists of stocks reaching 52-week lows.

To find out whether the company is reeling from only a temporary setback instead of a terminal problem, look for long-term debt that is no greater than 40 percent of the company's total capitalization and less than 10 percent of annual sales. New management, significant cost reductions and the introduction of potentially profitable products or services are additional signs that the corpse may be coming back from the grave.

Many successful investors have discovered that personal experience leads them to stock-market winners. But do not invest without finding more facts. Superb products can come from poorly run companies. And a close encounter with a single product tells you nothing about a firm's other lines of business. They may not be so terrific. In other words, use your experience, but do not be overimpressed.

Some of the most sought-after growth stocks, of course, are those of companies on the cutting edges of technology—and they often have high price-earnings and debt-equity ratios. The reason is that investors continue to believe that high technology will be the economy's major source of long-term growth. And they still have sound reasons to believe, even though young companies in overcrowded, highly competitive fields are especially risky.

You can reduce your risk by concentrating on underdeveloped industries where one or two companies have found a profitable market niche. One such field is the design of circuit-board assemblies for original-equipment manufacturers in the personal computer, communications, and automotive industries. Some companies like Jabil Circuit in St. Petersburg, Florida, have seen sales grow more than 50 percent a year.

The human side of technology is the speculative biotech industry. Biotech stocks are not for the timid. Most of the companies have yet to show *any* earnings. And profits could be a long time coming because years of clinical testing are required before a medical product can be sold. Safest bets are firms whose products are well along in the testing phase like Isis Pharmaceuticals with its "antisense" drugs for retinitis and Crohn's disease, or that improve the functioning of existing antibiotics (Xoma).

Keep in mind that when a company has high debt, it usually means that investors shy away from buying its common stock. To provide the physical plant and equipment that the company needs, management must issue bonds or preferred shares to attract investors. That can make it difficult for a small company to weather a downturn, let alone a full-blown recession. All or most of the gross profits will have to be used to pay interest, and there will be nothing or very little left over for the common shareholders.

By contrast, speculators look for high-debt situations when business is good. With hefty profits, interest can be paid easily, and the balance comes down to the common stock. Typically, airlines with heavy debt obligations for new planes do well in boom times: An extra 10-percent gain in traffic can boost profits by as much as 30 percent.

SPOTTING TAKEOVER CANDIDATES

Sometimes just reading a company's annual report and financial statements can help you spot a takeover candidate. Does the company have cash hoards, real estate, principal owners who want to sell, or other assets that might catch the eye of a takeover or buyout specialist? You can get added information from the *Value Line Investment Survey*.

Tens of thousands of investors have been blessed with bonanzas from the surge in corporate mergers and takeovers. And the stocks of the acquired companies have been bid up to giddy highs because many investors are trying to guess which firms will be acquired next so they can buy those companies' stocks and ride them up.

In a takeover deal, the acquiring company typically pays a premium of 30 percent or even more over the market price for each share of the company it wants to acquire. So it's small wonder that many investors are rushing to buy the stocks of companies that they think are candidates for takeovers. Here are some guidelines for finding them:

❏ *Look where the bargain-hunters do.* They prefer companies that have large cash holdings. The buying company then can recover part of the purchase price by using the selling company's very own cash. Acquisition-minded corporations also look for stocks selling appreciably below book value (or total assets minus liabilities per share).

❏ *Find out if owners are eager to sell.* Deal makers often search out companies whose principal owners have reasons to want a merger— for example, if they are elderly, own the controlling interest and have most of their eggs in that one corporate basket. A sellout would enable them to diversify their holdings and perhaps get some stock that is more readily marketable.

❏ *Look where takeover and merger activity are already strong.* Lately, it has been intense in the software industry, cable television, publishing, banks, and brokerage firms. But don't chase rumors. Having the right information about a company and knowing how to interpret it is more important than any of the other factors you might hear credited for the success of the latest market genius.

Takeovers, buyouts and other special situations aren't for everyone. If you think a new management team can work wonders for an ailing company, you'd better have the skills to judge just how sick the company is. That means you'll have to learn a lot more about securities analysis and accounting practices than you will pick up in this book. Fortunately, there's a lot of information out there, and a good deal of it is free.

INVESTOR INFORMATION

The danger of becoming well informed is that the more you learn, the more conflicting views you're bound to find about picking stocks. One skill that no book can teach is how to recognize the point at which you have to close the books and dive in.

For starters, obtain a copy of *Understanding Financial Statements* from the New York Stock Exchange, 11 Wall Street, New York, NY 10005 (212-656-3000); and the helpful booklet *How to Read a Financial Report* available from Merrill Lynch (800-637-7455).

Budding analysts or accountants can turn to several books on the subject, including *Financial Statement Analysis,* by Rose Marie Bukics. And *The Wall Street Journal Guide to Understanding Money & Markets.* Neither should leave you wanting to leave the room.

Finding the Right Broker

Face it: If you're going to buy individual issues of stocks you're going to need a broker—to execute trades if nothing else. A broker is your link to the exchanges where securities transactions take place and to the vastly larger Nasdaq and over-the-counter markets, where most of the new or emerging growth stocks are traded.

The first thing to know about brokers is that they are hardly ever called that anymore. They have much more impressive names: vice president, financial advisor, registered representative, account executive. Sometimes the title reflects extra schooling in the art and science of investing, or it just happens to be what the brokerage firm likes to call its brokers. Because the quality and experience of the individual matter more than the title on the business card, the best course is to ignore it and concentrate on discovering whether you've found a good match.

The worst scenario is when the broker picks the investor, rather than the other way around. Typically, it happens in one of two ways:

❑ You get a phone call from a representative of a national firm with a name you recognize. The broker tells you his firm is bringing to market a new issue of a promising software company and because they are one of the underwriters, the stock is available at no commission cost. Interested? You, who had been thinking about getting into small caps for some time, say "Yes." Bingo, you've got yourself a broker.

❑ You see a television commercial for Merrill Lynch and like what it has to say. So you stroll into the local office and tell the receptionist,

"I'd like to talk to someone about opening an investment account." The receptionist consults a piece of paper, picks up the phone and summons Mr. Jones. Again, you've got yourself a broker.

What's wrong with both of these examples is that you're trusting your fate to chance. In the first, the caller is probably fairly new on the job and prospecting for business using a list of area residents. In the second, the broker who is summoned to meet you is a random choice. You may get a good broker that way, or one whose recommendations are highly inappropriate for your investment goals.

Never sign on with someone who calls you cold over the phone, or walk into a branch firm off the street. Set up interviews with several candidates, and prepare a list of questions so you can compare answers. Andrew Lanyi, research director at Ladenburg, Thalman & Co., and author of *Confessions of a Stockbroker*, has these suggestions:

❏ Look for someone who has character and integrity, and is on the same wavelength as you. If you want a broker to help you find the next Microsoft, you're not going to be happy with someone who believes only in the *Fortune 100*.

❏ Ask the broker what he's putting his own money into. Don't be embarrassed, it's a fair question. He may own some of the stocks he's recommending to you and that can be a good thing. They may be companies he has the most faith in.

❏ Find out what research materials are available to the broker. A problem in many firms is the breakdown in communications between brokers and analysts. That determines how quickly you get answers to your questions.

CHOOSING A BROKER

Do you want investment advice and recommendations? If so, you're in the market for a full-service broker. Mostly, these are the high-profile national firms with armies of analysts who crank out buy and sell recommendations for a long list of stocks. And their fee structures reflect the expense of maintaining those research departments.

Commissions vary according to the number of shares and dollar amount involved, but on average you can expect to pay about 2 percent of the value of the shares each time you buy or sell. In general, the bigger the transaction the smaller the bite taken out of it by the broker's commission.

Full-service firms also pride themselves on their comprehensive asset-management services. They vary in details, but all include a money-market account into which the firm automatically "sweeps" idle funds (such as dividend payments), check-writing privileges, a substantial line of credit, and a comprehensive monthly statement. But such deluxe services may not benefit aggressive investors seeking greater returns with young, untested companies.

Just about everyone is familiar with Merrill Lynch's thundering herd, and recognizes Smith Barney as the brokerage firm that makes money "the old fashioned way, by earning it." But a growing number of investors are turning their ears instead to lesser-known regional brokers who follow the stocks of small local companies.

Regional firms often specialize in fast-growing companies with strong management. Some specialize in regions, and others in a single industry. Many have notable records of performance, as was mentioned in Chapter 4; for example, Legg Mason in Pittsburgh, Robinson-Humphrey in Atlanta, Prescott, Ball & Turben in Cleveland, and Rauscher Pierce Refsnes in Dallas.

These brokers tend to have strong and deep ties to their region and handle significant underwritings for new companies too small to be noticed by national firms. So, if you think the economic prospects are bright for companies in your state or in a specific part of the country, a phone call to a regional broker will get you a sampling of current research reports. If you like what you see, you can open an account, also by phone, and start receiving monthly market letters with forecasts and lists of recommended stocks.

To find other regional firms, one good source is Standard & Poor's *Security Dealers of North America*. It lists brokerage firms, their addresses and phone numbers, by city and state. A sampling is also given in Appendix C, Regional and Discount Brokers.

When these firms venture out of their regions, it usually is to cover the competitors of local companies. Their analysts keep turning up small companies that have fast-expanding markets and earnings. And gradually the glitter of these little stars will attract the attention of national firms. That's the regional analyst's dream: finding stocks, getting clients into them early, then waiting until a big national firm "discovers" them—and sends the price soaring.

If you make your own investment decisions and don't need or want advice or recommendations from your broker, there's no need to pay for them. Most *discount brokers* don't make specific buy and sell recommendations. What you get is fulfillment of your order, period (although some discounters offer a range of investor services).

You can save as much as 80 percent on commissions by dealing with a discount broker. But you pay some penalties for these huge price cuts. National Discount Brokers, for example, requires its customers to open an account with $2,000, and Brown & Co. asks for $15,000 up front to begin trading. But most discount brokers will pay interest an any money that isn't fully invested.

If you want cut-rate commissions but feel hesitant to end your relationship with a full-service broker, try asking for a discount. Your broker probably can offer as much as 30 percent off the typical full fee on any substantial transaction. That's close to what you would pay at Charles Schwab or Quick & Reilly. And just one winning stock recommendation from a full-service broker's research staff could more than make up the difference.

On the other hand, you might do well to move to a discounter if you feel confident enough to do your own stock picking. In choosing, it's paramount to select a company that can weather precipitous ups and downs in the stock market. If the firm has at least ten years of service, then it already has survived two market downturns, and you are probably safe.

UNCOVERING HIDDEN FEES

If you thought the only expense in trading stocks was the broker's commission, you may be in for a shock the next time you get your statement. Many brokerage houses are charging a variety of new fees.

For example, Smith Barney and Harris Upham & Co. charge investors a $50 fee when they transfer a securities account to another firm. Merrill Lynch charges $15 to supply you with a stock certificate. And if you tend to buy stocks and hold them, some brokerage houses will hit you with an inactive-account fee. At Prudential Securities an investor needs to generate $150 or more in commissions—a minimum usually satisfied with a single transaction—to avoid a $50 charge.

Confirmation slips, used to prove a purchase or sale of shares, come with an added postage-and-handling fee ($4.85 at Merrill Lynch), which is not deductible from taxable investment profits, the way a broker's commission is. And despite their claim to bare-bones order-taking, some discount brokers also have their share of "hidden" fees.

There are no regulations regarding how much brokerage houses can charge you for various services, but you can protect yourself. Keep in mind that brokers need your business and may be willing to negotiate fees and charges. "If your brokerage is on the high end, ask your broker to match the competition," advises Gerri Detweiler, policy director for the National Council of Individual Investors.

At Fidelity Brokerage, for example, there are no fees for confirmation slips, account transfers, or inactive accounts. Verify fees and commissions before you choose or change a brokerage firm, adds Detweiler. If you need some leverage, obtain a copy of the annual brokerage survey put out by the American Association of Individual Investors, 625 N. Michigan Ave., Chicago, IL 60611 (800-428-2244). Cost: $4.

When you've selected a broker, you'll be asked to fill out a new-account information form. On that form you'll have to make some choices about the kind of account you want.

Cash accounts are the most sensible choice for new customers. They require that all trades be settled on a cash basis, meaning if you want to buy $1,000 worth of stock, you've got to deliver the $1,000 to the broker within a few days of the transaction.

Margin accounts permit you to trade with money borrowed from the brokerage firm. The size of the loan depends on the current "margin requirement," which for some years has been 50 percent. Before you choose, review Chapter 9, Margin Trading and Options.

When you open your account, you'll also be asked whether you want the broker to hold your stock certificates in *street name* or send them to you, in which case you'll be responsible for their safekeeping. The main advantages of keeping your shares in street name are liquidity and convenience.

If you want to trade on margin, securities in street name easily serve as collateral. Meanwhile, the shares are stored safely in the firm's vault, and you receive up-to-date records on their value. The only drawback is that if the brokerage goes broke, your holdings will be tied up for months. You'll get them back eventually, because they are insured by the Securities Investor Protection Corporation.

DOLLAR-COST AVERAGING

It seldom fails. A first-time investor dives into the market on a hot tip, buying at the top. Then the stock tumbles and he sells—precisely at the bottom. You can avoid such expensive errors by investing a set amount each month—regardless of whether the market is headed up or down. This is a canny and profitable investment strategy called *dollar-cost averaging*.

Think of it as investing on the installment plan. If stock prices go up, you can congratulate yourself for having earned some profits. What if the price drops? Then you have a new opportunity to pick up some bargains. A few months earlier, your $500 would buy only 15 shares—now it can buy 20!

Many people find that a sound way to practice dollar-cost averaging is to buy shares of a mutual fund at regular intervals—particularly no-load funds that offer a diversified portfolio of securities for a small fee. But dollar-cost averaging also can be used to buy shares of individual stocks, if you avoid the prohibitively high brokerage fees on small transactions.

As mentioned, deep-discount brokers like Brown & Company and National Discount charge as little as $19 to buy 100 shares of a $10 Nasdaq or listed stock. By contrast, most full-service brokers charge a commission of 4 percent for such a transaction, or $40. Want it cheaper? Trade by personal computer at Scottsdale and the same transaction will cost you just $9! (More about on-line trading in Chapter 14, Investing by Computer.)

Look at dollar-cost averaging as a defensive strategy. It can keep you from getting crushed in some of the wild up-and-down market swings. And it helps you avoid two common errors: putting all your money into the stock market at a time when it may be due for a tumble and selling out at big losses when stocks are deeply depressed.

The strategy won't automatically improve the performance of your portfolio. But don't underestimate the value of the added discipline, organization, and peace of mind it gives you. It's natural to be frightened away from owning stocks when prices head down, even though experience has shown that such dips can be the best time to buy.

And while dollar-cost averaging lets you put your investments on autopilot, you shouldn't leave them there indefinitely. Don't continue to buy *any* stock merely out of habit. Reexamine the company's prospects on a regular basis—at least twice a year—and adjust your investments accordingly.

There's another difference between big and small stocks and that's liquidity. Thousands of shares of IBM change hands each day. But there are many days when not a single share of some small companies traded over-the-counter changes hands. And if you want to unload 1,000 shares of TechNext, it could require a few days for your broker to sell it, and probably not at your asking price.

That's the debit side of buying small cap stocks. The "spread" or gap between bid and ask prices on a small stock can top 3 percent, says Dick Syron, chairman of the American Stock Exchange. "People are very fussy about paying a 3 percent load on a mutual fund," he says, "but don't think twice about it when buying an individual stock."

A broker also may have an arrangement with the dealer under which he receives a payment for funneling orders through that dealer. Clearly, that's an additional cost to the dealer that may be recouped by increasing the bid and ask prices. If that's the case, you end up paying the extra amount.

The only way around this potential abuse is to ask your broker to execute over-the-counter transactions on Nasdaq's Small Order Execution System or to purchase stocks directly from the market maker (listed in the pink sheets directory available from most brokers). You can also buy small company stocks that are listed on the American or New York Stock Exchanges where you are more certain of getting the best price available at the moment the transaction takes place.

Eventually, a decimal system in which prices are quoted closer to the penny will replace archaic fractions on all markets and exchanges. The result will be to narrow the "spread" even further, says Syron, saving investors billions of dollars a year.

In the meantime, savvy investors try to keep trading costs down by avoiding the stocks that are the most expensive to buy, and by trading carefully in small amounts. Another cost-cutting strategy is to trade as little as possible, but holding small stocks can be risky unless you own a whole lot of them. They are more likely than large stocks to plunge all the way to zero.

To compensate for that risk, many analysts point to the historic fact that small stocks do return more than their big cousins. But you have to be certain that trading costs don't eat into that return, says Donald Keim, professor of finance at the Wharton School of the University of Pennsylvania. "At any point in time, it's hard to find the other side of a trade, so you usually need a dealer." And they want to get paid for the risks of holding stocks while they are looking for someone else to buy them.

ADVISERS AND PLANNERS

Make sure the broker you choose is *really* a broker. Actually, there are two other categories of professionals whose job it is to help you with your investments: financial planners and investment advisers.

Most financial planners work in a solo or group practice. Others are on the staffs of brokerage firms, banks, insurance companies, and mutual funds. At least 200,000 people call themselves financial planners, according to the Consumer Federation of America, but only 15 to 20 percent have ever completed a course in the complex field. And without federal regulations or national accreditation requirements, it's not easy to weed out the incompetents.

By contrast, investment advisers often manage billions of dollars for their clients and until recently wouldn't even talk to you unless you had investments of $100,000 or more. But competition has forced some to accept much smaller accounts, some as little as $10,000. Fees on the smallest accounts typically are about 2 percent of the assets being managed, and half of that for larger accounts.

Following are guidelines for selecting the best in each category, but before you do, check with your State Securities Administrator or the National Association of Securities Dealers (800-289-9999) to see if the planner or adviser has a history of securities-related complaints. And insist on visiting the office (even if it's in his home) and getting unbiased references.

Financial planners

Even planners themselves admit that too many who claim the title are incompetent or worse. Anyone can print up some business cards and stationery and call himself a financial planner regardless of education, experience or ethics. But first-rate planners are increasingly available if you know how to identify them. You can find some by asking for recommendations from accountants, lawyers, and business associates, or by attending free seminars that planners often hold to recruit clients.

There are fee-only planners, those who work on commission, and some who do both. For an explanation, write to the International Association for Financial Planning, 2 Concourse Parkway, Atlanta, GA 30328 (800-945-4237). The Institute of Certified Financial Planners (800-282-7526) will provide background information on up to three planners in your area who are licensed as CFPs, and whether they receive commissions from investments they recommend.

You are probably best off with a planner who also has experience as a broker, accountant, lawyer or insurance agent. Such credentials show that he or she has specialized training and can be made to answer to some body of regulators. Cross off any candidates who have not bothered to get any such training.

The Securities and Exchange Commission can tell you whether a financial planner is also registered with them as an investment adviser, and will provide educational materials on how to pick a planner or adviser. Call 800-732-0330, or check out the SEC World Wide Website on the Internet at www.sec.gov.

Before you hire a planner, ask some tough questions. That's the best way to separate the crack advisers from the quacks. Be sure to ask how the planner earns his or her money. The advantage of hiring a fee-only planner is that you know he will not recommend an investment to you just to collect a commission. But fee-only planners are costlier ($75 to $250 an hour) than those who accept commissions.

Investment advisers

A safer bet, if you can find one, is an investment adviser. They usually handle only well-heeled clients by the handful, but if you can find one, it may be the most profitable investment you can make.

Start by asking for recommendations from a lawyer, accountant or broker. If you are one of the fortunate few who have $1 million or more to invest, you also can write to the Investment Council of America, 20 Exchange Street, New York, NY 10005. This is a professional organization of top advisory firms, and it will mail you a free list of its members.

To determine whether or not any adviser is up to managing your money, check his or her record. Michael Price and Richard Driehaus are probably out of your reach. But you might find some up-and-comers who will handle your money for a reasonable fee, and whose high-growth investment philosophy is similar to yours.

If you hire an investment adviser, you generally will have to sign a contract giving him or her discretion over your account. The adviser then will be free to buy and sell stocks without further authorization from you. If that makes you at all uncomfortable, perhaps you should not have an investment adviser.

Once you have contracted with an adviser, be patient. Wait at least six months before you judge the record. If the value of your holdings drops 20 percent from the high of the previous quarter, and the adviser fails to take remedial action, it may well be time to fire him.

Remember, you can also buy shares of stock and even IPOs without the help of a broker or anyone else. A number of small companies are selling stock directly to investors through direct public offerings (see Chapter 5) and you can buy shares of local and foreign companies through DRIPs and ADRs (for Dividend Reinvestment Plans and American Depositary Receipts).

Buying stocks directly can save you a lot of money in brokerage commissions, but you won't get the advice, recommendations, and service that a broker would typically provide. And there's an added risk in foreign stocks because of currency swings that "can move up or down regardless of what's happening to the stock," says Rika Yoshida, associate editor of the *Morningstar International Stocks* newsletter.

John Markese, president of the American Association of Individual Investors, thinks the direct sales programs are great. "People can invest as little as $500 after the account has been established, and can contribute specific amounts rather than figuring out how many shares they can afford," he says. The minimum transaction cost for many brokers would eat up all your profits at the smaller investment level.

Brokers big and small are also getting into the business of new issues, or IPOs. But the number of shares that will be available to new investors is open to question. Whether a customer gets shares "depends on what the customer is worth to us," admits Robert Mazzarella, president of Fidelity Brokerage Services, which has an IPO program with Salomon Brothers.

Fidelity will not screen its two million brokerage customers, however, to find out whether they should invest in IPOs or not. "We are not in a position to determine the suitability of our customers," says Mazzarella. "How it fits into their portfolio is their choice."

No such qualms bother Charles Schwab, who markets IPOs underwritten by Credit Suisse, J.P. Morgan, and Hambrecht & Quist. Because buying new issues can be riskier than buying well-known stocks with long track records, Schwab will allocate IPO shares to its largest and most sophisticated customers. Ordinary customers will have a tough time getting their hands on any of them.

KEEPING RECORDS

If you've been investing for a while, you know that the paperwork can be confusing if you don't keep it sorted out. If not, you soon will. That white stuff accumulates like crazy. A first impulse is to stick it all into a shoebox or the circular file. Don't do it.

For starters, you'll want the information they contain at tax time, not to mention whenever you are faced with deciding whether to hold or sell a particular stock or mutual fund. By developing a simple record-keeping system, you can make it quick and easy to lay your hands on the papers you need when you need them.

Choose a system

One handy way to keep records is to use a three-ring binder with dividers for each stock or brokerage account. This will make trasaction slips, income statements, and other pertinent documents easy to find. When you receive your annual summary, you can toss the monthly statements. But keep confirmation slips in your active file for as long as you own the stock.

It's also a good idea to keep a copy of your brokerage account application on file. "It confirms the name the account was opened in, the account number, and your Social Security number," says David Strege, vice president of Bryton Financial Advisors. That information will prove useful if the brokerage makes a mistake, such as inadvertently transposing decimals.

What to keep

Besides lists of your investments, keep careful records of bank accounts, insurance policies or annuities, and the names of any financial advisers you might have. A personal financial file should list names and amounts of any money-market funds, as well as safe-deposit boxes, tax records, credit-card information, mortgages and wills.

Keeping records is not only a wise precaution, it's also a constant reminder of your financial position. If you know where your money is, you can take advantage of tax changes and map out new investment strategies. But storing stock certificates at home is foolish. "People have actually lost track of stocks when they've held the certificates themselves," says Strege. If you must, make photocopies and send the originals to your brokerage.

Computer programs

Another way to reduce the size of your files is to transcribe much of the information onto a computer software program such as Quicken

Deluxe or Microsoft Money. Some investors love the systems, and others hate them. "It definitely takes more time to enter the data than it does to stick a piece of paper in a binder or folder," says Strege. And you still need to hold on to most statements as backup.

Ultimately, the best record-keeping system is the one that you will use regularly. That means it should be simple, efficient and easily accessible. Otherwise you may not be able to document profits and losses or payments you make that are tax-deductible.

BROKER TROUBLES

The old joke attributed to Woody Allen has it that, "A broker is someone who invests other people's money until it's all gone." If you think your broker is underperforming or getting you to trade too much (thereby earning fat commissions), there are several things you can do.

The North American Association of Securities Administrators can tell you whom to contact in your state for a computer check of complaints against a broker or financial planner. Call NAASA at 202-732-0900. You can also get help or advice from your state attorney general's office or local Better Business Bureau.

To find out about a brokerage firm, write or fax the Securities and Exchange Commission, 450 Fifth St. NW, Washington, DC 20449 (202-628-9001). You must supply the company name to obtain a copy of the firm's filing, which includes a record of any complaints or lawsuits.

If you're thinking of suing, think again. Arbitration through a major stock exchange or the National Association of Securities Dealers may be your only recourse (unless you've crossed out the arbitration clause in your account contract). But that's not likely. "Most brokers won't take your account if you don't agree to the arbitration clause," says Richard Greenfield, a lawyer specializing in suing brokers for unhappy clients.

Other critics say arbitration panels are "stacked" against investors, compensation for losses is low, and punitive damages are almost nonexistent. But you may get lucky. Investors do prevail in about 54 percent of complaints filed against brokers, according to the *Securities Arbitration Commentator,* typically recovering about 40 percent of the losses within a year.

The Securities Investor Protection Corporation insures brokerage customers up to $500,000. If a firm fails, the SIPC asks the court to appoint a trustee who may transfer accounts to another firm. Otherwise, you will be sent stocks registered in your name. Any unsettled claims will then be met by the SIPC from its own funds of $1.5 billion.

"Investors can't complain about a broker's bad advice unless it was reckless or irresponsible," says the Amex's Syron. Pay attention to your monthly statement and confirmation slips when trades are executed. Some "red flags" to look for:

❏ Profits on your trades are consistently below the commissions you've paid. That could signal excessive trading in your account—called churning—just to create commissions for the broker.

❏ Your statement shows holdings that don't match your stated objectives or trades that you haven't okayed (unless you have a discretionary account). "If you talk to your broker about growth stocks and new issues and he comes back with ideas about mutual funds and municipal bonds, you probably have the wrong broker," says Syron.

INVESTOR INFORMATION

There's no shortage of information on how to choose a broker, much of it from brokerage firms or stock exchanges. Your best bet: *Invest Wisely: Advice from Your Securities Regulators,* available from the Securities and Exchange Commission (800-734-0330). It has advice on how to interview brokers and protect yourself against fraud.

For candid advice on how to work with your broker once you've found him, read the chapter "You and Your Broker" in Andrew Lanyi's *Confessions of a Stockbroker.* It's filled with funny and informative anecdotes told from an insider's vantage point—and can help make you rich, too.

Investing by Computer

Who can forget Netscape's awesome August 1995 initial public offering, which triggered the explosive Internet investing mania? The on-line pioneer's offering price had doubled to $14 a share leading up to its IPO and then, in the first frantic days of trading, shot up another 168 percent to nearly $38, before closing at $29.

No one seemed to mind that this start-up company was losing money. Netscape's first-day market value topped $2 billion, an unsustainable 100 times annual sales. By comparison, Standard & Poor's 400 index of large industrial companies traded at a mere 1.4 times sales. Of course, Netscape along with several other high-flyers flamed out, and are now trading below their initial IPO price. But even so, a new breed of investors became smitten with on-line investing.

And the sweep of technology will very soon affect the way we all invest—especially the sorts of people who use discount brokers. At Charles Schwab, on-line accounts have more than doubled to 750,000 in a single year, or 25 percent of all accounts. "A serious consumer of financial services would be crazy not to have a computer," says Paul Saffo, director of the Institute for the Future.

You'll still be able to monitor and change investments without the Internet, but it will take an increasingly longer route. Advances in technology are already making the Internet cheaper, faster, and easier to use. That makes the idea of on-line investing—even if it's just an occasional price quote—eminently sensible, says Saffo.

The big lure is pricing. Trade 500 shares of a $20 stock at Schwab through a broker and you'll pay a commission of $110. Do it on-line and you'll pay only $30. And it gets even cheaper. The same transaction will cost just $15 at E-Trade, $12 at Waterhouse Securities, and a mere $9 at Scottsdale.

But there's much more to computer investing than just low prices. Websites now offer you a wealth of tools, databases, and research materials "traditionally reserved only for brokers and investment advisers," notes Michael Gazala, senior analyst with Forrester Research in Cambridge, Massachusetts. You want free, real-time stock quotes? Muriel Siebert's got them. If you want to screen hundreds or thousands of stocks check out Aufhauser. And if you're into technical analysis, you can get "candlestick" charts at E-Trade.

Gazala expects more than 11 million additional accounts to go online in the next five years, for an annual growth rate of 40 percent. And that's only a small fraction of the estimated 80 million existing accounts nationwide. "As the Internet becomes easier to use the numbers could increase even more," he says.

Microsoft Money '98 and Intuit's Quicken Deluxe '98 on-line personal finance software allow users to retrieve price quotes, news, and analysis on their investments and update portfolios without even being aware that they are logging on and off of the Internet.

BIDS AND BYTES

Stephen Killeen, senior vice president of Fidelity Brokerage Services, thinks that the increasing use of the computer for investing is part of a broader, decade-long trend of individuals taking charge of their own investments—spurred by the rise of no-load mutual funds and self-managed retirement accounts. "The Internet has simply added more octane," he says.

In several ways, the Internet is an ideal technology for investment tasks such as picking small growth stocks, and has long been the backbone of Nasdaq and over-the-counter markets where most of them are traded. Some of the advantages:

- ❏ You can get stock quotes that are ahead of those on the "crawler" ticker at the bottom of your monitor screen, and daily net asset values (NAV) of stock funds before they are printed in the next day's newspaper.

- ❏ Brokerages offer lower commissions on-line because it's less costly for them to accept trades that way. (But they realize that a vast majority still want to talk with a broker before placing an order.)

❏ Normal office hours do not apply, or even time zones across the country or around the world. That can be crucial to investors in an era when nearly everyone leads fast-paced, hectic lives.

❏ You can find loads of free information that was once available only to well-heeled investors, analysts or brokers, and large corporations. And get on-line statements downloaded easily (with no typing!)

So while you don't have to use a computer or the Internet to make your trades, if you prefer to deal with the telephone or a full-service broker, you should know there are compelling reasons why the Internet makes good sense for self-directed investors.

The convenience of cyber-investing appeals to first-time investors like Bob Van Degna of East Greenwich, Rhode Island. "It's a timing issue. You can learn what you want to learn when you want to learn it. You don't have to make a telephone call in the morning to find out how your stocks did."

Van Degna relies on computers to stay up-to-date on his personal investments as well as his business ventures. "The technology lets me look up information about new companies, earnings reports, news releases, SEC filings, and track how my investments are doing," he says. "The newspapers are pretty limited to current prices, highs and lows. There's no way to check performance over 90 days or more."

The need to meet the demands of users like Van Degna is driving the Internet access companies to expand the company's "backbone"—the vast collection of information about companies, news releases, SEC reports, and actions against them by state or federal courts.

But enough about the future. Let's look at what you can do *now* with a home computer, a modem, and a decent piece of software. For starters, you can save on investments, uncover important tax deductions, find a great mortgage deal, and pay less for your insurance.

SOFTWARE PROGRAMS

Though computers can't do everything, one chore they can do very well is help you manage your money and become a more successful investor. But it's not enough just to buy a computer and modem, you also have to buy software programs to fit your own situation.

The simplest programs help you balance your checkbook and keep track of personal finances. You can get such software for as little as $30.

Other people are using computers increasingly to help keep track of their investments and analyze trends in the stock market. Within seconds, some of these programs will let you size up a buying opportunity or a must-sell situation.

But none of the programs does it all and no combination of them can replace sensible decision-making. Use them in conjunction with the basic investment principles you've learned from reading this book and other resources.

Following is an overview of some available software programs, starting with the simplest. Before purchasing any of them, talk with knowledgeable friends who use financial software, check your public library (many have programs you can practice with), and then obtain promotional materials that describe any special features.

QUICKEN DELUXE 98.   This best-seller is just about the easiest to learn and use. It's also compatible with Windows or Macintosh, and ready for the year 2000! In addition to managing your investments, it sorts financial information into tax categories for record-keeping, and can help you find the best mortgage or insurance deals around. Small businesses can add on a payroll program with extras like customized invoicing if wanted.

MICROSOFT MONEY 98.   Gives you on-line access to financial experts so you can make informed decisions, trade stocks and mutual funds, get instant market news, and track your stock portfolio. Monthly reports give you an overview of your activities and transactions so you can avoid common mistakes.

ANDREW TOBIAS'S MANAGING YOUR MONEY.   One of the most comprehensive and popular financial planning packages available. In addition to doing portfolio management, it tracks stocks, has an address keeper, a calendar, a to-do list, a simple word processor, and a tax planner that prints out IRS-approved forms on any printer (added cost).

VALUE LINE INVESTMENT SURVEY.   This Windows-compatible program offers a stock-picking strategy with years of proven success, as well as authoritative reports and projections from Value Line analysts on 1,700 or 5,000 stocks. Other features include screening, sorting, and charting functions for fast-growing companies. Current subscribers to Value Line can obtain special pricing (800-634-3583).

MORNINGSTAR STOCKTOOLS.   This time-saving program helps you screen, rank, and compare information on 8,000 stocks quickly and profitably. Unique Field Builder lets you create custom data you think essential for uncovering growth companies. And *Stock Ideas* electronic newsletter can lead you to new opportunities you might want to add to your portfolio. Free demo disk available (800-735-0700).

Keep in mind that programs that help you choose stocks to buy or suggest when you should sell must stay current, so they tend to rely on the Internet or an investment service such as Dial/Data for constantly updated information. These stock monitoring services are an additional cost, so you may be paying a monthly service fee.

MAJOR DATABASES

With a personal computer and a modem, you can tap into the telephone lines and an amazing amount of up-to-date financial information including stock prices, mutual fund values, earnings estimates, analysts' opinions, historical data, research reports, and trading volume.

Or you can place stock orders through on-line discount brokers. Charles Schwab, for example, uses real-time quotes for every trade but doesn't do a lot of hand-holding. You get only one free call to customer service per month. And while it costs brokers $1,640 a month to rent one of those Bloomberg machines, you can get a reasonable facsimile a lot cheaper.

There are hundreds of investment-related Websites and most of them are free. Even those that charge a subscription fee, like Microsoft Investor (www.investor.msn.com) and James Cramer's irreverent but popular TheStreet (www.thestreet.com), provide some valuable information gratis.

Pick your "virtual" Bloomberg machine from among these Websites, or check those listed by *U.S. News & World Report* at www.usnews.com.:

YAHOO!FINANCE (WWW.QUOTE.YAHOO.COM).   Lacks state-of-the-art graphics, but delivers quick stock updates that are easy to read and use. Quotes pop up quickly and the formats can be customized to include performance data. Other features include Zacks Investment Research ratings of stocks by industry, and Reuters news coverage of world markets.

Also contains abundant information on mutual funds, including top portfolio holdings. Free.

BigCharts (www.bigcharts.com). Sophisticated site lets a technically inclined investor use charting tools to compare the performance of one stock or several. Daily list of "momentum" stocks traded on the Amex and Nasdaq can tip you off to stocks rising sharply in price on large increases in trading volume. Free.

Wall Street Journal Interactive (www.wsj.com). This might be the single best site on the Internet. It offers the daily *Wall Street Journal* including Asian and European editions, the *Barron's* weekly, and the monthly *SmartMoney*. Briefing books of 10,000 publicly traded companies and real-time data on individual stocks are added features. Cost: $49 annual fee ($29 if you subscribe to any of the periodicals mentioned).

IPO Intelligence (www.ipo-fund.com). Offered by Renaissance Capital, this service tracks and analyzes initial public offerings including market comments, deals worth watching, and a guide to investing in IPOs. Browsers can search for IPOs by company name, industry, underwriter or region. Free (reports cost $50).

The only danger of Net-based stock tickers is that you can't keep your eyes off them. But if you're prepared for financial mood swings, Yahoo's search engine can select the stocks you want to monitor and provide market recaps (great for anyone who holds stock options).

On-line Services

Surfing the Web is easy, but putting it to work is anything but. The sheer volume of material can distract anyone, so it's tough to know where to begin. Let the four sites above be your guide, then you can check out any others that offer services you may want. Among them:

❏ Hoover's Online (www.hoovers.com). Snapshot information on a company (free; charges for detailed reports). Web visitors may also type in criteria such as location, size or industry to see a list of all competitors.

❏ Securities and Exchange Commission (www.sec.gov). You can get the full text of reports that public companies are required to file, including detailed financial statements and any proxy materials.

❏ White House Briefing Room (www.whitehouse.gov). This site draws together data from a variety of government departments, including an abundance of financial and economic data as well as industry trends.

❏ Federal Reserve Bank (www.stls.frb.gov). Websites of Federal Reserve Banks like this one in St. Louis include a useful database of exchange rates, gross domestic product figures, and other economic statistics.

❏ *New York Times* (www.nytimes.com). If you don't have the *Wall Street Journal*, this Website offers financial news updated throughout the day—and you don't have to wait for a "news wheel" to find the top stories.

Mutual Funds

There are also Websites devoted to mutual funds—and frankly some of them are a little weird. Those in the following list share two important characteristics: They're packed with useful information, and they're free! You don't even have to register. Use them to keep an eye on funds you own or to search for new ones.

❏ Quicken (www.quicken.com). Favorite of those who love to play with numbers, but can't afford a fund database. You can screen funds, including small caps, based on criteria including fees and performance.

❏ Morningstar (www.morningstar.net). Respected mutual fund tracker's Website is updated daily, offers analyst commentary, portfolio makeovers, and helpful fund facts from a massive database. No in-depth analysis or comparisons (that goes to paying subscribers).

❏ FundAlarm (www.fundalarm.com). This cranky Website tells investors when to *sell* their funds (a heretical notion in mutual fund circles). Even if you're happy, site can help you identify funds to avoid.

ON-LINE TRADING

Thanks to the computerization of our world, you can now tap into a number of on-line brokerage services that plug you into the floors of the major stock exchanges or the Nasdaq and over-the-counter markets. Fees start as low as $9 per trade, but the sites are best left to those who don't need a lot of handholding.

They are not perfect, and as mentioned there are reports of hidden fees, as well as higher prices than advertised. But the firms that offer on-line trading say it keeps their labor costs down and eliminates a lot of mistakes. The only hitch is that you'll need an Internet account like CompuServe, Prodigy, America Online, or Dow Jones, which will cost $10 to $30 a month.

To place a trade on-line, you must have an account with a brokerage company plus a user name and password or personal identification number. Once inside, you can get immediate real-time quotes, call up your own transaction history, check account balances, switch mutual fund shares, and place orders to buy and sell stocks at any time. Users can also browse through news and background information, and take advantage of fund evaluation and stock selection tools.

The leading brokers offering reasonably priced on-line trading, are shown in Appendix C. Access is by browsers like Netscape Navigator, or Microsoft's Internet Explorer, which are pretty good at protecting security breaches.

But you don't have to rely on brokers or financial advisers for your information about stocks or funds. Now that personal computers are as common as microwave ovens, you can surf the Internet for stock tips, fund choices, economic data, and much more. There are some caveats, however.

❑ *Many of the more popular sites charge a fee.* And, those that offer free information, usually reserve the best stuff for subscribers. Some Websites start out free to generate interest, then switch to a subscription-only format. If that's the case, ask the provider if they offer a free trial before making a commitment.

❑ *Don't fall in love with a particular Website.* It may not be there when you turn your computer on tomorrow. Websites come and go with breathtaking frequency, and many links are exit ramps to dead-end streets.

❑ *Watch out for bad or dated information.* In addition to lots of really useful advice and recommendations, the Internet also contains in-fomercials from stock promoters, con artists, and other types looking to sell bogus products. They can disappear into cyberspace before you can register a complaint.

❏ *Protect your assets.* If you like chat rooms, stick to those monitored by someone. *Morningstar,* for example, lets analysts join in its chat room and screens comments from participants. There are also Websites designed to expose scams (mentioned in Chapter 15, Penny stocks and Other Scams).

There's also no shortage of Websites offered by mutual fund companies if you'd rather let them do the stock picking. All of them are free, but offer mostly cookie-cutter approaches to investing, says Ken Fisher, money manager and columnist for *Forbes* magazine. Here's what three offer:

CHARLES SCHWAB (WWW.SCHWAB.COM). Extensive worksheets for rebalancing your portfolio, test for risk tolerance, and types of stock suggestions, such as small caps. Free booklets, but painfully slow if you don't have a fast Internet connection.

FIDELITY INVESTMENTS (WWW.FIDELITY.COM). Asset allocation program is easy to understand, but you have to download it (takes 15 minutes). Little help on picking stocks, except for retirement.

VANGUARD GROUP (WWW.VANGUARD.COM). Fast, simple program that bases recommendations on age, risk tolerance and financial situation. Helps estimate how much you should be saving and how to allocate investments.

These high-tech delivery services won't necessarily make you a better investor. But they will make you better informed, if you use them judiciously. Give each Website a test run with a few securities from your portfolio before deciding whether to sign on for an extended period.

Yahoo!Finance is my favorite, but you may like the opinions of James Cramer, who says he started tracking stocks as a second-grader. He now manages about $352 million for wealthy clients and has posted an annual return of 22 percent versus 15 percent for Standard & Poor's 500 (and 45 percent in the most recent year).

Cramer is obsessive about the market and wants you to be the same way. "It's not brain surgery," he says. "People ought to be better investors. That's the only way most of them will ever be rich." A stock market junkie, Cramer says that between trades he keeps an ear glued to CNBC's *Squawk Box* Wall Street show on a nearby screen.

"People think if you write about stocks and you trade stocks you are inherently corrupt," he says. "But look at the writers who have never bought a share of stock and were urging caution during the sell-off in October 1987." Cramer, 43, concedes that trading is a young person's game, but thinks the young-at-heart may enjoy that adrenaline rush as well.

The only caveat: the Internet is also a medium for possible misinformation and subterfuge, particularly in chat rooms. One "stock service" issued report after report about "unheard of" stocks destined to double or triple in value. More often than not, such reports are a way for insiders to dump their stocks at above-market prices (if there is a market!) So when using Websites, always be alert to the possibility of being seriously, or even disastrously misinformed.

The two internet sites that post warnings and help the SEC expose cyberscams or investment frauds are the National Fraud Information Center (www.proud.org) and the National Association of Securities Dealers (www.nasdr.com).

FUNDAMENTAL OR TECHNICAL ANALYSIS?

Not even glitches can stop the Internet stampede, and it's easy to understand why. There's no broker or financial planner, and not even a phone call to a discount broker. By 2002, one in five will be investing on-line, or 14 million accounts, says Forrester Research.

"This is a sea change in personal investing," notes John Markese, president of the American Association of Individual Investors, which recently published a list of 254 Websites for personal investors. "You still don't have as much information as the big investors, but the gap is closing," he says. And this has made cyber-investors bold enough to feel they can do the same kind of financial analysis as a professional trader. The only question is whether to look at fundamental or technical factors.

Examining the financial balance sheets of individual companies to determine their strengths and weaknesses is the hallmark of *fundamental* stock analysis because it looks to numbers for clues to a company's prospects for growth. But another school of thought, called *technical* analysis, looks at patterns created by the movements of the market itself for indications of what's going to happen next.

Decide what you want, and find a broker or Website that delivers it. Once you have a list of priorities, shop around for the perfect match.

Some on-line sites include access to IPOs and other public offerings, as well as extensive fundamental or technical research.

Brokerage firms have technicians on their staffs of analysts and their reports are available on request. The better-known technical analysts publish their own newsletters, and the successes of a few, such as Martin Zweig's *Performance Ratings Report* and Stan Weinstein's *Professional Tape Reader,* have earned them celebrity status. (See Appendix B for a list of investment newsletters and advisory services.)

Technical analysts usually try to make money on short-term moves in the market rather than on the long-term potential of a particular stock. Many use the Dow theory, named after one of the founders of Dow Jones. It holds that a significant market move up or down is underway when a change in the direction of the Dow industrial average is "confirmed" by the Dow transportation index moving in the same direction. Disciples claim that the theory will confirm a change in market direction in time for attentive investors to take advantage of the trend.

The rise of on-line trading is like manna from heaven for technical investors, who trade a lot and want to lower costs. And the trend could have serious consequences for Wall Street, says Michael Gazala, senior analyst at Forrester, who follows technology and investing trends. "Traditional brokerage firms will discover they have no choice but to look to the Internet to generate new business among younger investors who enjoy surfing the Web."

COMPUTER INVESTING

Access at any time gives investors in small stocks increased opportunities to use software and Websites to slice, dice and graph a portfolio. And if you don't have a personal computer (fewer than 40 percent of households do), the Internet may soon be as close as your cable television.

Microsoft, the world's largest software company, spent $425 million in 1997 to acquire WebTV Networks, and $1 billion for a stake in Comcast Corp., a cable television company. The bet is that television screens will be increasingly used for Internet access in the future. "Ease of use still has a way to go," says Paul Saffo. But a television set instead of a home computer seems a less daunting means of tackling the Internet.

Whether you've got just the basic equipment or don't even own a computer (the library does), it's relatively easy to get started investing by computer. And you can get all the help you'll need in simple-to-understand language from many of the free Websites mentioned.

For example, my favorite search engine, Alta Vista, was asked to search for "Investing and Personal Finance." A minute or two turned up forty references from the American Stock Exchange to the *Wall Street Journal Lifetime Guide to Money* and Wired News Stocks (www.wired.com).

You get the idea. The nicest thing about the Internet is that you don't have to deal with pushy salespeople, and the information is virtually limitless. My search produced scores of resources containing nearly a million words! Don't be alarmed. Think what you can do if you're less vague and more specific—about stocks or anything else.

WHERE TO START.   Begin with any one of the Websites that were mentioned earlier in this chapter, or click on Digital Think (www.digital-think.com), a guide to using the Web for those who have a basic understanding of investment terms and principles.

In order to place a trade, you must have an account with an on-line brokerage plus a user name and password or personal identification number. (Some firms allow investors to open accounts on the spot, provided they send a check to settle trades within three days).

FINANCIAL PLANNING.   If you have the name of an individual company or mutual fund, you can place orders to buy, sell or exchange shares at anytime. Otherwise you can browse through targeted news and background information, and get investment ideas from electronic newsletters like *Yahoo!Finance* and *Morningstar StockTools.*

If you're tracking a large number of investments, go for the Quote Track service available from America Online (AOL). It costs extra ($3 an hour), but you get a lot more options than the basic service. Other pluses include an investment bulletin board and company or mutual fund profiles.

PORTFOLIO MONITORING.   Updates are just a click away on a number of Websites which let you eliminate unnecessary risks and uncover useful diversification strategies. They can also help you control sector exposure and ensure that new stocks will fit with current holdings.

In this way, you can custom-tailor a portfolio to your needs, limit volatility while you build wealth, and see how well you've balanced your portfolio against market shifts. But look on the computer as an additional way to improve your financial bottom line, not as a substitute for thinking.

SELECTING YOUR COMPUTER

Because computers are great organizers and calculators, they can save you money and time not only on your portfolio of investments, but with financial planning and preparing tax returns. And you can deduct at least part of the cost of the computer and software—as long as you use both for those purposes (and not to play games!).

What's more, computers have gotten much more affordable. You don't need to spend much more than $1,500 for a machine that can handle most of the programs mentioned in this chapter (see Figure 14.1). There's no point in spending more unless you work in the industry or your office is paying.

Salespeople will likely steer you toward more expensive computers with extra power, but most of the slowness in starting programs or getting stuff off the Internet results from pokey modems, operating systems, and telephone lines—things a faster microprocessor may not do much to fix.

For some, managing their investments is not enough of a reason to invest $1,500 plus $30 a month. Many investors don't trade often enough to be lured by the discount brokers with online services. Others dislike the idea of putting personal or financial information where nefarious types might try to grab at it. But credit cards, telephones, even the mail are in many ways more susceptible to theft or fraud.

"People do have to be skeptical about the on-line tips that show up in chat rooms or on computer bulletin boards," cautions John Stark, spe-

---

FIGURE 14.1. WHAT YOU NEED TO GET STARTED

You don't need a high-powered personal computer to use on-line services effectively. These are the *minimum* system requirements:

Hardware	486 microprocessor, with 16 megabytes of RAM (random access memory). Color monitor. 14.4 baud modem.
Software	Windows 3.1
Web browser	Netscape Navigator or Microsoft Internet Explorer

cial counsel for Internet projects at the Securities and Exchange Commission. "There's a lot of junk out there and you need to cut through it."

Even so, the SEC has filed fewer than 15 cases of on-line investment fraud in the past two years, usually involving "touting" or the spreading of false information in order to get a stock price to move. And not a single example of someone hacking into a brokerage account has been reported.

Still, the wealth of financial information the Web provides, the power it offers investors, and the promise of easier and faster systems may soon induce even the most reluctant investors to take their first steps into the future of investing by computer. The most aggressive may never come back to the old way.

INVESTOR INFORMATION

I guess this is not the place to mention something as old-fashioned as a book, but there are a number of them out there on choosing and using personal computers for managing your portfolio.

Cyber Investing: Cracking Wall Street with Your Personal Computer by David L. Brown shows how to turn your PC into an investment tool using data services, newsletters, reports and search tools. *Stock Traders' Almanac* called it the "best investment book of 1997."

The Savvy Investor's Internet Resource by Bryan Pfaffenberger and Claire Mencke takes you through every type of investing and shows you how the Websites can help. For pro or novice, either book may be the best site of all.

Penny Stocks
and Other Scams

The surging stock market has spawned widespread investment fraud across the country. Investors lost $12 billion in 1997 alone, according to the North American Securities Administrators Association. And NASAA regulators expect the ranks of the ripped-off to grow—the legacy of economic good times and current low interest rates and inflation. Overconfident investors are susceptible to pitches for all sorts of investments, legitimate and otherwise.

There are plenty of widows among the victims, but you'll also find congressmen, news anchors, baseball players and retired generals. "Anyone's vulnerable," says Denise Crawford, NASAA president. "And we're not talking about $200 for coins, but $20,000 or $50,0000—whatever swindlers can soak you for."

Even though the majority of brokers and financial planners are honest, investors are well-advised to stay on guard against those who might misrepresent the facts, sell bogus financial products, or simply take the money and run. Be on the lookout for phony investment and Ponzi schemes operating over the Internet as well as the telephone.

Crawford says people should be alert for telltale signs of fraud when they are called by telemarketers, particularly those who urge them to make quick decisions. "That's a sure sign that a person is up to no good." And she urges victims or potential victims to assist regulatory agencies in curtailing confidence crimes. "People sometimes don't think an encounter is a crime," she says. "Or they're so embarrassed that they won't come forward."

Exploiting our hopes of getting rich quick, telemarketers often sell questionable or illegal securities, stock in gold mines or oil wells, or phony IPOs in unseen "new" inventions or high-technology ventures such as broadcast licenses, cellular telephone projects and wireless cable television.

Clearly, con artists are hitting new lows while the Dow Jones is hitting new highs. State securities regulators estimate that fraud involving the sale of marginal companies' low-priced stocks to novice investors amounted to $6 billion, and complaints about stock swindles and unsolicited telephone calls from brokers is up 37 percent according to the Securities and Exchange Commission.

The victims are usually told that the company in question is the next Microsoft or Starbucks, but the shares they buy too often turn out to be worthless. The scope of the illegal activity also appears to be soaring along with the numbers of people making financial gains. In 1997, the broad stock market had gains of almost 30 percent—despite turmoil in Asia and other world markets. Historically, stocks have risen about 10 percent a year.

The shares of some small or new companies have soared even higher, particularly IPOs or new issues for technology companies, where returns of 350 percent in just a few months are not unheard of. Publicity about such "hot stocks" has only fueled interest in such investments. "There's so much money in the market, and so much belief that everything will go up, that people are much more predisposed to throw dollars at get-rich-quick schemes," says William McLucas, SEC enforcement director, who has a task force to consider ways to root out fraud in the small-stock marketplace.

DIALING FOR DOLLARS

Telephone investment fraud has touched too many households. In one recent rip-off, more than 4,000 people paid $5,000 to $8,000 for low-grade rubies and emeralds of little value. The telemarketer delivered them sealed in plastic cases and promised to buy them back at a markup—but only if the seal had not been broken. Ultimately, the seller disappeared.

Make it a rule never to make a purchase or an investment based solely on a cold call. Always request more information in writing. And be sure to check out any company before sending any money, especially by overnight service. Some other investment scams du jour:

❑ A father-and-son accounting team in Illinois who claimed to be investment advisers ripped-off a dozen investors for $1.7 million. The money was supposed to go to stocks and other investments, but went instead to the family accounts. Father and son did eventually go to jail.

❑ A company claiming to have a device that could predict a person's blood sugar by passing infrared light through a finger was charged with fraud by the SEC. But not before it had raised $1.9 million from private investors and planned an $18 million public offering.

If you think you're too smart for the telephone pitchmen, think again. Even experienced Wall Street professionals, along with lawyers, accountants and bankers have fallen for the siren call. One reason is that the best of the scam artists tie their pitches to current events, thereby improving their credibility and creating a sense of urgency.

According to NASAA's Crawford, cold callers are enticing investors to replace CDs with higher-yielding stocks at much greater risk, even when there are costly penalties for early withdrawal of certificates. The majority of victims are people on fixed incomes who can hardly afford the losses.

OVERSEAS SCAMS.   Until recently, investors have been in love with foreign stocks—part of the peace dividend and emerging world markets. "People have been investing overseas because of perceived opportunities," says Rika Yoshida of *Morningstar International Stocks.*

"That's blinded them to the risks," he says, including volatility, corruption and currency fluctuations, a fact that's not lost on con artists, who are astute trend watchers. Phone and mail fraud has gone global, from fake platinum mines in South Africa to gemstones in Brazil.

In one example, investors took the advice of a "representative" of the Dai-Ichi Kangyo Bank in Tokyo. The bank is real, but the agent wasn't. He promised 14-percent interest in passbook savings accounts that didn't exist.

BLIND POOLS.   A sort of investment partnership in shell companies with no assets or stated business purposes, "blind pools" are frequently vehicles for stock manipulation. After selling stock to gullible partners, a blind pool often merges with a private firm to bypass regulatory review.

They may play off something you've seen in the news. Real auctions of artworks (Van Gogh, Picasso) spawned pools selling bogus prints "signed" by well-known artists. And stories about the appreciation of rare coins have fueled scams involving misgraded or inferior items, including the Clinton inaugural coin.

A temporary fuel shortage caused by Mideast tensions may lead to a flurry of risky oil and gas leases and swindles involving precious metals or foreign currencies. Tens of thousands of investors lost $250 million in "dirt pile" gold mines, according to the Council of Better Business Bureaus. Their advice: If someone calls with a deal that sounds phony, hang up.

BOILER-ROOM SCAMS.   Telemarketers often work from gypsy offices or "boiler rooms" that also lure clients by advertising on cable television shows or "infomercials" that dispense news and financial advice. Typically, swindlers push one scam for a short time, close down and reopen somewhere else. If you're retired, they'll tout safety and security. Otherwise, they'll promise big gains with little risk.

They look for prestige by naming a well-known person or firm, or by claiming to have "inside information" about stocks they're offering. They purchase their lists of people to call from financial magazines, newsletters or advisory services, and will inform the person called that he or she has been specially selected to participate in an "unusual" investment opportunity with virtually no risk. Large profits are guaranteed, but the investor must move quickly to get in on the deal.

If the person called isn't hooked by a "can't miss" investment opportunity, the con artist will work on family financial concerns. When cajoling doesn't work, telemarketers resort to shame, anger or blatant threats. Or the initial caller may bring in a more-experienced high-pressure "closer" to steamroll the customer into a hasty decision. Once hooked, the customer is asked for the money right away. And if he can't get a credit card number, the caller will offer to send a courier to pick up the payment. "They know once you start thinking things over, you just might figure out it's a scam," says NASAA's Crawford.

You can find legitimate investments, as well as honest coin dealers, but it's not likely you'll do so through high-pressure telemarketers. "Be wary of strangers," warns Crawford. "If you're interested, have them send you information in the mail.

MAIL FRAUD

Con artists often balk at using the postal service because of the stiff penalties for mail fraud, and the fact that United States postal authorities have one of the best records for convictions. "Inspectors have struck such terror that swindlers are using private carriers like Federal Express," says John Barker of the National Consumers League.

Even so, mail scams take in nearly $2 billion annually. Several that have been brought to the attention of postal officials include unscrupulous newsletter writers touting investments in phony coal mines, offshore banks, medical insurance, and even vineyards. Life insurance companies sell annuities without the assets to secure them. And other scams offer bogus municipal bonds, living trusts, and timeshares.

Law enforcement officials are becoming increasingly concerned that con artists and swindlers are turning to what they see as easy pickings in the stock market. But regulators across the country have banded together to go after people they accuse of small-stock scams. Their target: small stock manipulators who hire people to drive up the price of the stock.

A public relations firm may receive free shares in exchange for issuing glowing releases about the company's prospects. An analyst may recommend the stock in a newsletter, on the television or over the Internet, also in return for free stock which he could sell when the price started to rise. Investors buy these phony investments from salespeople who describe themselves as senior executives of legitimate-sounding firms with a Wall Street address.

In fact, those addresses turn out to be dingy offices, one-bedroom apartments or even mail drops. And the "executives" are young men whose only training is in the hard sell and whose previous jobs may have been at tire stores or pizza parlors. They receive huge commissions which may take the form of stock, cash or even drugs.

The big problem for regulators is those operations that appear on the surface to be legitimate. There are brokerage firms that consider multimillion dollar fines to be part of doing business. Regulators urge prospective investors to check out people who try and sell them investments by calling state officials or the North American Association of Securities Administrators, which keeps records of complaints about brokers and disciplinary actions against firms.

Investors are also told to ignore brokers' pleas, threats or claims of once-in-a-lifetime opportunities for those who send money right away. Regulators suggest that investors insist on receiving a prospectus or registration statement that describes the company, and get a second opinion from a financial professional or trusted adviser.

PENNY STOCKS

The success of today's boiler rooms can be explained in part by the clever use of new marketing techniques, cheap long-distance rates, and automatic phone dialers. In addition, respected brokerage firms, mutual funds, and insurance companies have unintentionally helped the con artists by marketing new and unusual financial products by telephone and through the mail in recent years.

Another problem that regulators call "pump and dump" is when stock promoters gain control of a marginal or struggling brokerage firm and turn to boiler-room tactics to market penny stocks or initial public offerings. In 1997, Stratton Oakmont agreed to pay about $2 million to investors after it was accused of using high-pressure sales tactics, manipulating stock prices, and making unauthorized trades in customer accounts, according to the Securities and Exchange Commission.

Despite the name, an issue needn't cost mere pennies to qualify as a penny stock. Both NASAA and the Securities and Exchange Commission define penny stocks as those selling for less than $5 a share. Of course, many substantial and legitimate stocks sell for low prices. But too many of these micro-caps are fraught with risk.

Some investors figure that it's bound to be easier to score big with a minipriced issue than a high-priced one. It stands to reason that even in a powerful bull market it will take years for IBM, at $115 a share, to double or triple in price. But a $5 stock? Or better yet, a $1.50 stock? They have been known to double in less than a week. Any list of top percentage gainers—for a day, month or year—is bound to be dominated by stocks selling at or near single digits. By the same token, the biggest percentage *losers* also tend to be low-priced stocks.

Another attraction is that cheap issues allow investors to buy 100 shares with small outlays. Buying such "round lots" can be psychologically soothing and, in many cases, can give you a break on commissions. But it's no indication of value (as you may recall from Chapter 3). All else being equal, a $1 stock of a company that earns 10 cents a share is no better than a $10 stock that earns $1 a share.

"In penny stocks, very rarely is there a pot of money at the end of the rainbow," says the SEC's McLucas. And it's not just con artists who are picking investors' pockets. Small companies have been involved in misrepresentations and making false profit claims to investors.

Be extra vigilant before investing in a low-priced stock that's not listed on an exchange or on the computerized Nasdaq market. Prices for thousands of these over-the-counter issues can be found only on the "pink sheets"—printed lists that are updated just once daily and are generally available only to brokers. Pink-sheet stocks are especially ripe for abuse because investors cannot get price quotes easily and because the companies don't have to issue regular financial reports, as do Nasdaq and exchange-listed companies.

To counter this, the Securities and Exchange Commission has a "cold call" rule designed to protect investors from high-pressure tactics involving pink-sheet stocks. Before a broker unfamiliar to you can sell you a penny stock, you must sign a suitability agreement, plus a purchase agreement, the first three times you buy shares covered by the rule. For a copy, write to the SEC, 450 Fifth St. NW, Washington, DC 20549 (202-272-7560).

In addition, the National Association of Securities Dealers is considering removing some 3,400 stocks from its OTC Bulletin Board though they could still be listed on the pink sheets. Barry Goldsmith, NASD executive vice president, says the move is aimed at "unscrupulous operators who perpetuate the notion that the over-the counter market is the same as Nasdaq. The two are separate and distinct."

Regulators estimate that investors are being defrauded of some $6 billion annually through penny stock scams, and are looking to close more loopholes in the rules governing pinksheet stocks. Before you write a big check, look for these red flags:

❏ *The stock has a large spread.* Some high-risk stocks have a spread of 30 percent or more, meaning if you had to sell it, you would lose nearly a third of the price you paid. A big spread can also indicate that people are trying to manipulate the stock price to their gain.

❏ *Big change in trading volume.* Ask your broker for a price-volume chart on the stock in question. If it suddenly shows an increase in trading, watch out. Scam artists may be buying shares to drive up the price.

❏ *Reverse stock splits.* Solid companies often split their stock, making more shares available at a lower price. Small, risky companies sometimes do the opposite to reduce the number of shares and inflate the price.

❏ *Broker insists you buy right away.* If you can't get a prospectus or financial report, and the broker balks at your questions, forget about the stock. "That's an immediate red flag," says NASD's Goldsmith.

ROGUE BROKERS

Fraud is not limited to boiler rooms or brochures touting gemstones, rare coins or penny stocks. Hundreds of millions of dollars disappear from broker-managed customer accounts each year due to negligence or theft, says William Donoghue, Seattle investment adviser and author of *The Donoghue Strategies*. His advice:

Make sure you get a monthly statement, then read it carefully. Don't trade options or futures (contracts on everything from soybeans to Japanese yen), or buy stocks on margin unless you completely understand these strategies. "Even good brokers give bad advice," says Donoghue. Find someone who can give you advice that truly meets your investment needs. And get in writing all claims, promises and guarantees made by your adviser. If you bet right, you can make a bundle. Buy schlock stocks and you can quickly lose a fortune.

Even professional investors get taken by con artists or "rogue brokers" when there's a thriving bull market. "There's lots of money to be made, and that is precisely when you get the crooks," says historian Robert Sobel. His theory: The brightest, most creative criminal minds in finance flock to Wall Street when business is booming—as it has been for seven years.

They are also getting harder to police. At any given time, more than 5,000 investment messages are posted on Prodigy, one of the major on-line services. This way stock promoters or other con artists can reach hundreds of thousands of investors at one time and do it anonymously. "There's no one who can save you but yourself," cautions Jared Silverman, chief of New Jersey's Securities Bureau.

If you have doubts about a telephone sales pitch or think you've been the victim of mail fraud, contact your state securities agency, attorney general or local Better Business Bureau. Other ways to investigate bogus claims: federal law enforcement or consumer protection agencies, congressmen or senators, and postal inspectors.

The need to exercise good financial sense doesn't stop once you've decided to invest. It's also important to be alert for any telltale signs that things aren't quite the way they should be. Remember, you don't have to be a swindler's "mark" if you use caution.

The National Fraud Information Center collects public information about investment swindles and other scams from government and private watchdog groups, and is maintained by the Federal Trade Commission and National Association of Attorneys General. If the person or firm you're checking up on is in the computer data bank, you'll be told on the phone. Call or write: NFIC, Box 65868, Washington, DC 20035 (800-876-7060).

"Victims think a fraudulent telemarketer's actions are not crimes, but simply hard sells," says John Barker of the National Consumers

League. Others believe they can match wits with suspect callers, but that's usually a mistake. Research shows that people who think they are too smart to be taken are among those most likely to fall for a scam.

PONZI SCHEMES

In some scams, early investors are paid bogus gains put up by later investors, who end up with zero when the balloon breaks and the swindler pockets the remaining huge sums of money. These "Ponzi schemes" are named after an Italian immigrant who bilked $10 million from some very proper Bostonians who were promised profits from trading international postage coupons.

Typically, Ponzi schemes masquerade as tax shelters, deals in gold or diamonds, real estate and collectibles (like baseball cards), as well as putting together unique, tailor-made portfolios of stocks or hedge funds. Many are "big-ticket" items: One scheme involving trusts and real estate partnerships promised investors more money after retiring than while they were working. Federal investigators report that thousands of investors put in $45 million before the scheme was exposed. Here's how ponzi schemes work:

1. The con artist promises big returns to investors, typically 30 to 40 percent or more a year. Investors begin sending money.

2. Phony financial statements are sent to investors. If someone demands cash payments, he is paid with money other investors have sent in.

3. More investors flood in as news spreads about big returns on their investment. They show friends the financial statements.

4. If enough investors demand their original investments back, the scheme collapses because the con artist has spent the money—or fled with it.

Surprisingly often, wealthy people who are assumed to know better have been caught up in these fast-money schemes that guarantee far higher interest rates or returns than the prevailing market is paying. Laurance Rockefeller, Estee Lauder, William Simon, Woody Allen, Erica Jong, Bob Dylan, and Elvis Presley have been victims of Ponzi schemes.

Why did these otherwise shrewd investors (William Simon is the former Secretary of the Treasury) fall prey to a phony, even primitive get-rich scheme? "The rich and powerful are human like everyone else," says Dr. Richard Budson, professor of psychiatry at Harvard Medical School. "They can be gullible at times."

As the stock market runs to record highs, financial fraud is thriving and claiming gullible new victims all the time. "The crooks are moving away from the phony sweepstakes offers to investment scams," says William McLucas, SEC enforcement director. "It's just the pitch that changes."

Take, for example, the charges against Bennett Funding Group, which sold office equipment leases to investors, who were supposed to earn profits on the income stream. The only problem: The Bennett brothers, Patrick and Michael, sold the same lease contract to more than one investor, sold phony lease contracts, and sold leases that had already been pledged to banks, for a total of $700 million. "This may well be the largest Ponzi scheme in history," says McLucas.

In another scheme, the promoter offered what he called a "fully hedged arbitrage" program in stocks and options listed on the New York Stock Exchange. It was billed as a can't-lose mutual fund with returns as high as 50 percent and virtually no risk. Again, initial investors were paid with new investors' money to create the illusion of big profits to attract still more investors.

(*Arbitrage* is the simultaneous purchase and sale of the same or an equivalent security in order to make a profit from the price discrepancy. Often, the difference is only a few cents, so arbitrageurs must trade a huge number of contracts at a time.)

The fund was exposed when the promoter was convicted of fraud and money laundering, but not before investors lost $7 million. The up-shot is, you can determine quickly if you're dealing with a real mutual fund, legally known as a "registered investment company." By law, funds must register with the SEC and file financial statements at least twice annually. You can get that information by calling the SEC Public Reference Branch (202-272-7450).

Ponzis aren't the only scams making a comeback. Investors have heard about people getting rich from initial public offerings of stock in tiny technology companies. And con artists have found that if the technology is exciting enough, people will buy anything. It makes sense. After all, young software engineers can become millionaires overnight these days. Even tame investments like stock mutual funds have given investors returns of 30 percent or more in a year. So all kinds of people are looking for easy ways to strike it rich.

"People who aren't willing to believe they have won a sweepstakes prize, are willing and ready to believe they can make huge returns through investment scams," says John Barker. This lack of skepticism has regulators and enforcers shaking their heads. "There are still plenty of legitimate investments out there," adds SEC's McLucas.

MINDING THE STORE

If you believe the adage, "You can't cheat an honest man," you may be headed for an expensive lesson. Today's con artists are equal-opportunity swindlers. No one is immune. And if like most of us, you're not opposed to making or saving a buck when opportunity knocks, you may be more vulnerable than you think.

Everyone who has a telephone or mailbox is a prospect. Whether you become a victim is largely up to you. No matter what questions you ask, skilled swindlers have ready answers. That's why sales calls from persons or businesses that are unknown to you should always be checked out before you actually invest in anything. For starters, ask for a phone number to call back and verify the existence of the company.

Con artists are likely to know more about you than you know about them. Depending on the source of their prospect list, they may know your age and income, health and hobbies, occupation and marital status, education, whether you own or rent, what magazines you read, the church or synagogue you attend, and which charities you support.

"The high-tech, sophisticated scam artists are experts at obtaining and using information," says Robert Carbone, assistant district attorney in Kern County, California. "Names of your doctor and close relatives, medical history, property ownership, and the rest are all available through public records." And they are all skilled liars and experts at verbal camouflage.

Perpetrators of phone and mail fraud are also extremely good at sounding and looking like legitimate businesses. They will steer potential clients to "singers" who have been paid to lie about the deal's attractiveness. So never assume you'll "know a scam when you hear or read about one." Even if you've heard about the kinds of schemes mentioned in this chapter, be warned that expert swindlers are constantly devising new ones.

If you want to put an end to annoying cold calls from anyone, legitimate or otherwise, get an unlisted number. Otherwise, follow these precautions spelled out in *Avoiding Phone Fraud*, a brochure available from the National Fraud Information Center (800-876-7060):

Ask for *written* information about the company and check it out with a consumer protection agency or the state attorney general where the business is located. Never send cash by mail or private delivery service. Be highly skeptical of offers that sound too good to be true; they usually aren't true. Also, don't accept calls from third-party callers (they can be billed to your telephone number).

If you don't mind getting catalogs by mail, but could live without all those sweepstakes offers, write or phone the offending company and ask that your name be removed from its mailing list. For more drastic action, there's a free service that can significantly reduce unsolicited mail:

Write to the Direct Marketing Association Mail Preference Service, which will remove your name from many national mailing lists. When you register, the DMA places your name on a mail-removal file. To apply, address letters indicating your wish to: DMA, Box 9008, Farmingdale, NY 11735. Include your full name and address, with any spelling variations you've noticed on direct mail you've received.

INVESTOR INFORMATION

There's much more you should know about investor rip-offs, and a good place to start is with the free booklet *Investment Swindles: How They Work and How to Avoid Them*, available from the Consumer Information Center, Pueblo, CO 81009.

Published annually, the *Consumer's Resource Handbook* tells what steps to follow if you suspect an investment fraud and how to avoid one, including hot lines and addresses of government agencies. It's available free from the Office of Consumer Affairs (800-664-4435).

For those who just want to learn more about scam artists and their schemes, or enjoy hearing about other people being ripped off, read *Chuck Whitlock's Scam School*. The author is a prominent consumer advocate and scam-buster who has exposed many of the tricks of con artists.

CHAPTER 16

Thinking About Taxes?

Congress has passed historic tax legislation with the most far-reaching tax cuts in sixteen years. The sweeping new tax bill, officially known as the Taxpayer Relief Act of 1997, will provide more than $90 billion in taxpayer relief over the next five years, and enhance opportunities to save and invest for the future.

The deal includes big tax breaks for children, education expenses, health insurance, inheritances and individual retirement accounts. Also being cut are capital gains taxes on the sale of assets such as stocks, mutual funds and real estate. What the changes will mean to you as an investor:

CAPITAL GAINS. Everyone, regardless of income, can now qualify for a lower tax on profit from the sale of stock or other investments held 18 months or longer. Under the new law, the capital gains tax rate drops from 28 to 20 percent in the top bracket, and from 15 to 10 percent in the bottom bracket. That could result in a huge tax savings.

But timing is everything. If you don't pay attention to the new holding periods and the effective dates for the changes, your gains could still get taxed at the 28 percent rate. Even lower rates go into effect for securities bought after December 2000. But you don't have to worry about that yet.

RETIREMENT ACCOUNTS. Employees covered by a 401(k) or other retirement plan at work may find it easier to make tax-deductble IRA deposits. For 1998, the maximum adjusted gross income (AGI) rises from

$40,000 to $50,000 on a joint return ($30,000 on a single) and will climb to $80,000 and $50,000 over the next eight years.

Couples in which both spouses work but only one has a retirement plan will be treated more fairly (as long as joint income is below $150,000). And investors who are eligible can contribute to the new Roth IRA where you never pay taxes on the earnings, allowing a more aggressive approach to choosing investments.

HOME SALES.   If you're thinking of selling, the new tax law could be of tremendous value. Until now, to defer tax on any profit, sellers had to buy a replacement home of at least equal value within two years.

Now, up to $500,000 of current and deferred profit is free from capital gains taxes for joint filers ($250,000 for singles) This could free investment capital tied up in a home, and enable taxpayers to trade down to a smaller home without having to pay any tax on the profit.

ESTATE TAXES.   Another break is a higher value at which estates begin to be taxed. The new law raises the biting point to $625,000 for 1998, gradually lifting it to $1 million by 2006. And estates that include family-owned businesses and farms can now escape taxes on $1.3 million in assets.

Previously, anything over $600,000 was taxed at a federal rate that could go as high as 55 percent. A good way to reduce the value of a taxable estate: You can give $20,000 a year ($10,000 if single) tax free to each child or grandchild you designate.

The rest of this chapter shows how else you as an *investor* can save on taxes and invest more profitably. Tax considerations are always important when it comes to investing—but they should never be allowed to eclipse the basic reasons for investing given in earlier chapters.

NEW RULES FAVOR INVESTORS

The change in the capital gains tax rate is good news for investors, if you know how to use it. The last two times the rate fell, in 1978 and 1981, some distinct patterns emerged: The stock market sank but ultimately staged a powerful recovery. And there was a noticeable flow of cash into the stocks of small companies.

The problem is that in this new-era economy, such historical benchmarks have not always been useful. But no one is complaining. Inflation is under control and employment is at an all-time high. Demand for goods and services is also expected to increase, according to the National Association of Business Economists.

The tax cuts could have some modest short-term effect on the economy. But the potential impact isn't enough to change the general outlook, says Allen Sinai, chief global economist at Primark Decision Economics. "And the dollar amounts are very small potatoes compared to the last tax cut in 1981."

Okay, but couldn't the lower tax rate pave the way for even more speculation? Not necessarily. Unlike the past two reductions, this one comes amid a sizzling affair with the stock market. "This market needed a stimulus like Einstein needed a higher education," notes Thomas McManus, strategist at Nat West Securities.

Another departure from the past has to do with the stocks of small companies. They typically do not pay a dividend—the payoff is in capital appreciation. That makes them all the more desirable when the capital gains rate falls, because dividends get taxed as ordinary income—a higher rate for most investors. But nothing is certain, except that the old tools just don't work exactly the way they're supposed to.

Capital gains aren't just for the rich anymore. The new rules give everyone—not just the top 5 percent—a tax break on profits from selling stocks or funds, bonds, real estate, and other assets.

Not since 1986 have investors enjoyed such favorable treatment (forgetting the crash of 1987). And in the year 2007, long-term investors could benefit from the lowest possible capital gains rate ever: zero, zip! The potential savings for long-term investors are huge.

For example, if you invested $1,000 in Microsoft at the end of July 1987, it would be worth about $54,000 right now. And if you cash in under the lower rate, you could save $4,240 in taxes compared with the old rate. Why the change? Investing has surged with about 40 percent of households having investments in the stock market, many through employee stock mutual funds. And they have all made money in the over seven-year-old bull market that has sent the Dow Jones industrial average soaring nearly 250 percent.

Rich or not, the lower capital gains rate should prompt a flurry of portfolio review and planning among investors. Some of the ways you can make the tax cut work for you:

❏ Don't base investment decisions on taxes. Investment advisers and financial planners tell their clients to look at whether buying or selling makes economical sense. But that advice is widely ignored.

❏ Sell if you get stock as part of your pay. Corporate executives' investments might be substantial, but they are exposed to greater risk than someone with a more diversified portfolio of stocks.

❏ Sell if you're holding an investment that is up sharply but is beginning to underperform. Sheldon Jacobs, publisher of the *No-Load Mutual Fund Investor,* plans to tell his readers to sell subpar holdings.

❏ Buy stocks instead of bonds. That's because most earnings from stocks come from price increases and are capital gains. Bond earnings come from interest payments and are taxed as ordinary income.

❏ Look into mutual funds that minimize annual distributions in favor of long-term capital gains. Each year, a fund has to distribute any dividends to shareholders who then pay taxes on them.

❏ Consider index funds that don't do any trading. Active trading by management could cost you more under the new tax rules. Investments must be held for 18 months rather than a year to qualify for the lower tax.

❏ Forget about shorting. Until now, a popular way to avoid capital gains taxes on stock has been to borrow identical shares and sell them short. This tactic had not been treated as a sale. Now it will be.

PLANNING IS TOUGHER

Investors have struck gold with the last year's capital gains tax cut, and there are other valuable nuggets in the new federal tax law. But to mine them, you'll have to dig through some complicated rules. Some may call into question conventional tax strategies.

"The old rules about deferring income and accelerating deductions may get turned around," says Greg Jenner, tax policy director at Coopers & Lybrand. In deciding whether to sell appreciated stock or mutual funds, you should first consider your overall goals.

Just because you qualify for the 20- or 10-percent capital gains rate is no reason to rush out and sell. "Money has been lost trying to save on taxes," says Jenner. "That's when people lose sight of investment fundamentals." But the lower rate does make it more attractive to take some gains that might not be offset by losses in other investments.

According to an analysis by T. Rowe Price, investors who are eligible to contribute to a Roth IRA could earn significantly more after-tax income during retirement from that account than from a traditional IRA. And you won't have to be concerned about the tax consequences of a stock fund with high turnover that throws off a lot of capital gains.

In general, the younger you are, the longer the period of time until you start withdrawing the money and the higher the expected rate of return, the more advantageous it is to convert to a Roth IRA. And in 1998, there is a special one-time opportunity to spread taxes on earnings so far over four years. The only hitch: Married couples who file separate returns aren't eligible at all.

Now may also be the time to sell your home—if you have occupied it for at least two of the last five years. Home sales are booming, says David Lereah of the Mortgage Bankers Association. And skyrocketing rents in many areas are giving consumers even more incentive to buy along with those wanting to trade up to more expensive homes.

The age requirement has also been eliminated on home sales, and there is no one-time use of the tax break as there was previously. Taxpayers who have a principal residence and a vacation home may find this provision especially appealing: They can sell their principal residence and start living in the vacation home and after two years time, sell the vacation home and not pay tax on the gain (if less than $500,000).

Despite all the changes, some tax advice remains the same for investors:

❏ Don't buy mutual funds before the end of the year without checking to see if they've already made their capital gains distribution. If you do, you'll get stuck paying the same taxes as shareholders who have owned the fund the entire year.

❏ Think twice before giving stock or mutual funds to a child or charity to avoid the capital gains tax. There is slightly less incentive to give away securities now, because your tax bill on the gains has declined sharply and will decrease even more in the future.

❏ Avoid taking short-term gains on any stocks, even those that have appreciated considerably in the past year. They continue to be taxed at regular rates, currently as high as 39 percent. Keep them at least until they qualify as long-term gains and are taxed at the 20 percent rate.

❏ Forget about short-selling "against the box" in order to postpone the capital gains tax. In such a transaction, an investor sells borrowed securities while holding onto stock owned a long time. This rule no longer applies.

INVESTING MATTERS

How else might tax changes affect your investing decisions in the future? Put simply, investors who buy and hold stocks will get to keep more of their gains when they sell. Those who focus on dividends and interest won't. Here are some answers to questions you may have, not all by any means.

Should you sell?

If your investments have peaked or you want to rebalance a portfolio with big and small stocks, the cut in capital gains is a strong incentive. But if you have held them only a short time, you may want to factor in the "downside protection" that can result from waiting for long-term rates.

For example, assume that you purchased shares for $2,500 that ten months later are worth $5,000. You want to sell, but will lose the protection of waiting eight more months. You should consider this before taking any short-term gain. Take state income taxes into account as well. The downside protection in Massachusetts would be almost 12 percent.

Should you switch assets?

The new tax rules do favor small stocks that pay no dividends over those that do, as well as other income investments such as bonds (taxed as ordinary income). But should you get into small stocks in a really big way?

Not necessarily. You may still want to maintain a diversified portfolio with a mix of asset classes to reduce risk while you seek higher returns. And if you're invested in municipal bonds, you'll most likely want to continue to take advantage of their tax-free income (though a portion may be subject to alternative minimum tax).

What about tax-deferred accounts?

Some experts have been quick to suggest that stocks and stock funds should be held in taxable rather than tax-deferred accounts because of the lower capital gains taxes. But the longer the time frame, and the higher the anticipated rate of return from an equity, the more tax deferral can work to your advantage.

As the numbers show, if the money is withdrawn in a lump sum after just five years, the value of the taxable account is well ahead of the tax-deferred account. But after 25 years, the results are quite different.

"Every investor's situation is different," says Michael Carona, CPA, tax partner with Coopers & Lybrand in Boston. "But a little knowledge now about how the numbers work may help you get a head start this tax season with the investment moves that may be most favorable for you."

SEIZE YOUR SHARE

As we've seen, investors can save thousands a year with the new tax law. But it will take smart planning, starting now. Though disproportionate benefits will flow to some taxpayers—mainly wealthy investors and inheritors, and big families with middling incomes—the new law will still allow investors and savers to keep more of their income.

The only problem: Finding your share of the savings will take more work than ever. Most of the tax breaks are narrowly targeted and phased in and out over so many timetables that you may feel like a circus tiger jumping through hoops at the crack of the tax collector's whip, says Peter Sepp, spokesman for the National Taxpayers Union, a tax-cutting advocacy group. "This bill brings to the average investor a level of complexity once reserved for the very rich," he says.

In general, for your gain to qualify as "long term" under the new law you must hold the assets for more than 18 months before selling (versus 12 months under the old law). Stocks you buy and hold for at least five years will be taxed at only 8 percent (18 percent in the top income bracket). Here's what you can do to seize the opportunity:

Go for growth. The new law makes long-term investment in growth stocks the most attractive option for your taxable accounts. That's because the returns for such shares come almost exclusively in the form of capital gains, which are taxed at the new low rate when you sell.

Stock fund investors can also take advantage by choosing growth stock funds that keep taxable short-term capital gains to a minimum. To find such funds, look for a tax-efficiency ratio of at least 80 percent. Or check out a fund's turnover rate, which at 50 percent indicates that a manager holds stocks an average of two years.

Ask for options. If you are among the millions of employees who are offered stock options, take them. But ask for incentive options instead of unqualified ones if they are available. You generally owe no tax when you exercise an incentive option, and the gain is considered long-term.

By contrast, when you exercise nonqualified options, you owe ordinary income tax on the difference between the option price and fair market value of the stock on the day you sell. You only have to hold an incentive option for six months before selling.

MATCH LOSSES AND GAINS. When the capital gains tax rates were closer to the rates on ordinary income, investors were advised to comb through their portfolios in search of unpromising stocks they could sell at a loss to offset any gains, short or long, that they planned to realize.

Now your best tax strategy is to sell your losers only in years when you have short-term capital gains and other income to offset. The reason: If you're in the 28 percent income tax bracket, you save on taxes and offset short-term gains.

BEWARE OF ALTERNATIVES. The new law virtually guarantees that most of us will pay a stiff penalty initially intended to hit only the wealthiest taxpayers. What it does is trigger an alternative tax if you realize a big capital gain and outsize the deductions on your federal return.

See a tax adviser before you sell any stocks or options, since avoiding or mitigating the alternative tax may take multiyear planning. By 2007, this rule will grab an estimated $9 million from unsuspecting taxpayers.

LEGITIMATE SHELTERS

Although the federal government has softened the blow, you will obviously take a hit if you sell a stock and make a huge profit. But there's one way to avoid capital gains taxes, and probably state and local income taxes as well.

If you give generous sums to charities each year, consider donating appreciated securities instead of cash, by asking your broker to switch ownership of your shares to a needy organization. "By transferring the stock and letting the charity decide whether and when to sell, you don't have to pay capital gains taxes," says Donald Korn, author of *Audit-Proof Tax Shelters.*

Let's say you bought $5,000 worth of stock and your investment has appreciated in 18 months to $10,000. Under the new law, if you sell the stock you have to pay a 20 percent tax, or $1,000. But if you transfer the stock to a charity instead, you avoid the capital gains tax and deduct $10,000.

While "tax shelters" are mostly remembered as cattle breeding or other limited partnerships from the late 1970s and early 1980s, there are still investments you can make that will cut your tax bill—now more than ever. Consider the following:

HOUSING CREDITS.   With the Dow Jones passing 8,000, many investors are sitting on gains they are reluctant to take because of the taxes they would owe. But there are money-making investments such as low-income housing that actually reduce taxes.

Tax credits (not deductions) are available to people who invest in such projects, and syndicators offer private placements in these projects. "Affordable housing today is privately owned and managed with a profit potential," says Richard Agazio, executive vice president of Boston Capital, which offers such investments.

MUNICIPAL BONDS.   Less profitable than housing credits, municipal bonds also can be used to shelter investment income. Like all bonds, they pay interest, but it's exempt from federal and state income taxes. That means no tax is due, ever. With other types of investments, the taxes are deferred, which means they will have to be paid later.

But there are risks. If you are forced to sell the bond before redemption, you might get a lower price than you paid, taking a loss. And the longer the time until maturity, the greater the market risk.

DEFERRED ANNUITIES.   They make sense if you pay a hefty tax each year on investment income. Otherwise, you're better off paying the 15 percent each year and doing what you want with the after-tax dollars.

But if you're willing to live with illiquidity for several years, while you let your money compound, the greater the value of your account will be. The shelter is in the tax deferral— $360,000 compared to $196,000 for a 20-year taxable account where both pay 10 percent annually.

GIFT SHARES.   These are mutual funds for a child set up as irrevocable trusts for at least 10 years and would not be appropriate if you need tuition money sooner. If not, the advantage is that you shift any tax to the lowest income bracket.

One that invests primarily in small growth stocks is Royce Gift-shares, which has had an annual return of 21 percent, according to *Morningstar Investor*. Minimum initial investment is $2,000.

OFFSHORE BANKS.   Got a million? Then you might want to investigate the pros and cons of popular tax havens in the Bahamas, Cayman Islands, Liechtenstein, and elsewhere. They fall into two categories: those that levy no tax at all (Bahamas), and those that levy very low taxes (Liechtenstein).

But just mention "tax havens" and many people get anxiety attacks. Questionable ones are more likely than ever to draw the IRS's attention. "But if your goal is tax planning and not tax evasion, offshore banks are perfectly legal," says Anthony Ginsberg, international analyst and author of *Tax Havens.*

AVOIDING AN AUDIT

Only a small fraction of taxpayers is audited each year, but the number should grow as more auditors begin prowling through returns. Some areas of special concern are self-employed workers and charitable deductions. The tax returns of proprietorships and partnerships are audited at a far higher rate than other returns. But if you find that dreaded notice in your mailbox, don't panic—and definitely don't ignore it.

A series of savvy moves can help cut through the red tape of an IRS examination and challenge extra taxes. One thing is certain: The damage will be minimal, unless you have engaged in outright fraud.

"As the tax shelter wars wind down, the IRS has been shifting audit resources to self-employment, an area they consider rife with abuses," says Robert LeBaube, a former IRS official now with the accounting firm of Coopers & Lybrand.

A particular target is the individual who files a profit or loss statement as a sole proprietor (Schedule C). Legal and medical practices, restaurants, and small retail stores are businesses likely to come under scrutiny. But anyone who has a home office can expect to feel the heat as rookie auditors hone their write-off bashing skills on personal returns. If you have your own business and make at least $100,000 a year, the chance of being audited more than doubles, according to IRS statistics.

Large expenses, late payroll tax payments, and lavish salaries are some ways to attract attention. The government also hates sloppy and incomplete records. "Anyone who has poor records just may get audited every year," says LeBaube.

Tax collectors are also turning up the heat on charitable deductions for which they suspect inflated receipts have been used to pad write-offs.

One example: A taxpayer who bids on antique furniture at a charity auction and then deducts the full amount rather that subtracting the fair-market value from the purchase price. If you're caught making this mistake you'll have to come up with the under-paid tax, plus a penalty on the tax due and interest of another 10 percent on the shortfall.

"If you pay tax on $100,000 in income, and you have a $10,000 contribution to charity, that can seem out of line," says IRS spokesperson Gail Ellis. "But if your income is, say, $500,000 it doesn't seem out of line at all." But charitable contributions should be well documented, she adds.

The IRS won't tell individuals specifically what triggers an audit, but accountants know there are "red flags" you should keep in mind as you complete your tax return, to prevent common—and costly—mistakes. Aside from charitable and home-office deductions, expect trouble if you:

❑ Take tax-shelter losses or those from a hobby or sideline. These are causes of many audits and are closely scrutinized. And once a return is questioned for any one item, it's possible to be questioned on other items, warns Ellis.

❑ Omit income from your return that has been reported to the IRS by banks, brokerages, mutual funds, or others, concerning savings interest, dividends, sale of property, and capital gains or losses on the sale of stocks and mutual funds. Or, if you fail to attach Schedule E to report income from rents, royalties, partnerships, estates, and trusts.

❑ Make math errors or there is a problem with information matching. The math test is simply a question of the IRS crunching the numbers to make sure everything is correct. Information is that received from third parties such as banks, mutual funds and brokerage firms.

The IRS computers use a formula with built-in alarms for deductions, tax shelters, and types of income at every level. A high score makes a tax return an audit candidate. But a mail and phone audit for a tax deficiency is more common and less intimidating. Challenge or pay it and you can avoid paying quite a bit of interest.

Even if the notice calls for an office audit, and the issues involved are easy to document, you may be able to send copies and request a mail audit. The last thing you want is a field audit, because the examiner could be in contact with more records. Request a change in location from your home or office to that of an accountant or lawyer.

If at all possible, try to avoid IRS enforcement actions, which include dipping into bank accounts, garnishing salaries, or taking houses and cars if you don't pay up. And bankruptcy won't help much because it doesn't eliminate tax liability.

To avoid a tax audit, beware of tax shelters that promise suspiciously high write-offs. They will almost surely provoke the IRS. Often, the safest and best tax shelters can be found right where you work or in retirement plans for self-employed people and small-business owners.

If you want to calculate how much you are likely to owe the IRS under provisions of the new 1997 tax rules, you'll get accurate answers fast by logging on to accounting firm Ernst & Young's Website: www.ey.com/tax. Some tidbits you'll find there are the 50 most overlooked deductions and 25 most common mistakes on tax forms. Not surprisingly, math errors top the list.

Tips for a winning audit

Whatever the reason you're chosen for an audit, it's a chilling experience even if you've done nothing wrong. There are steps you can take that will make the procedure more anxiety-free:

- ❏ *Get help.* Ask the person who prepared your return for tips and advice on how to get ready. You usually don't have to go at all, if you hire an accountant or lawyer and provide him or her with power of attorney.

- ❏ *Don't volunteer information.* Answer questions to the best of your knowledge, but supply only those documents (copies) needed to substantiate the items questioned.

- ❏ *Keep your cool.* If the examiner asks questions you can't answer, explain that you will need additional time to provide accurate answers. Avoid off-the-cuff replies. If the agent gives you a hard time, ask that an IRS supervisor participate in the audit.

- ❏ *Audit yourself.* If you haven't been keeping records, you can often reconstruct them to prove questionable deductions. Ask for statements from airlines, travel agencies, and credit-card companies.

- ❏ *File an appeal.* During the hearing you'll have the opportunity to state your case before an appeals officer who'll make a ruling based on your additional information. It may seem a bit bothersome, but it can be worth it.

INVESTOR INFORMATION

Admittedly, reading an annual consumer guide such as J.K. Lasser's *Your Income Tax* is not like reading Tom Clancy or John Grisham. But most of us have to worry about only a few parts of the new tax rules. Unless you have exotic investments, the law is no harder to decipher than other important financial reading.

It also helps to get an accountant's view of the rules, in addition to the booklet you'll get in the mail from the Internal Revenue Service. For a complete list of all IRS booklets, ask at your local office for the *Guide to Free Tax Services* (Publication 910) or call 800-829-3676.

And if you still can't get tax shelters out of your mind, and really do have a million dollars, invest first in a copy of *Tax Havens,* by Anthony Ginsberg. It helps separate the legal shelters from vacation and investment traps for the unwary.

Leading Indexes and Indicators

STOCK INDEXES

These indexes contain stocks of small cap companies and less well-known issues.

Amex Market Value. Measures changes in the aggregate market of over 800 issues including resources, technology, services, and consumer goods.

Nasdaq Composite. Weighted measure of all small cap stocks and national market securities sold over-the-counter via the National Association of Securities Dealers Automated Quotations.

Nasdaq Small Cap. Smaller capitalization tier of stocks with lower listing requirements than those of national market companies.

NYSE Composite. Capitalization-weighted average of 1,500 stocks listed on the New York Stock Exchange.

Russell 2000. Weighted measure of the 2,000 smallest companies in the Russell universe of 3,000 stocks.

S&P Mid Cap. Capitalization-weighted index of 400 stocks with a median value of about $1 billion.

S&P OTC 2500. Like the Nasdaq index, indicates the overall direction of over-the-counter issues.

S&P Small Cap 600. Market-weighted average of 600 issues ranging from roughly $50 million to $950 million.

Value Line Composite. Equally weighted index of 1,700 stocks traded over-the-counter and on both exchanges (Amex, NYSE).

Wilshire 5000. Value-weighted index derived from 5,000 stocks traded on both exchanges and over-the-counter.

KEY INDICATORS

Statistical composites that indicate the rate of change in the economy and financial markets.

Consumer Confidence. A measure of people's feelings about the economy in general.

Consumer Price Index. Measures price changes for goods and services and the direction of inflation.

Corporate Profits. Earnings growth for all companies listed in Standard & Poor's 500 stock index.

Dow Jones Industrial Average. Price-weighted index of 30 major companies that exert influence on stock market action.

Gross Domestic Product. Measures goods and services produced on an annual basis and can predict business trends and economic activity.

Inflation. Measures rate of inflation from high to low—good for business and good for the stock market.

Industrial Production. Index that shows amount of business volume as a percentage of the average.

Leading Indicators. This index represents 11 components of economic growth from stock prices to housing starts.

Standard & Poor's 500. Broader average than DJIA includes market-weighted stocks sold on both exchanges and over-the-counter.

Unemployment Rate. Statistic that reflects the overall status of the economy and economic trends.

Workers' Hourly Wage. Increase in 1997 (to $12) was the biggest since 1990.

Newsletters and Advisory Services

NEWSLETTERS

This list includes financial newsletters that cover stocks and/or mutual funds. Specialty newsletters (bonds, single funds, conservative) are excluded.

Addison Report
Box 402
Franklin, MA 02038
508-528-8678
Cost: $250

Adrian Day's Investment Analyst
824 E. Baltimore St.
Baltimore, MD 21202
800-433-1528
Cost: $49

AgBiotech Stock Letter
Box 40460
Berkeley, CA 94704
510-843-1842
Cost: $165

Analyst Watch
115 N. Wacker Dr.
Chicago, IL 60606
800-399-6659

BI Research
Box 133
Redding, CT 06875
203-270-9244
Cost: $90

Beating the Dow
Box 2069
River Vale, NJ 07675
800-477-3400
Cost: $125

Bowser Report
Box 6278
Newport News, VA 23606
757-877-5979
Cost: $48

Cabot Market Letter
Box 3067
Salem, MA 01970
508-745-5532
Cost: $295

California Technology Stock Letter
Box 308
Half Moon Bay, CA 94019
415-726-8495
Cost: $295

Chartist
Box 758
Seal Beach, CA 90740
310-596-2385
Cost: $150

Dines Letter
Box 22
Belvedere, CA 94920
800-845-8259
Cost: $195

Equities Special Situations
160 Madison Ave.
New York, NY 10016
800-237-8400
Cost: $150

Executive Stock Report
Box 85333
Richmond, VA 23293
800-446-7922
Cost: $475

FXC Investors Report
62-19 Cooper Ave.
Queens, NY 11385
800-392-0992
Cost: $190

Forbes Special Situations
60 Fifth Ave.
New York, NY 10011
212-620-2210
Cost: $495

Ford Investment Review
11722 Sorrento Valley Rd.
San Diego, CA 92121
800-842-0207
Cost: $120

Garzarelli Outlook
7811 Montrose Rd.
Potomac, MD 20854
800-804-0939
Cost: $149

*Gerald Perritt's Mutual Fund
   Letter*
12514 Stancey Rd.
Largo, FL 33773
800-326-6941
Cost: $89

Global Investing
Box 1945
Ft. Collins, CO 80522
800-388-4237
Cost: $245

Ground Floor
Box 2069
Rivervale, NJ 07675
800-477-3400
Cost: $114

Growth Fund Guide
Box 6600
Rapid City, SD 57709
605-341-1971
Cost: $99

Growth Stock Outlook
Box 15381
Chevy Chase, MD 20825
301-654-5205
Cost: $195

Growth Stock Winners
1750 Old Meadow Rd.
McLean, VA 22102
800-832-2330
Cost: $105

Growth Stocks Report
107 Edinburgh S.
Cary, NC 27511
919-461-3960
Cost: $199

Harry Browne's Special Reports
Box 5586
Austin, TX 78763
800-531-5142
Cost: $225

*Individual Investor Special
    Situations*
1633 Broadway
New York, NY 10019
212-843-2777
Cost: $195

Insiders
2200 SW 10th St.
Deerfield Beach, FL 33442
800-442-9000
Cost: $49

Invest with the Masters
7811 Montrose Rd.
Potomac, MD 20859
800-211-8559
Cost: $119

Investing with Barry Ziskin
1217 St. Paul St.
Baltimore, MD 21202
800-433-1528
Cost: $79

InvesTech Market Analyst
2472 Birch Glen
Whitefish, MT 59937
800-955-8500
Cost: $175

Investor's World
7811 Montrose Rd.
Potomac, MD 20854
800-804-0942
Cost: $195

LaLoggia's Special Situations
Box 167
Rochester, NY 14601
716-232-1240
Cost: $230

Louis Rukeyser's Wall Street
1750 Old Meadow Rd.
McLean, VA 22102
800-892-9702
Cost: $79

Low Priced Stock Survey
7412 Calumet Ave.
Hammond, IN 46324
219-852-3210
Cost: $82

Low Priced Stocks
4016 S. Michigan St.
South Bend, IN 46614
800-553-5866
Cost: $45

MPT Review
1 E. Liberty
Reno, NV 89501
800-454-1395
Cost: $225

Margo's Small Stocks
Box 642
Lexington, MA 02173
617-861-0302
Cost: $125

Mark Skousen's Forecasts
7811 Montrose Rd.
Potomac, MD 20854
301-424-3700
Cost: $177

Medical Technology Stock Letter
Box 40460
Berkeley, CA 94704
510-843-1857
Cost: $320

Mini-Cap Analyst (Pro Trader)
Box 28011
Harbor Center, Vancouver
   Canada V6B 5L8
604-669-8270
Cost: $120

Motley Fool
918 Prince St.
Alexandria, VA 22314
703-838-3665
Cost: $104

Mutual Fund Strategist
Box 446
Burlington, VT 05402
800-355-3863
Cost: $95

National Trendlines
14001 Berryville Rd.
North Potomac, MD 20874
800-521-1585
Cost: $75

New Issues
2200 SW 10th St.
Deerfield Beach, FL 33442
800-442-9000
Cost: $95

Next Super Stock
4800 Hampden Lane
Bethesda, MD 20814
888-278-6252
Cost: $69

Ney Stock and Fund Report
Box 92223
Pasadena, CA 91109
818-441-2222
Cost: $195

No-Load Fund Investor
1 Bridge St.
Irvington-on-Hudson, NY 10533
800-252-2042
Cost: $129

OTC Insight
Box 5759
Walnut Creek, CA 94596
800-955-9566
Cost: $295

Oberweis Report
951 Ice Cream Dr.
North Aurora, IL 60542
800-323-6166
Cost: $139

Peter Dag Portfolio Strategy
65 Lakefront Dr.
Akron, OH 44319
800-833-2782
Cost: $195

Portfolio Advisor
320 Arizona St.
Hollywood, FL 33019
954-923-3553
Cost: $245

Professional Tape Reader
Box 2407
Hollywood, FL 33022
800-868-7857
Cost: $395

Prudent Speculator
Box 1438
Laguna Beach, CA 92652
714-497-7657
Cost: $175

*Richard Band's Profitable
   Investing*
7811 Montrose Rd.
Potomac, MD 20854
301-424-3700
Cost: $100

Ruff Times
Box 887
Springville, UT 84663
801-489-8681
Cost: $97

Scientific Investment
1521 Alton Rd.
Miami Beach, FL 33139
800-232-8197
Cost: $129

Sector Selector
Box 642
Lexington, MA 02173
617-861-0302
Cost: $233

Savvy Investor
1619 Sam Houston Ave.
Huntsville, TX 77340
409-291-8004
Cost: $135

Special Investment Situations
Box 4254
Chattanooga, TN 37405
615-886-1628
Cost: $160

Special Situations
17 Battery Place
New York, NY 10004
212-425-7500
Cost: $150

Strategic Investment
824 E. Baltimore St.
Baltimore, MD 21202
410-234-0691
Cost: $59

US Investment Report
25 Fifth Ave.
New York, NY 10003
212-460-9200
Cost: $228

Wall Street Digest
1 Sarasota Tower
Sarasota, FL 34236
813-954-5500
Cost: $150

World Investor
1217 St. Paul St.
Baltimore, MD 21202
410-234-0691
Cost: $99

Zweig Performance Ratings
Box 360
Bellmore, NY 11710
516-223-3800
Cost: $225

ADVISORY SERVICES

These provide reports, charts and/or newsletters as well as market information and investment advice on stocks and mutual funds.

Argus Research Corp.
17 Battery Place
New York, NY 10004
212-425-7500

Argus Viewpoint; Economy at a Glance; Portfolio Selector; Special Situations

Chartcraft Inc.
30 Church St.
New Rochelle, NY 10801
914-632-0422

Charts available for all common stocks sold over-the-counter and on both exchanges (Amex, NYSE).

Dow Jones & Co.
Box 300
Princeton, NJ 08543
609-452-1511

News/retrieval service for professionals and serious investors providing quotes and news on selected stocks or mutual funds.

Institute for Econometric Research
2200 SW 10th St.
Deerfield Beach, FL 33442
800-442-9000

Fidelity Insight; Fund Watch; Insiders; Investor's Digest; Market Logic; Mutual Fund Forecaster; New Issues

Lipper Analytical Service
25 Broadway
New York, NY 10004
800-221-5277

Ranks the performance of more than 3,000 stock mutual funds in thirty categories.

Media General Financial Services
Box 85333
Richmond, VA 23293
800-446-7922

Database Service; Executive Stock Report; Price and Volume; Screen and Select

Morningstar Inc.
225 W. Wacker Dr.
Chicago, IL 60606
800-876-5005

Database Service; Morningstar Investor; Morningstar Mutual Funds

National Association of Investors Corp.
Box 220
Royal Oak, MI 48068
810-583-6242

Advisory service for individual investors and member investment clubs.

Securities Industry Association
120 Broadway
New York, NY 10271
212-608-1500

Foreign Activity Report; Securities Industry Trends

Standard & Poor's Corp.
25 Broadway
New York, NY
800-852-1641

Emerging & Special Situations; 500 Directory; Market Month; Outlook; Security Dealers; Surveys by Industry; Trendline Charts

Value Line Inc.
220 E. 42nd St.
New York, NY 10017
800-634-3583

Convertibles Survey; Investment Survey; Mutual Fund Survey; OTC Special Situations

Vickers Stock Research Corp.
601 Indiana Ave.
Washington, DC 20004
800-645-5043

Facts on Funds; Institutional Portfolios; Weekly Insiders Report

Sources: Hurlbert Financial Digest; Select Information Exchange

Regional and Discount Brokers

REGIONAL BROKERS

Advest Inc.
90 State House Sq.
Hartford, CT 06103
800-243-8115

J.C. Bradford & Co.
330 Commerce St.
Nashville, TN 37201
800-251-1060

Alex Brown & Sons Co.
135 E. Baltimore St.
Baltimore, MD 21202
800-638-2596

Crowell, Weedon & Co.
624 S. Grand Ave.
Los Angeles, CA 90017
213-620-1850

Dain Bosworth Inc.
600 S. 6th St.
Minneapolis, MN 55402
612-371-2711

D.A. Davidson & Co.
Box 5015
Great Falls, MT 59403
800-332-5915

Edward D. Jones & Co.
201 Progress Pkwy.
Maryland Heights, MO 63043
314-851-2000

A.G. Edwards & Sons Inc.
1 N. Jefferson Ave.
St. Louis, MO 63103
314-515-3000

Interstate/Johnson Lane
121 W. Trade St.
Charlotte, NC 28202
704-379-9000

Janney Montgomery Scott Inc.
1801 Market St.
Philadelphia, PA 19103
800-526-6397

Legg, Mason Wood Walker
111 S. Calvert St.
Baltimore, MD 21202
800-368-2558

McDonald & Co.
800 Superior Ave.
Cleveland, OH 44114
800-553-2240

Piper, Jaffray Inc.
222 S. 9th St.
Minneapolis, MN 55402
800-333-6000

Raymond James Financial
800 Carillon Pkwy.
St. Petersburg, FL 33716
800-248-8863

Rauscher Pierce Refsnes Inc.
2700 N. Haskell
Dallas, TX 75204
214-989-1000

Sutro & Co.
201 California St.
San Francisco, CA 94111
800-652-1030

Van Kasper & Co.
600 California St.
San Francisco, CA 94108
800-652-1747

Wheat First/Butcher Singer
901 E. Byrd St.
Richmond, VA 23219
800-627-8625

DISCOUNT BROKERS

Accutrade
10825 Harney St.
Omaha, NE 68154
800-882-4887

American Express
Box 59196
Minneapolis, MN 55459
800-297-7378

K. Aufhauser & Co.
140 Broadway
New York, NY 10005
800-368-3668

Baker & Co.
1940 E. 6th St.
Cleveland, OH 44114
800-321-1640

Bidwell & Co.
209 SW Oak St.
Portland, OR 97204
800-547-6337

Brown & Co.
1 Beacon St.
Boston, MA 02108
800-822-2021

Discover (Lombard)
333 Market St.
San Francisco, CA 94105
800-566-2273

E-Trade Group
4 Embarcadero Pl.
Palo Alto, CA 94303
800-786-2573

Fidelity Brokerage Services
Box 770001
Cincinnati, OH 45277
800-544-7272

Kennedy Cabot Inc.
9470 Wilshire Blvd.
Beverly Hills, CA 90212
800-252-0090

National Discount Brokers
7 Hanover Sq.
New York, NY 10004
800-888-3999

PC Financial
1 Pershing Pl.
Jersey City, NJ 07399
800-825-5723

Pacific Brokerage Services
5757 Wilshire Blvd.
Los Angeles, CA 90036
800-421-8395

T. Rowe Price
100 E. Pratt St.
Baltimore, MD 21202
800-225-5132

Quick & Reilly
26 Broadway
New York, NY 10002
800-672-7220

Charles Schwab & Co.
120 Kearny St.
San Francisco, CA 94120
800-435-4000

Scottsdale Securities
12855 Flushing Meadow Dr.
St. Louis, MO 63131
800-619-7283

Securities Research Inc.
830 Azalea Lane
Vero Beach, FL 32963
800-327-3156

Muriel Siebert & Co.
885 Third Ave.
New York, NY 10022
800-872-0711

StockCross Inc.
1 Washington Mall
Boston, MA 02108
800-225-6196

USAA Brokerage Services
9800 Fredricksburg Rd.
San Antonio, TX 78284
800-531-8343

Vanguard Brokerage Services
Box 2600
Valley Forge, PA 19482
800-992-8327

Waterhouse Brokerage Services
100 Wall St.
New York, NY 10005
800-934-4410

Jack White & Co.
9191 Towne Center Dr.
San Diego, CA 92122
800-233-3411

Wilmington Brokerage Services
1100 N. Market St.
Wilmington, DE 19801
800-345-7550

Small Cap Mutual Funds

AAL Small Cap Stock A
222 W. College Ave.
Appleton, WI 54919
414-734-7633

AARP Small Company
2 International Place
Boston, MA 02110
800-322-2282

AIM Aggressive Growth
11 Greenway Plaza
Houston, TX 77046
713-626-1919

Academy Value
4455 E. Camelback Rd.
Phoenix, AZ 85018
817-751-0555

Accessor Small to Mid Cap
1420 Fifth Ave.
Seattle, WA 98101
800-759-3504

Acorn; Acorn USA
227 W. Monroe St.
Chicago, IL 60606
800-922-6769

Aetna Ascent
Aetna Small Company
151 Farmington Ave.
Hartford, CT 06156
800-367-7732

Alliance Quasar A
Box 1520
Secaucus, NJ 07096
800-227-4618

American Cent Giftrust
4500 Main St.
Kansas City, MO 64141
816-531-5575

American Heritage
1370 Ave. of Americas
New York, NY 10019
212-397-3900

American Performance
   Aggressive Growth
3435 Stelzer Rd.
Columbus, OH
800-762-7085

Apex Mid Cap Growth
1270 Ave. of Americas
New York, NY 10020
800-845-8405

Aquila Rocky Mountain
   Equity A
380 Madison Ave.
New York, NY 10017
800-762-5955

Arch Small Cap Equity Trust
Box 78069
St. Louis, MO 63178
800-551-3731

Ariel Appreciation
Ariel Growth
307 N. Michigan Ave.
Chicago, IL 60601
800-292-7435

Ark Special Equity
680 E. Swedesford Rd.
Wayne, PA 19087
800-624-4116

Armada Mid Cap Regional
680 E. Swedesford Rd.
Wayne, PA 19087
800-342-5734

Artisan Small Cap
1000 N. Water St.
Milwaukee, WI 53202
800-344-1770

Avesta Small Cap
Box 1555
Houston, TX 77251
713-216-4643

BB&T Small Company
   Growth A
3435 Stelzer Rd.
Columbus, OH 43219
800-228-1872

BNY Hamilton Small Cap
   Growth
125 W. 55th St.
New York, NY 10019
800-426-9363

BT Investment Small Cap
6 St. James Ave.
Boston, MA 02116
800-730-1313

Babson Enterprise
2440 Pershing Rd.
Kansas City, MO 64108
800-422-2766

Baron Asset
Baron Growth & Income
767 Fifth Ave.
New York, NY 10153
212-583-2000

Barr Rosenberg U.S. Small Cap
237 Park Ave.
New York, NY 10017
800-527-6026

Bear Stearns Small Cap Value C
245 Park Ave.
New York, NY 10167
800-766-4111

Benchmark Small Company
   Index A
207 E. Buffalo St.
Milwaukee, WI 53202
800-621-2550

Berger New Generation
Berger Small Cap Value
Berger Small Company Growth
210 University Blvd.
Denver, CO 80206
800-960-8427

Berwyn
1189 Lancaster Ave.
Berwyn, PA 19312
302-324-0200

Biltmore Special Value A
Federated Investors Tower
Pittsburgh, PA 15222
800-994-4414

Bonnel Growth
Box 8987
Wilmington, DE 19899
800-426-6635

Brazos/JMIC Small Cap
  Growth
1100 N. Market St.
Wilmington, DE 19890
800-336-9970

Bridgeway Aggressive Growth
Bridgeway Ultra Small
  Company
5650 Kirby Dr.
Houston, TX 77005
800-336-9970

Brown Capital Small Company
105 N. Washington St.
Rocky Mountain, NC 27802
800-525-3863

Bull & Bear Special Equities
11 Hanover Square
New York, NY 10005
212-363-1100

CRM Small Cap Value
2 Portland Square
Portland, ME 04101
800-276-2883

California Investment S&P Sm
  Cap
44 Montgomery St.
San Francisco, CA 94104
800-225-8778

Calvert Cap Accumulation A
4550 Montgomery Ave.
Bethesda, MD 20814
301-951-4820

Cappiello-Rushmore Emerging
  Growth
4922 Fairmont Ave.
Bethesda, MD 20814
301-657-1500

Chesapeake Growth
Drawer 69
Rocky Mountain, NC 27802
800-525-3863

Clover Equity Value
Clover Small Cap Value
11 Tobey Village Office Park
Pittsford, NY 14534
800-932-7781

Colonial Small Cap Value A
1 Financial Center
Boston, MA 02111
617-426-3750

Columbia Small Cap
1301 SW Fifth Ave.
Portland, OR 97207
503-222-3606

Compass Small Cap Growth
Compass Small Cap Value
259 Radnor-Chester Rd.
Radnor, PA 19807
800-441-7764

Consulting Group Small Cap
  Growth
Consulting Group Small Cap
  Value
222 Delaware Ave.
Wilmington, DE 19801
212-816-8725

Corner Cap Growth
Box 8687
Richmond, VA 23226
404-240-0666

Cowen Opportunity A
Box 41911
Kansas City, MO 64141
800-262-7116

Crabbe Huson Small Cap
Crabbe Huson Special
121 SW Morrison
Portland, OR 97204
503-295-0919

Crest Funds Special Equity
680 E. Swedesford Rd.
Wayne, PA 19087
800-273-7827

DFA U.S. 6-10 Small Company
DFA U.S. Small Cap Value
1299 Ocean Ave.
Santa Monica, CA 90401
310-395-8005

DG Opportunity
Federated Investors Tower
Pittsburgh, PA 15222
800-748-8500

Dean Witter Capital Appreciation
Dean Witter Special Value
2 World Trade Center
New York, NY 10048
800-869-6397

Delafield
600 Fifth Ave.
New York, NY 10020
800-221-3079

Delaware Trend A
Delaware Value A
90 Washington St.
New York, NY 10006
800-523-4640

Diversified Investors Special
  Equity
4 Manhattanville Rd.
Purchase, NY 10577
914-697-8779

Dreyfus Aggressive Growth
Dreyfus Emerging Leaders
Dreyfus New Leaders
Dreyfus Premier Small Company
Dreyfus Small Company Value
1 Exchange Place
Boston, MA 02109
800-645-6561

ESC Strategic Small Cap D
Box 182487
Columbus, OH 43218
800-261-3863

Eastcliff Regional Small Cap Value
225 E. Mason St.
Milwaukee, WI 53202
800-595-5519

Eclipse Financial Asset Equity
Box 2196
Peachtree, GA 30269
770-631-0414

Emerald Small Cap Ret
3435 Stelzer Rd.
Columbus, OH 43219
800-637-3759

Enterprise Small Company
Value A
3343 Peachtree Rd.
Atlanta, GA 30326
404-396-8118

Evergreen Limited Market
Evergreen Small Cap Equity
Income
Federated Investors Tower
Pittsburgh, PA 15222
800-807-2940

Excelsior Early Life Cycle
Excelsior Environmental
Products & Services
114 W. 47th St.
New York, NY 10036
212-852-3969

FAM Value
111 N. Grand St.
Cobleskill, NY 12043
800-932-3271

FBL Managed
5400 University Ave.
Des Moines, IA 50266
515-225-5586

FBR Small Cap Growth/Value
1001 19th St. N.
Arlington, VA 22209
888-888-0025

FPA Capital
11400 W. Olympic Blvd.
Los Angeles, CA 90064
310-473-0225

Fairmont
1346 S. Third St.
Louisville, KY 40208
800-262-9936

Fairport Midwest Growth
4000 Chester Ave.
Cleveland, OH 44103
800-332-6459

Fasciano
190 S. LaSalle St.
Chicago, IL 60603
312-444-6050

Federated Index Trust Mini Cap
Federated Small Cap Strategies B
2 World Financial Center
New York, NY 10281
800-341-7400

Fidelity Export & Multinational
Fidelity Low-Priced Stock
Fidelity Small Cap Stock
82 Devonshire St.
Boston, MA 02109
800-544-8888

Fiduciary Capital Growth
225 E. Mason St.
Milwaukee, WI 53202
414-226-4555

Fiduciary Management Growth
Box 1520
Secaucus, NJ 07096
800-221-5672

59 Wall Street Small Company
6 St. James Ave.
Boston, MA 02116
212-493-8100

First American Emerging
Growth
First American Regional Equity
680 E. Swedesford Rd.
Wayne, PA 19087
800-637-2548

First Investors Special Situations
95 Wall St.
New York, NY 10005
800-423-4026

First Omaha Small Cap Value
Box 419022
Kansas City, MO 64141
800-662-4203

First Source Monogram Special
    Equity
3435 Stelzer Rd.
Columbus, OH 43219
800-766-8938

Flag Investors Emerging Growth
135 E. Baltimore St.
Baltimore, MD 21202
800-767-3524

Fortis Advantage Capital
    Appreciation
Box 64284
St. Paul, MN 55164
800-800-2638

Founders Discovery
2930 E. Third Ave.
Denver, CO 80206
800-525-2440

Franklin Balance Sheet
    Investment
Franklin Micro Cap Value
Franklin Small Cap Growth
Franklin Value
700 Central Ave.
St. Petersburg, FL 33701
800-342-5236

Fremont U.S. Micro Cap
50 Beale St.
San Francisco, CA 94105
800-548-4539

Frontier Equity
101 W. Wisconsin Ave.
Milwaukee, WI 53072
800-231-2901

GT Global America Small Cap
    Growth
50 California St.
San Francisco, CA 94111
800-824-1580

Gabelli Small Cap Growth
19 Old Kings Hwy. S.
Darien, CT 06820
914-921-5100

Galaxy Small Cap Value
Galaxy Small Company
    Equity
290 Donald Lynch Blvd.
Marlboro, MA 01752
800-628-0414

Gateway Small Cap Index
400 TechCenter Dr.
Milford, OH 45150
513-248-2700

Glenmede Small Cap
    Equity
1 Exchange Place
Boston, MA 02109
800-442-8299

Goldman Sachs Small Cap
    Equity
4900 Sears Tower
Chicago, IL 60606
800-526-7384

Govett Smaller Companies A
1 Parkview Plaza
Oakbrook, IL 60181
800-225-2222

HSBC Small Cap
600 17th St. S.
Denver, CO 80202
800-634-2536

Harris Insight Small Cap
  Opportunity
1 Exchange Place
Boston, MA 02109
800-982-8782

Heartland Small Cap
  Contrarian
Heartland Value
790 N. Milwaukee St.
Milwaukee, WI 53202
800-432-7856

Henlopen
400 W. Ninth St.
Wilmington, DE 19801
302-654-3131

Heritage Small Cap Stock A
880 Carillon Pkwy.
St. Petersburg, FL 33716
813-573-8143

HomeState Growth
1857 William Penn Way
Lancaster, PA 17605
717-396-1116

Hotchkis & Wiley Small Cap
800 W. 6th St.
Los Angeles, CA 90017
800-346-7301

IAI Capital Appreciation
IAI Value
3700 First Bank Place
Minneapolis, MN 55440
800-945-3863

IDS Progressive A
Box 59196
Minneapolis, MN 55459
612-671-3733

ITT Hartford Small Company
Box 8416
Boston, MA 02266
888-843-7824

Insightful Investor Growth
175 Great Neck Rd.
Great Neck, NY 11021
800-424-2295

Invesco Small Company Growth
Invesco Small Company Value
1315 Peachtree St. NE
Atlanta, GA 30309
800-525-8085

Ivy Emerging Growth A
700 S. Federal Hwy.
Boca Raton, FL 33432
800-456-5111

JPM U.S. Small Company
6 St. James St.
Boston, MA 02116
800-766-7722

Janus Enterprise
Janus Venture
100 Fillmore St.
Denver, CO 80206
800-525-8963

John Hancock Discovery
John Hancock Emerging Growth
John Hancock Fundamental
  Value
John Hancock Global
  Marketplace
John Hancock Small Cap Equity

John Hancock Special Equities
John Hancock Special Value
101 Huntington Ave.
Boston, MA 02199
800-225-5291

Jundt U.S. Emerging Growth
1550 Utica Ave. S.
Minneapolis, MN 55416
800-370-0612

Jurika & Voyles Mini Cap
1999 Harrison St.
Oakland, CA 94612
800-584-6878

Kaufmann
140 E. 45th St.
New York, NY 10017
800-237-0132

Keeley Small Cap Value
401 S. LaSalle St.
Chicago, IL 60605
312-786-5050

Kemper Small Cap Equity
Kemper Small Cap Value
120 S. LaSalle St.
Chicago, IL 60603
800-621-1048

Kent Small Company Growth
290 Donald Lynch Blvd.
Marlboro, MA 01752
800-633-5368

Keystone Emerging Growth
Keystone Small Company
   Growth
200 Berkeley St.
Boston, MA 02116
617-338-3400

LKCM Small Cap Equity
301 Commerce St.
Forth Worth, TX 76102
817-332-3235

Landmark Small Cap Equity
6 St. James St.
Boston, MA 02116
800-721-1899

Lazard Bantam Value
Lazard Small Cap
30 Rockefeller Plaza
New York, NY 10020
800-823-6300

Legg Mason Special
   Investment
111 S. Calvert St.
Baltimore, MD 21203
410-539-0000

Lexington Small Cap Value
Box 1515
Saddle Brook, NJ 07662
201-845-7300

Lindner Growth
Lindner Small Cap
7711 Carondelet
St. Louis, MO 63105
314-727-5305

Longleaf Small Cap
6075 Poplar Ave.
Memphis, TN 38119
800-445-9469

Loomis Sayles Small Cap
   Growth
Loomis Sayles Small Cap Value
1 Financial Center
Boston, MA 02111
617-482-2450

Lord Abbett Developing Growth
Lord Abbett Research Small Cap
767 Fifth Ave.
New York, NY 10153
800-874-3733

Lutheran Opportunity Growth
625 Fourth Ave. S.
Minneapolis, MN 55415
612-339-8091

MAS Small Cap Value
Box 2798
Boston, MA 02208
800-354-8185

MFS Aggressive Small Cap
MFS OTC
500 Boylston St.
Boston, MA 02116
800-887-8671

Managers Special Equity
40 Richards Ave.
Norwalk, CT 06854
800-835-3879

Marshall Small Cap Stock
Federated Investors Tower
Pittsburgh, PA 15222
800-236-8560

Mason Street Aggressive Growth
Box 419419
Kansas City, MO 64141
888-627-6678

MassMutual Small Cap Value
Box 5143
Denver, CO 80231
413-788-8411

Matrix Emerging Growth
300 Main St.
Cincinnati, OH 45202
513-621-2875

Matterhorn Growth
301 Exford Valley Rd.
Yardley, PA 19067
800-637-3901

Mentor Growth B
Box 1357
Richmond, VA 23211
804-649-2311

Meridian
Meridian Value
60 E. Sir Francis Drake Blvd.
Larkspur, CA 94939
800-446-6662

Merrill Lynch Phoenix
Merrill Lynch Small Cap Index
Merrill Lynch Special Value
1 Financial Center
Boston, MA 02111
800-637-3863

Montgomery Micro Cap
Montgomery Small Cap Oppor-
    tunities
Montgomery Small Cap
101 California St.
San Francisco, CA 94111
415-248-6000

Morgan Grenfell Micro Cap
Morgan Grenfell Smaller Com-
    panies
680 E. Swedesford Rd.
Wayne, PA 19087
800-814-3401

Morgan Stanley American Value
Morgan Stanley Small Cap Value
Box 2798
Boston, MA 02208
800-548-7786

Mosaic Mid Cap Growth
1655 Fort Myer Dr.
Arlington, VA 22209
703-528-6500

Munder Small Company
    Growth
480 Pierce St.
Birmingham, MI 48009
800-438-5789

NI Growth
NI Micro Cap
400 Bellevue Pkwy.
Wilmington, DE 19809
800-686-3742

Nations Small Company
    Growth
1 NationsBank Plaza
Charlotte, NC 28255
800-321-7854

Navellier Aggressive Growth
920 Incline Way
Incline Villa, NV 89450
800-887-8671

Needham Growth
445 Park Ave.
New York, NY 10022
800-331-3186

Neuberger & Berman
    Genesis
605 Third Ave.
New York, NY 10158
800-877-9700

Nicholas II
Nicholas Limited Edition
700 N. Water St.
Milwaukee, WI 53202
800-227-5987

NA Emerging Growth
NA Mini Cap Growth
Box 82169
San Diego, CA 92138
800-551-8043

Northern Small Cap
207 E. Buffalo St.
Milwaukee, WI 53202
800-595-9111

Norwest Small Cap
    Opportunity
Norwest Small Company
    Stock
61 Broadway
New York, NY 10006
612-667-0250

ORI Growth
Box 701
Milwaukee, WI 53201
800-407-7298

ONE Small Cap
237 William Howard Taft Rd.
Cincinnati, OH 45219
800-578-8078

Oak Hall Equity
Box 446
Portland, ME 04112
800-625-4255

Oakmark Small Cap
2 N. LaSalle St.
Chicago, IL 60602
800-625-6275

Oberweis Emerging Growth
Oberweis Micro Cap
1 Constitution Dr.
Aurora, IL 60506
630-897-7100

One Group Gulf South
  Growth
3435 Stelzer Rd.
Columbus, OH 43219
800-480-4111

Oppenheimer Discovery
Oppenheimer Quest
Box 5143
Denver, CO 80231
800-525-7048

Overland Express Strategic
  Growth
111 Center St.
Little Rock, AR 72201
800-525-9612

PBHG Emerging Growth
PBHG Limited
PBHG Strategic Small
  Company
680 E. Swedesford Rd.
Wayne, PA 19087
800-433-0051

PIMC Micro Cap Growth
PIMC Small Cap Growth
PIMC Small Cap Value
2187 Atlantic St.
Stamford, CT 06902
800-927-4648

Pacific Advisors Small Cap
215 N. Marengo Ave.
Pasadena, CA 91101
800-989-6693

Pacific Horizon Aggressive
  Growth
125 W. 55th St.
New York, NY 10019
800-332-3863

PaineWebber Small Cap
1285 Ave. of Americas
New York, NY 10019
800-647-1568

Parkstone Small Cap
3435 Stelzer Rd.
Columbus, OH 43219
800-451-8377

Parnassus
1 Market Stewart Tower
San Francisco, CA 94105
800-999-3505

Pasadena Small & Mid Cap
  Growth
600 N. Rosemead Blvd.
Pasadena, CA 91107
800-648-8050

Pathfinder
Box 75231
Los Angeles, CA 90075
800-444-4778

Penn Mutual
1414 Ave. of Americas
New York, NY 10019
212-355-7311

Perkins Opportunity
730 E. Lake St.
Wayzata, MN 55391
612-473-8367

Perritt Capital Growth
680 N. Lake Shore Dr.
Chicago, IL 60611
800-338-1579

Pillar Mid Cap Value
680 E. Swedesford Rd.
Wayne, PA 19087
800-932-7782

Pioneer Capital Growth
Pioneer Micro Cap
Pioneer Small Company
60 State St.
Boston, MA 02109
800-225-6292

Portico Mid Cap
777 E. Wisconsin Ave.
Milwaukee, WI 53202
800-228-1024

Preferred Small Cap
Box 8320
Boston, MA 02266
800-662-4769

Principal Preservation Select
    Value
215 N. Main St.
West Bend, WI 53095
800-826-4600

Princor Emerging Growth
Box 10423
Des Moines, IA 50306
515-247-6833

Prudential Small Companies
1 Seaport Plaza
New York, NY 10292
800-225-1852

Putnam OTC & Emerging
    Growth
1 Post Office Sq.
Boston, MA 02109
617-292-1000

Quaker Aggressive Growth
Quaker Small Cap Value
1288 Valley Forge Rd.
Valley Forge, PA 19482
800-220-8888

Qualivest Small Companies
    Value
3435 Stelzer Rd.
Columbus, OH 43219
800-743-8637

Quantitative Disciplined
    Growth
Quantitative Numeric
Lincoln N.
Lincoln, MA 01773
800-331-1244

RCM Small Cap
4 Embarcadero Center
San Francisco, CA 94111
415-954-5400

Revest Growth & Income
1414 Ave. of Americas
New York, NY 10019
212-774-7455

Rimco Monument Small Cap
    Equity
Federated Investors Tower
Pittsburgh, PA 15222
800-934-3883

RSI Emerging Growth Equity
317 Madison Ave.
New York, NY 10017
800-772-3615

Rembrandt Small Cap
680 E. Swedesford Rd.
Wayne, PA 19087
800-443-4725

Riverside Capital Value Equity
3435 Stelzer Rd.
Columbus, OH 43219
800-874-8376

Robertson Stephens Emerging
  Growth
Robertson Stephens Micro Cap
  Growth
Robertson Stephens
  Partners
555 California St.
San Francisco, CA 94104
800-766-3863

Rockwood Growth
11 Hanover Sq.
New York, NY 10005
208-522-5593

Royce Equity Income
Royce Global Services
Royce Low-Priced Stock
Royce Micro Cap
Royce Premier
Royce Total Return
Royce Value
1414 Ave. of Americas
New York, NY 10019
800-221-4268

SEI Small Cap
SEI Small Cap Growth
SEI Small Cap Value
680 E. Swedesford Rd.
Wayne, PA 19087
800-342-5734

SSGA Small Cap
2 International Place
Boston, MA 02110
617-654-6089

STI Classic Sunbelt
  Equity
680 Swedesford Rd.
Wayne, PA 19087
800-428-6970

Safeco Growth
Safeco Northwest
Safeco Small Company
Box 36480
Seattle, WA 98124
206-545-5530

Schroder Small Cap Value
Schroder U.S. Small Companies
787 Seventh Ave.
New York, NY 10019
800-464-3108

Schwab Small Cap Index
101 Montgomery St.
San Francisco, CA 94104
800-526-8600

Schwartz Value
3707 W. Maple Rd.
Bloomfield, MI 48301
810-644-2701

Scout Regional
2440 Pershing Rd.
Kansas City, MO 64108
816-471-5200

Scudder 21st Century Growth
Scudder Development
Scudder Micro Cap
Scudder Small Company Value
2 International Place
Boston, MA 02110
800-225-2470

Seligman Frontier
100 Park Ave.
New York, NY 10017
212-850-1864

Sentinel Small Company
National Life Dr.
Montpelier, VT 05604
802-229-3900

Shadow Stock
2440 Pershing Rd.
Kansas City, MO 64108
800-422-2766

Shelby
3435 Stelzer Rd.
Columbus, OH 43219
800-752-1823

Sierra Emerging Growth
9301 Corbin Ave.
Northridge, CA 91328
800-222-5852

Sit Small Cap Growth
90 S. 7th St.
Minneapolis, MN 55402
612-334-5888

Skyline Secial Equities
311 S. Wacker Dr.
Chicago, IL 60606
800-458-5222

Small Cap World
4 Embarcadero Center
San Francisco, CA 94120
800-421-4120

Smith Barney Managed Growth
222 Delaware Ave.
Wilmington, DE 19801
212-723-9218

Stagecoach Aggressive Growth
111 Center St.
Little Rock, AR 72201
800-222-8222

Standish Small Cap Tax-
    Sensitive
Standish Small Cap Equity
1 Financial Center
Boston, MA 02111
800-729-0066

State Street Aurora
State Street Emerging Growth
1 Financial Center
Boston, MA 02111
800-882-0052

Stein Roe Special Venture
Box 804058
Chicago, IL 60680
312-368-7800

Stratton Small Cap Yield
610 W. Germantown Pike
Plymouth Mills, PA 19462
800-634-5726

Strong Small Cap
Box 2936
Milwaukee, WI 53201
414-359-1400

SunAmerica Small Company
    Growth
733 Third Ave.
New York, NY 10017
800-858-8850

T. Rowe Price Small Cap Stock
T. Rowe Price Small Cap Value
100 E. Pratt St.
Baltimore, MD 21202
800-638-5660

TCW Galileo Earnings
    Momentum
TCW Galileo Small Cap Growth
865 S. Figueroa
Los Angeles, CA 90017
213-244-0000

TCW/DW Small Cap Growth
2 World Trade Center
New York, NY 10048
212-392-2550

Target Small Cap Growth
Target Small Cap Value
1 Seaport Plaza
New York, NY 10292
800-442-8748

Texas Capital Value & Growth
Box 141849
Austin, TX 78714
512-451-7905

Tocqueville Small Cap Value
1675 Broadway
New York, NY 10019
800-697-3863

Touchstone Emerging
    Growth
311 Pike St.
Cincinnati, OH 45202
800-669-2796

Trent Equity
2002 Pisgah Church Rd.
Greensboro, NC 27455
910-282-9302

Turner Small Cap Equity
680 E. Swedesford Rd.
Wayne, PA 19087
800-224-6312

UAM FMA Small Company
UAM ICM Small Company
UAM RHJ Small Cap
UAM Sirach Special Equity
100 Oliver St.
Boston, MA 02110
800-638-7983

USAA Aggressive Growth
USAA Building
San Antonio, TX 78288
800-382-8722

Value Line Small Cap Growth
Value Line Special Situations
220 E. 42nd St.
New York, NY 10017
800-223-0818

Van Kampen Amer Cap
    Aggressive Growth
1 Parkview Plaza
Oakbrook, IL 60181
800-421-5666

Van Wagoner Emerging
    Growth
Van Wagoner Micro Cap
Box 1628
Milwaukee, WI 53201
800-228-2121

Vanguard Explorer
Vanguard Extended Market
    Index
Vanguard Small Cap Stock
    Index
Vanguard Selected Value
Box 2600
Valley Forge, PA 19482
800-662-7447

Victory Special Growth
Box 9741
Providence, RI 02940
800-539-3863

Virtus Style Manager
Federated Investors Tower
Pittsburgh, PA 15222
800-723-9512

Vista Small Cap Equity
Box 419392
Kansas City, MO 64179
800-648-4782

WPG Growth
WPG Tudor
1 New York Plaza
New York, NY 10004
212-908-9582

Wall Street
230 Park Ave.
New York, NY 10169
800-443-4693

Warburg Pincus Post-Venture
Warburg Pincus Small Company
   Value
Warburg Pincus Emerging
   Growth
Warburg Pincus Small Company
   Growth
466 Lexington Ave.
New York, NY 10017
800-927-2874

Wasatch Aggressive Equity
Wasatch Growth
Wasatch Micro Cap
Wasatch Mid Cap
68 S. Main St.
Salt Lake City, UT 84101
800-551-1700

Weitz Hickory
1125 S. 103rd St.
Omaha, NE 68124
402-391-1980

Westcore Small Cap Opportunity
370 17th St.
Denver, CO 80202
800-392-2673

Wilshire Target Small Company
   Growth
Wilshire Target Small Company
   Value
Box 9770
Providence, RI 02940
888-200-6796

Winthrop Small Company Value
277 Park Ave.
New York, NY 10172
800-225-8011

Wright Junior Blue Chip
   Equities
1000 Lafayette Blvd.
Bridgeport, CT 06604
203-333-6666

Source: Morningstar, Inc.

Index